AF473855

Joan Eardley A Sense of Place

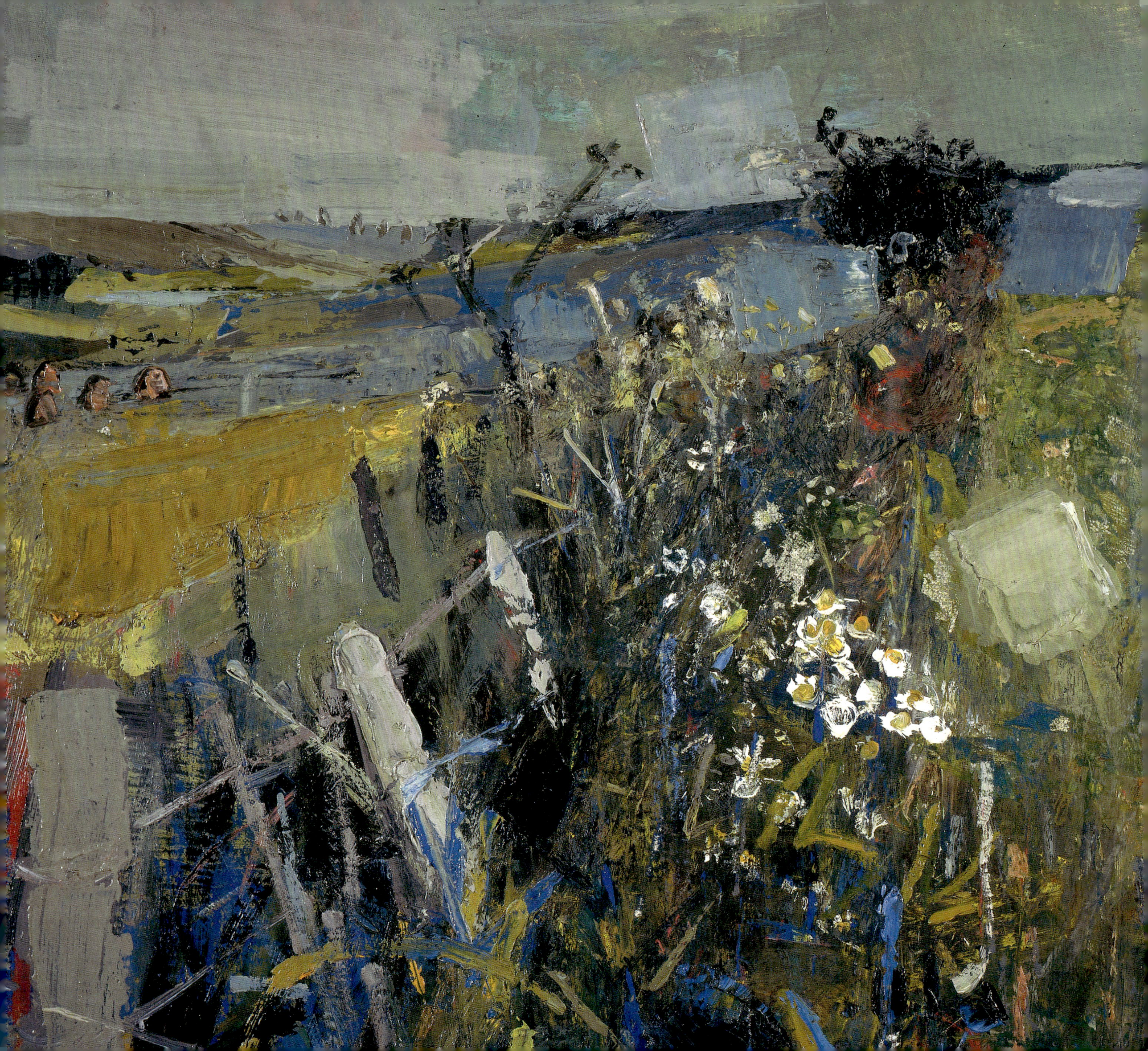

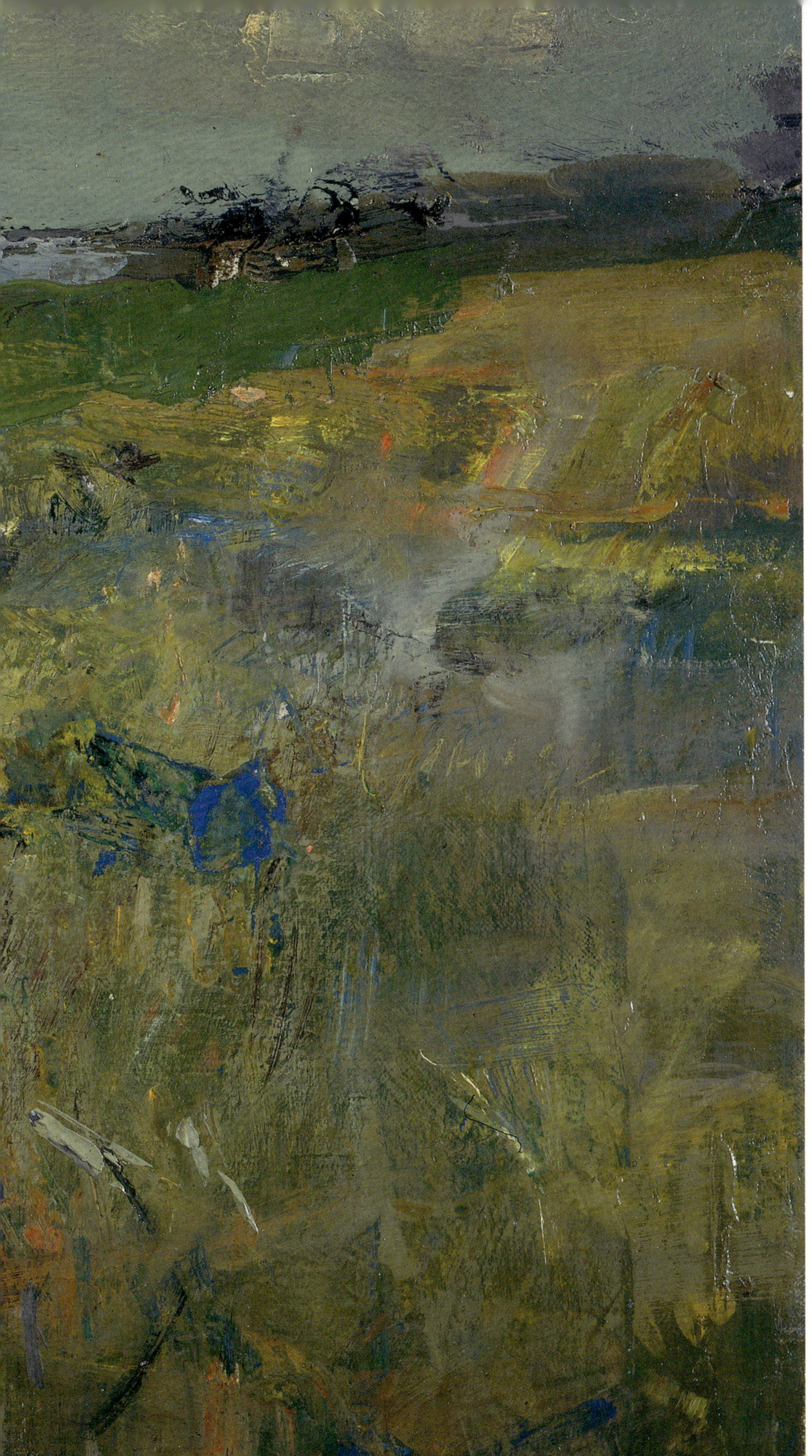

Patrick Elliott *with Anne Galastro*

Joan Eardley
A Sense of Place

National Galleries of Scotland
Edinburgh · 2016

Published by the Trustees of the National Galleries of Scotland to accompany the exhibition *Joan Eardley: A Sense of Place,* held at the Scottish National Gallery of Modern Art, Edinburgh, from 3 December 2016 to 21 May 2017.

Reprinted 2018, 2023

ISBN 978 1 911054 02 3

Designed and typeset in Adobe Text and Sweet Sans by Dalrymple
Printed in Italy on 150gsm Gardamatt Ultra by Conti Tipocolor

Front cover: *Hedgerow with Grasses and Flowers*, *c*.1962–63 (detail of plate 73)
Scottish National Gallery of Modern Art, Edinburgh
Back cover: *Red Haired Girl*, *c*.1960 (detail of plate 43)
Private collection
Frontispiece: *July Fields*, *c*.1959 (detail of plate 70)
City Art Centre, Edinburgh Museums and Galleries

All plate illustrations are works by Joan Eardley and feature in the exhibition, unless stated otherwise.

This exhibition has been assisted by the Scottish Government and the Government Indemnity Scheme.

The proceeds from the sale of this book go towards supporting the National Galleries of Scotland. For a complete list of current publications, please write to: NGS Publishing at the Scottish National Gallery of Modern Art, 75 Belford Road, Edinburgh EH4 3DR or visit our website: www.nationalgalleries.org

National Galleries of Scotland is a charity registered in Scotland (no.SC003728)

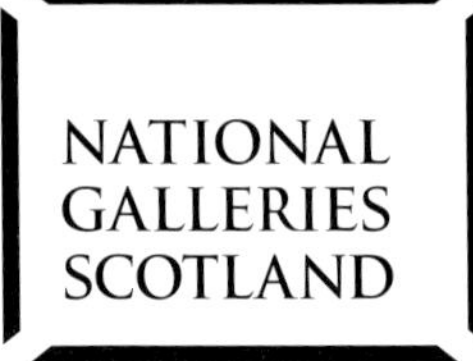

Contents

Directors' Foreword

Joan Eardley is one of Scotland's most admired artists. During a career that lasted barely fifteen years, she had two main subjects: the slums of Townhead in Glasgow and the fishing village of Catterline, about 100 miles north-east of Glasgow, which she first visited in 1950. She moved regularly between the two places, drawing and painting apparently contrasting imagery – street kids and tenement buildings in the one, stormy landscapes and boiling seas in the other. The two subjects contrast, but are not, at heart, so very different. Both had a peculiar sense of place that attracted her.

Like John Constable at East Bergholt, Eardley did not need to, or want to, roam far from her home: she found everything she needed for her painting close to her front door – or rather doors, for she had homes in both places. Constable's assertion that 'My limited and abstracted art is to be found under every hedge, and in every lane, and therefore nobody thinks it worth picking up' is a phrase that could have come from Eardley's lips.[1] Our aim here is to plot, as closely as possible, her movements in both places and to explore her working methods, from rough sketches to detailed pastels, from compositional designs and photographs through to large, resolved oil paintings. We can do this thanks to the remarkable gift of over 250 drawings and photographs, given to the Scottish National Gallery of Modern Art by Pat Black, Joan Eardley's sister, in 1987.

We are grateful above all to Anne Morrison-Hudson, Pat Black's daughter and the artist's niece, for her full commitment and support and for granting permission to reproduce all the works. We are also very thankful for the support of Walter and Norma Nimmo.

For assistance regarding Eardley and Catterline, we are especially indebted to Ron Stephen, who grew up in the village during the 1950s when Eardley painted there: his detailed knowledge of the village, its inhabitants and their lives has been of vital significance. Ann Steed's help has likewise been invaluable. We also thank Dave and Dorothy Ramsay, Stuart Buchanan, Ian Macintosh and Brian Watt, for their warm welcome and hospitality and for sharing their knowledge of Catterline.

We thank Ann McKenna and Pat McLean (née Ann and Pat Samson) and Andrew Samson for their memories of Eardley, who drew and painted them on many occasions in her Townhead studio, and Peter and David Sandeman, for their help and for permission to quote from letters sent to their mother Margot Sandeman. We also thank our lenders and those who have helped secure loans, including Jill Gerber (Cyril Gerber Fine Art, Glasgow); Guy Peploe, Christina Jansen and Tommy Zyw (The Scottish Gallery, Edinburgh); Helen Watson, Director of Exhibitions & Collections, Lakeland Arts, Kendal; Joanna Meacock and Ed Johnson (Glasgow Museums); Adrian George, Deputy Director, Government Art Collection; Jacky MacBeath, Head of Museums and Neil Lebeter, Deputy Head of Museums, University of Edinburgh; Dr Helen Scott, Curator (Fine Art), City Art Centre, Edinburgh; Mungo Campbell, Deputy Director, and Malcolm Chapman, Head of Collections Management, Hunterian Museum & Art Gallery, Glasgow; Alison Fraser, Lead Curator (Art), Museums and Galleries, Aberdeen; Arthur Watson, President, Joyce W. Cairns, Chair, Loans Committee, and Sandy Wood, Collections Curator, Royal Scottish Academy of Art & Architecture, Edinburgh; Ewan Mundy (Ewan Mundy Fine Art); Hilary Burwell, Art Collection Manager, Royal Bank of Scotland; and the private collectors who wish to remain anonymous. We are also grateful to Sebastian Galastro for tracking down information on Eardley's homes in Catterline; to Andy Phillipson for photography; to Jane Walker; and to Dan Hay for producing the maps of Townhead and Catterline.

Within the National Galleries of Scotland, we thank Patrick Elliott, curator of the exhibition, and Anne Galastro, for her research; Sarah Worrall, Publishing Project Manager and Gillian Achurch, Publishing Coordinator; Kirstie Meehan, Archivist; Claire Walsh, Curatorial Assistant; Graeme Gollan, Senior Paper Conservator; Charlotte Park, Paper Conservation Technician; and Cassia Pennington, Exhibitions Registrar.

SIR JOHN LEIGHTON
Director-General, National Galleries of Scotland

SIMON GROOM
Director, Scottish National Gallery of Modern Art

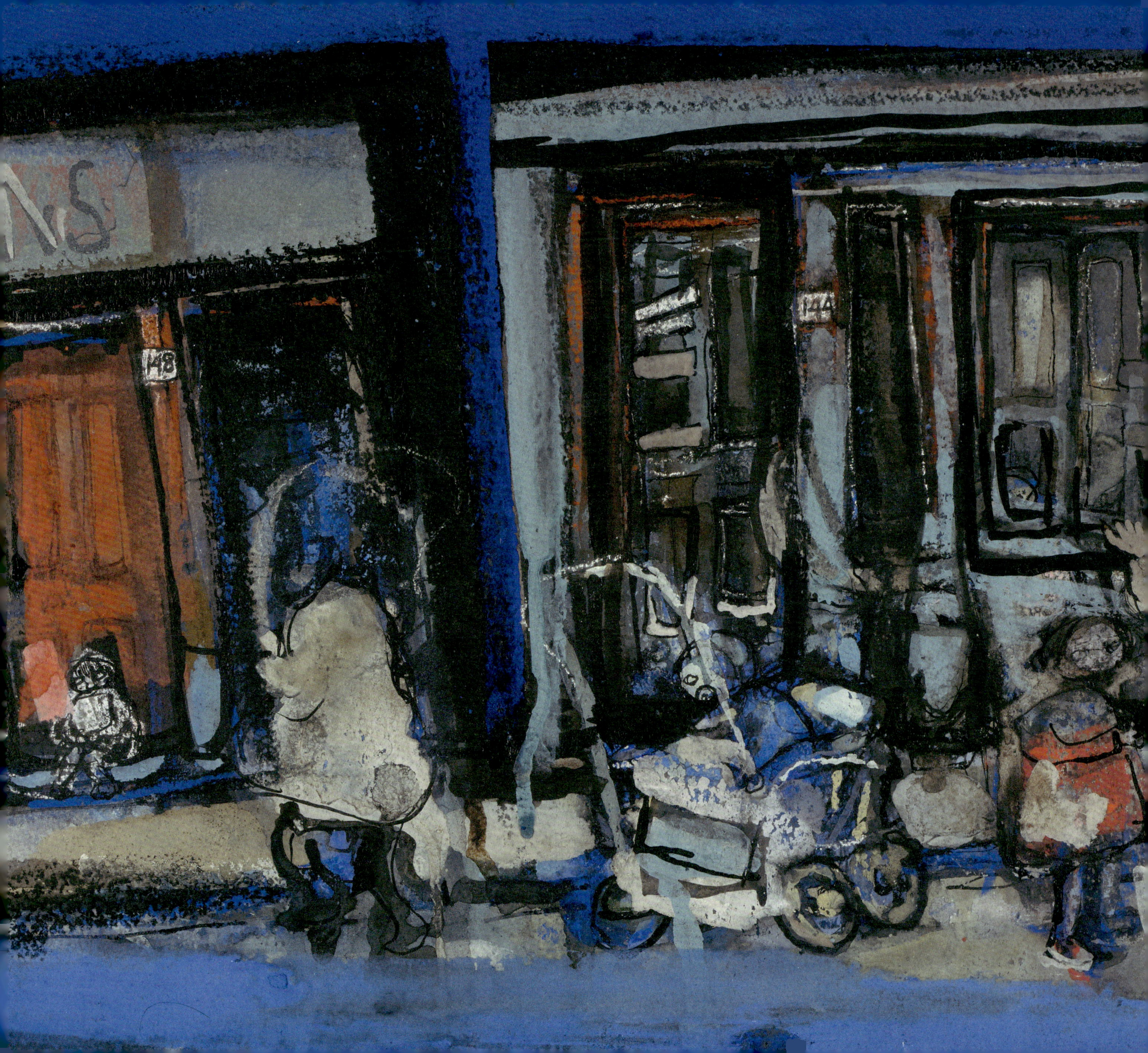
NS
148
144

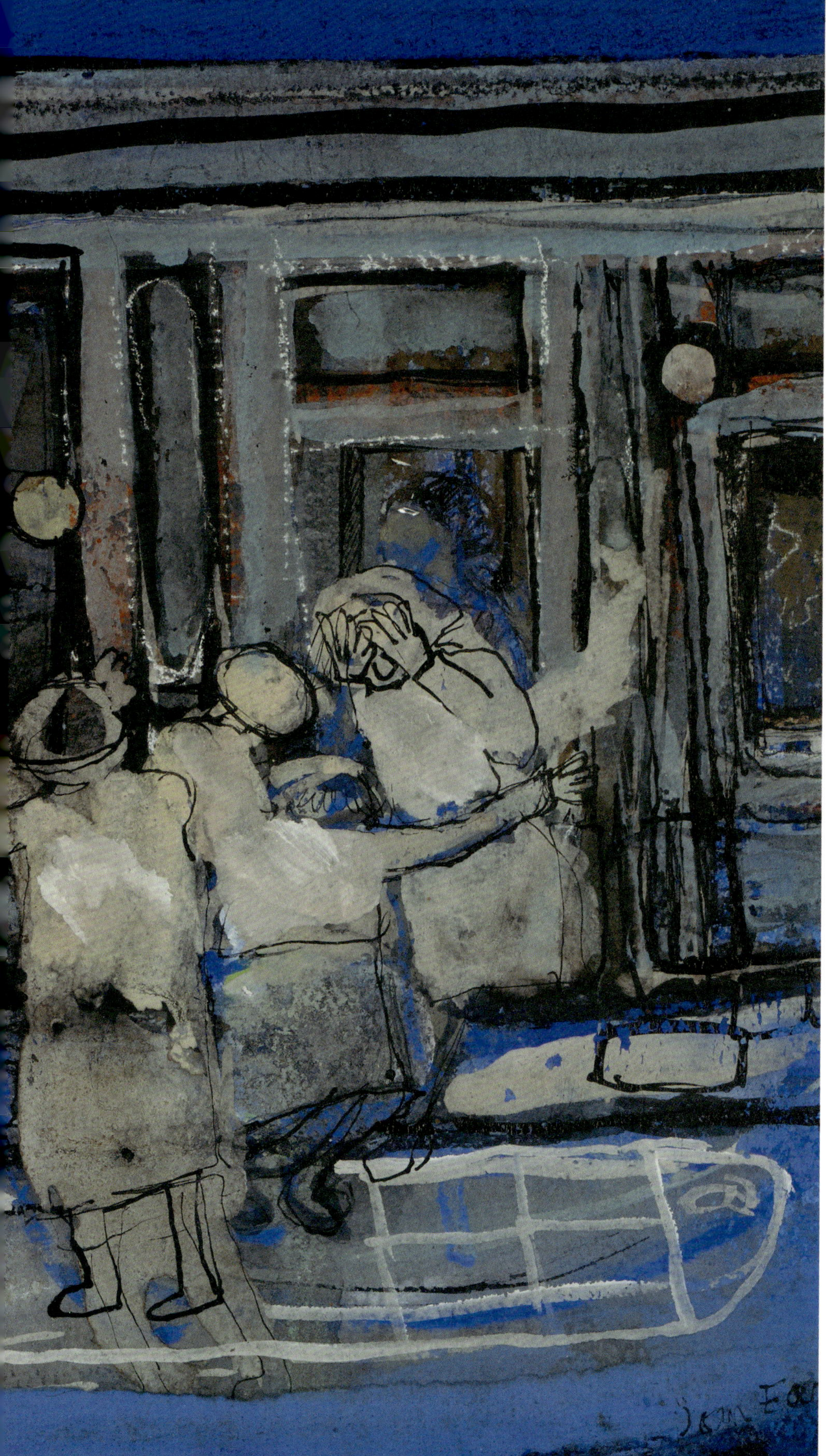

Introduction

Asked to comment upon the contrasting nature of her main subjects – Glasgow children and wild, coastal landscapes – Joan Eardley preferred to draw attention to their similarities rather than their differences: 'The children seem to be no more aware that I'm painting them than the sea and the cliffs are aware of me', she said.[2] This was at the end of her life, in 1963, but the two interests – city and rural life – had existed side by side in her work right from the start.

Joan Eardley was born in Sussex in the south of England in 1921 and grew up on a dairy farm. Her father suffered from severe depression and in 1926, when the farm was sold, Eardley, her sister and their mother moved into their grandmother's house in Blackheath in south-east London. Eardley's father took his own life in 1929. The threat of bombing in 1939 led the family to Auchterarder in Scotland, where they had relatives. In January 1940 they settled in a house at 170 Drymen Road in Bearsden, an affluent, almost rural suburb on the north-west side of Glasgow. Eardley enrolled at the Glasgow School of Art shortly afterwards. Although she divided her time between the Townhead area of Glasgow and Catterline, on the coast about twenty miles south of Aberdeen (see maps pp.124–25), she gave the Bearsden house as her home address until the last couple of years of her life.

Eardley first visited Catterline in 1950 and returned regularly thereafter. She borrowed a friend's cottage there from 1952 and rented a cottage herself from 1954. Before she had even settled in Catterline, she was conscious that two separate and contrasting places of

Detail from *Glasgow Street, Rottenrow*, *c.*1955–56 [plate 21]

work suited her. In 1951 she spent several months in the little town of Cologne, west of Toulouse in the south of France. From there, she wrote to her closest friend, the artist Margot Sandeman, who had evidently reached an impasse in the work she was doing in Glasgow. Eardley advised her to take a long break and work instead in the little bothy at Corrie on the Isle of Arran, where they often stayed together:

> *If you were not to stay* [in Corrie] *you would be denying yourself something which is necessary to every person who creates. ... It is the reason that I go dashing off to places like this so often. You don't need it so often perhaps – But now I think you do. ... anybody who paints needs a rest sometimes – but it is not the kind of rest an ordinary person thinks of – a holiday for 3 weeks and then back again. But a rest in the way that you now should go to Corrie and paint what you feel like there – anything so long as you feel satisfied doing it, lots and lots of not so important things – perhaps – but things just the same – that in itself puts up your morale. And go on and on until you don't want to anymore – until you actually want to come home ... These kind of goings away are entirely necessary for me.*[3]

The 'goings away' implied a coming back, which Eardley always did. She rarely dated her letters, or indeed her paintings, so it is impossible to construct an exact chronology of her movements. But we can say that at first she lived in Glasgow and made trips to Catterline, while by the early 1960s she was living in Catterline and making trips to Glasgow. She clearly needed both places, the one providing respite from the other. Wildly different on the surface, the two places did in fact have much in common. They were small, poor, close-knit communities, where a spirit of social cohesion existed.

By the early 1960s Townhead was destined for complete demolition to make way for a motorway interchange; and Catterline was semi-abandoned, owing to the decline in the fishing industry. Catterline was not a picturesque Highland village, with lochs, cattle and mountain streams, but a working harbour with boats, fishing nets, and fields of wheat, barley and oats. People may be absent from Eardley's Catterline paintings, but their presence is felt. She explored the point where man meets nature, epitomised in the paintings of hedgerows at the edges of crops, and the views of stormy seas and skies, pounding in upon the tiny, fragile cottages. Catterline and Townhead were the same, only different. As Eardley said:

> *Catterline has such a terrific clarity and terrific light, whereas Glasgow feels as though it has a sort of lid on the top of it, but at the same time it's a little community and the place that I chose to paint in Glasgow is also really a little community in a certain district, a little backstreet, where everybody knew everybody else. The same thing seems to be the case obviously in the village where I live in the north-east. It's the sort of intimate thing I like, and I think you've got to know something before you paint it. ... I suppose I'm essentially a romantic, I believe in the sort of emotion that you get from what your eyes show you and what you feel about certain things. Well I don't really know what I'm painting, I'm just trying to paint.*[4]

Fig.1 | Joan Eardley in the studio, working, 1962
Joan Eardley Archive, Scottish National Gallery of Modern Art, Edinburgh

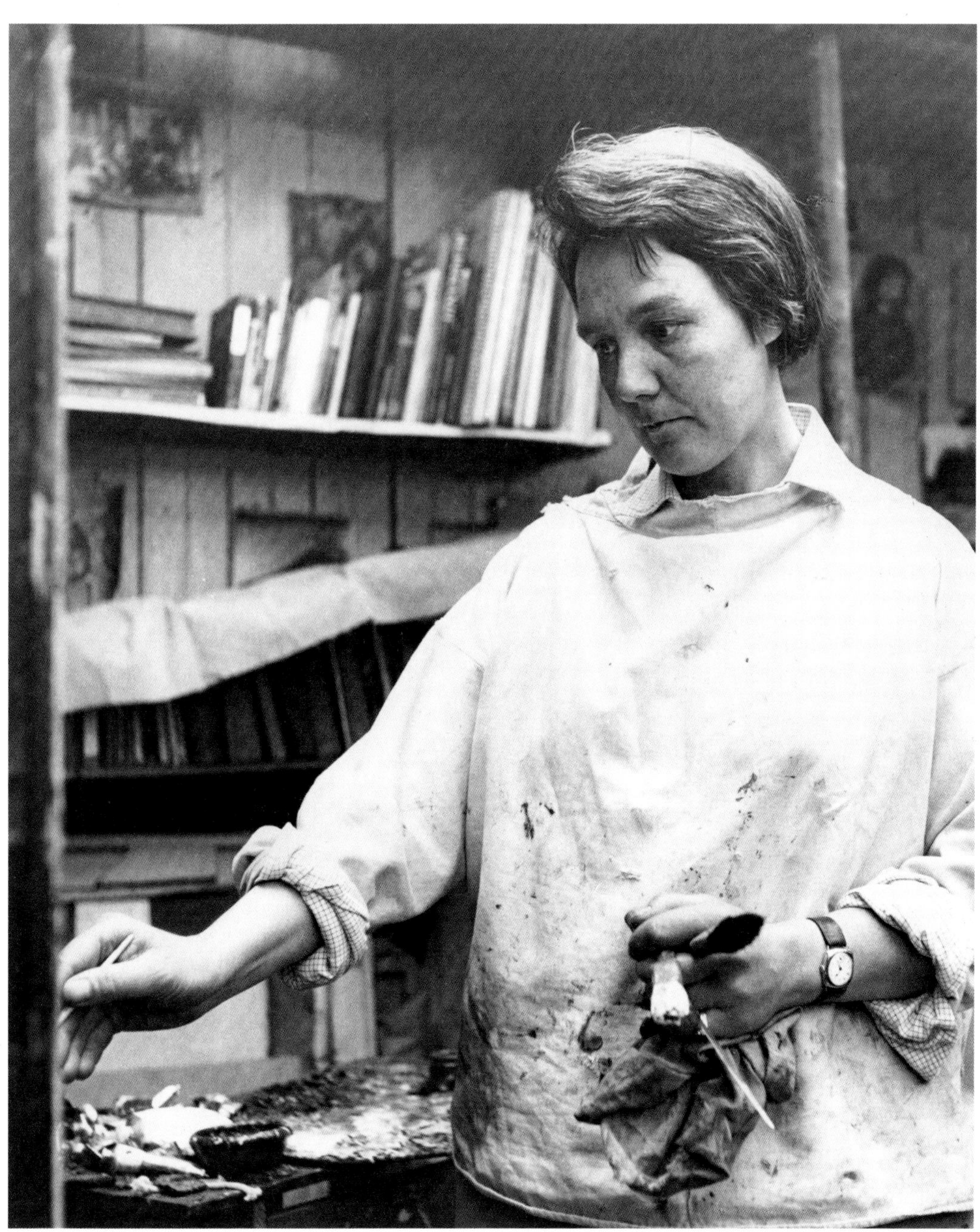

When I'm painting in the north-east I hardly ever move out of the village, I hardly ever move from one spot; I find that the more I know of the place, or of one particular spot, the more I find to paint in that particular spot. I do feel the more you know of something, the more you can get out of it, the more it gives to you. I don't think I'm painting what I feel about scenery, certainly not scenery with a name; because that is the north-east, just vast wastes, vast seas, vast areas of cliff ... well – you've just got to paint it.

I very often find I will take my paints to a certain place which has moved me and I begin to paint there and I find, by perhaps the end of the summer, I haven't moved from that place. My paints are still there, I've worn a kind of mark in the ground, there's no grass left; generally a sort of studio seems to have arrived outside. This seems to me how I work, once I've started in a place I don't find I want to move because I'm trying to do something and you're never really satisfied with what you're doing so you keep on trying and the more you try the more you keep on thinking of new ways of doing the particular subject and so you just go on and on. You might even turn round in the middle of doing a certain painting and you see something else, so, you run back and get another canvas and try and do that, but it's still the same spot, really, and it's probably the same feeling you are trying to grasp.

JOAN EARDLEY
Interview conducted by the Arts Council, 1961

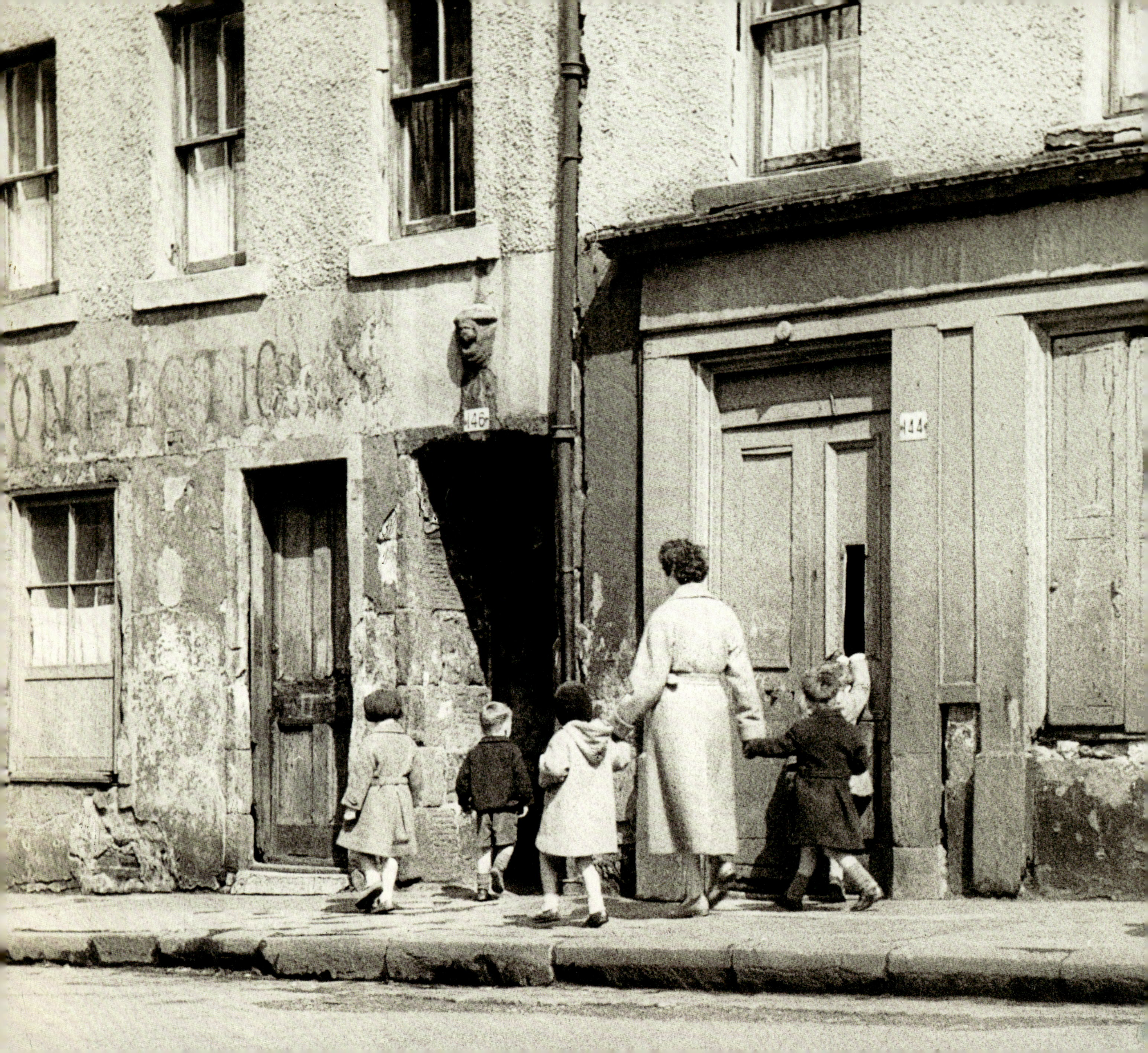
146
144

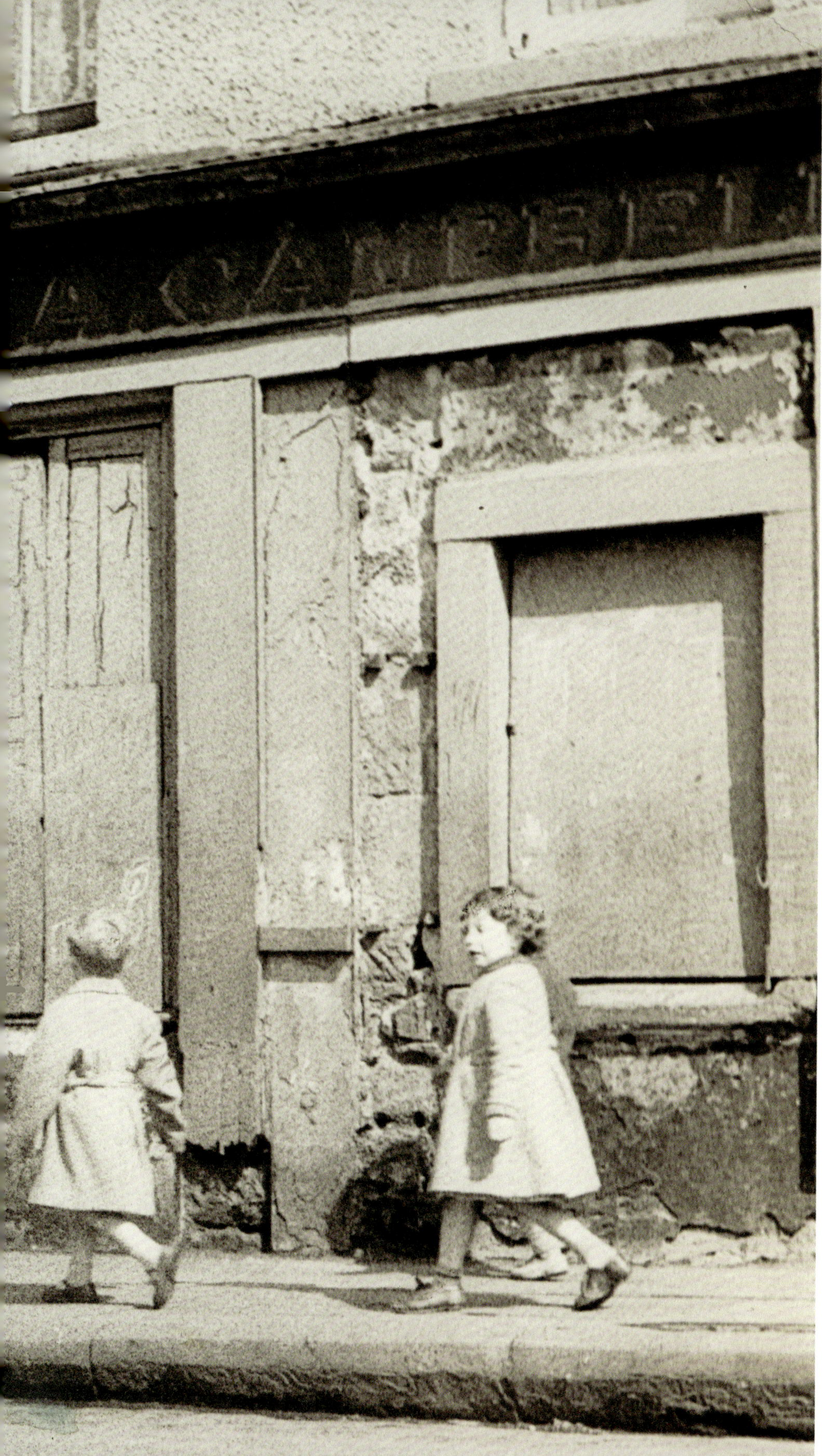

I TOWNHEAD

Eardley lived with her mother and sister in the comfortable suburb of Bearsden from 1940, taking the train into the city to study at the Glasgow School of Art. Robert Colquhoun, Robert MacBryde, Benjamin Creme and Margot Sandeman were among her contemporaries. She graduated in 1943 [fig.3] but continued to attend evening classes. She spent two years as an apprentice joiner at a construction firm in Bearsden, a 'reserved occupation', which she preferred to a teacher training course.

Eardley returned to the Glasgow School of Art in 1947 for post-diploma studies and the following year won scholarships that enabled her to travel to Italy and France. She was already someone to watch by this date. In 1948, when she was just twenty-seven, she was elected a member of the Society of Scottish Artists. Glasgow Museums and the Glasgow School of Art bought drawings by her.[5] In 1949 the Glasgow School of Art staged an exhibition of the work she had done on her travelling scholarship, and this led, in April 1950, to a solo show in Aberdeen. In the catalogue Hugh Adam Crawford, who had been her tutor in Glasgow but had recently been appointed Head of Gray's School of Art in Aberdeen, wrote that she was 'widely considered to be one of the most important young Scottish artists today.'[6]

Many of her Scottish contemporaries, including Colquhoun, MacBryde, Alan Davie, William Turnbull and Eduardo Paolozzi, headed to London as soon as they could, but Eardley chose to rent a small studio on the fourth floor at 21 Cochrane Street, near the City Chambers in Glasgow (see map p.124). She seems to have found the studio before heading off on her

Fig.2 | Rottenrow, Glasgow, *c.*1955–56

Joan Eardley Archive, Scottish National Gallery of Modern Art, Edinburgh. Photo by Audrey Walker

Fig.3 | Joan Eardley (seated at the left end of the second row) at the diploma awards ceremony, the Glasgow School of Art, 1943
Joan Eardley Archive, Scottish National Gallery of Modern Art, Edinburgh

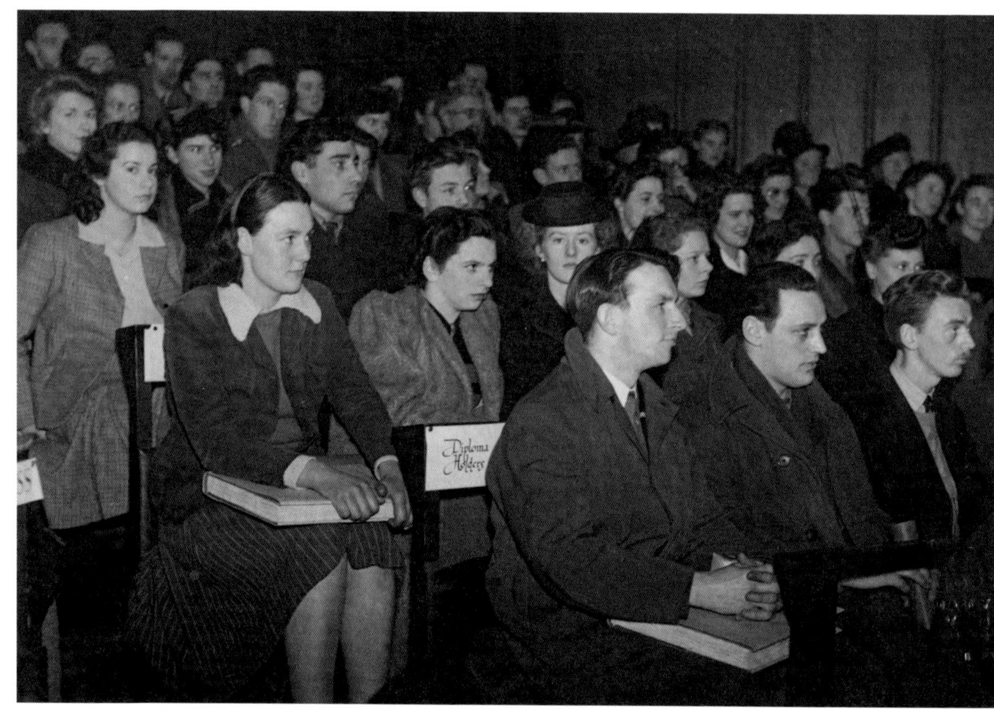

scholarship travels in September 1948, and in letters to her mother, written while she was abroad, she asked her to collect various things from the studio.[7] By this date Townhead was seriously overcrowded, with many buildings in a dilapidated state and thousands of families living in unsanitary conditions. Many of the tenements had been built in the second half of the nineteenth century as a result of the Glasgow City Improvement Trust scheme, established to provide better housing for the vastly increased population. As the city continued to grow in the early years of the twentieth century, the area provided both housing and industry, with all kinds of manufacturing businesses existing side by side with the overcrowded tenements. This gave the area a vibrant character that persisted into the 1950s, when Eardley began recording its young inhabitants. She explained her affection for this subject matter, and her interest in the run-down surroundings:

> *I like the friendliness of the back streets. Life is at its most uninhibited here. Dilapidation is often more interesting to a painter as is anything that has been used and lived with – whether it be an ivy covered cottage, a broken farm-cart or an old tenement.*[8]

Eardley's first biographer, William Buchanan, describes the Cochrane Street studio as 'an attic studio, four storeys up ... reached by an extremely steep set of stairs that passed several manufactories, one of which, a bookbinder, accounted for the strong smell of glue that pervaded the place.'[9] Records for the period tell us that the building was used as a warehouse, office and workshops (one of them by Robert Baillie, the bookbinder; Eardley made a few drawings on his old invoice forms), and that the only stable resident was the Neptune Club.[10] *Street Kids* [plate 5] was painted around this time and exhibited at the Royal Scottish Academy in 1951. Several related sketches exist [plates 2–4], which suggest her working method: drawing in chalks and pastels outdoors, concentrating on many details as well as figure studies, and then working the composition up on canvas in the studio. Smaller paintings were sometimes done outdoors. Which artists were inspiring her at this time? In letters to Margot Sandeman she scoffed at the idea, suggested by one critic, that her work was inspired by Colquhoun and MacBryde; instead she mentions her admiration for Paul Gauguin and Graham Sutherland.[11]

When Eardley was staying in the south of France in 1951, her mother informed her that the landlord of the studio might sell it. The price of £200 was beyond

Fig.4 | Eardley's studio, 204 St James Road, on the junction with McAslin Street, Townhead, Glasgow, *c.*1965
Joan Eardley Archive, Scottish National Gallery of Modern Art, Edinburgh
Photo by George Oliver

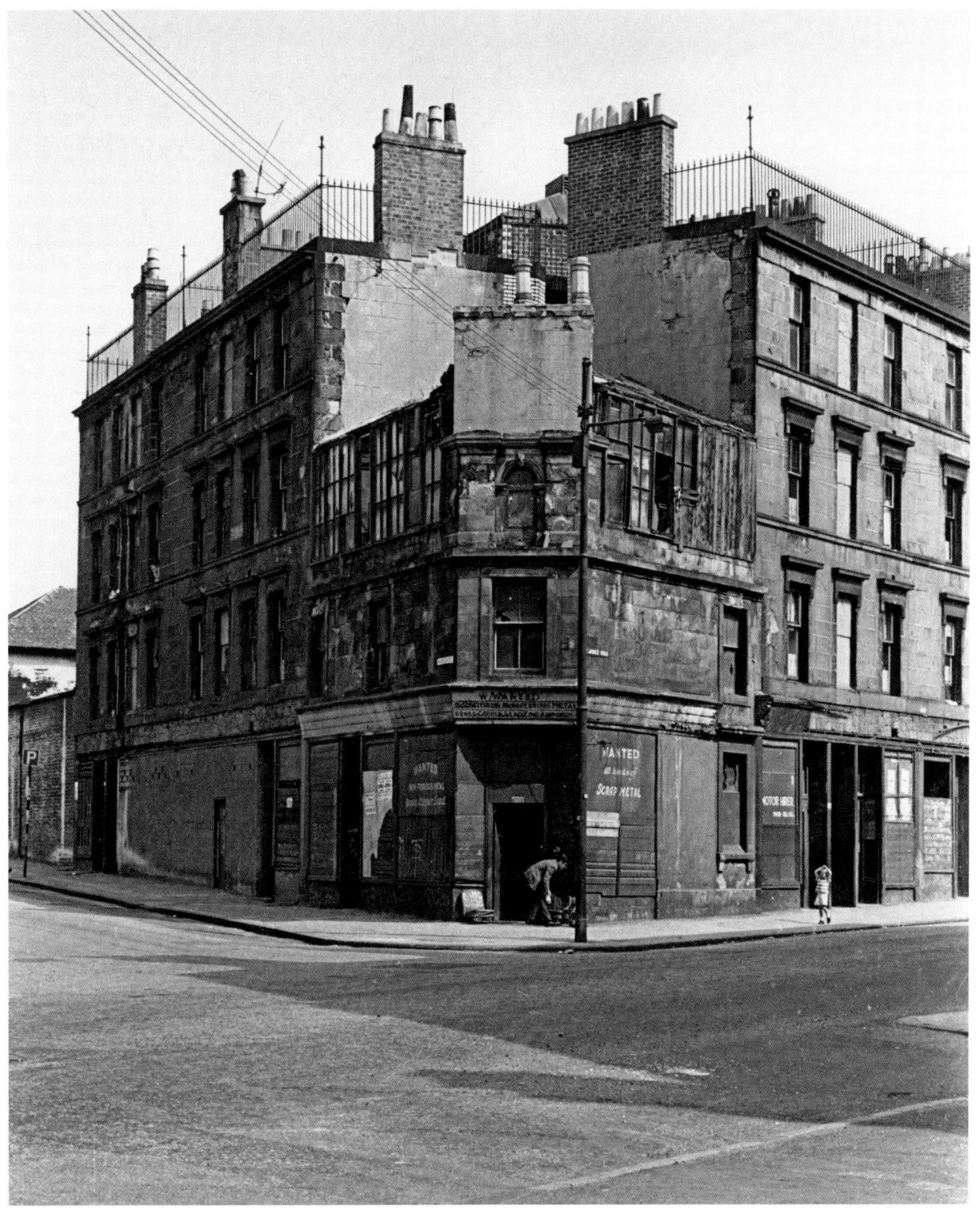

Eardley's means and the news caused her considerable anxiety, as she explained to her mother:

> *It's desperate to lose the studio ... because I had become attached to it, and it has been so useful to my work in that it is so near the slum parts that I draw. And so easy to get the slum children to come up. And I have become known in the district, in George St, and all the streets round about. So that I would regret very much losing it, as I think it would be impossible to get another one in this type of district. ... my work is among the towny things, particularly places like the tenements which are around my studio. I know that now – much as I love the country and country things my work does lie in the slummy parts – unfortunately!*[12]

In 1953 Eardley did in fact find another studio just a few streets north-east of the first one, at 204 St James Road, on the junction with McAslin Street, in Townhead [fig.4].[13] Two floors up, the studio had belonged to a photographer and was glazed on the roof and along two sides. It was above a scrap-metal merchant's and was rudimentary, as can be seen from photographs taken by Eardley's friend, Audrey Walker. William Buchanan describes it as a wedge-shaped room, divided by a wooden wall down the centre, with a kitchen sink, a large stove, and a bed against the partition wall.[14] The gallery-owner Robert Henriques visited her there and described the studio as 'a place of excessive squalor in a slum tenement, filled with pictures, sketches and drawings of the neighbourhood and its occupants.'[15]

Eardley's star continued to rise: Glasgow Art Gallery purchased one of her earliest Catterline paintings, *Catterline Coastguard Cottages*, 1951 [plate 49], while *A Carter and his Horse* [plate 6], exhibited at the Royal Scottish Academy in 1952, was bought by the

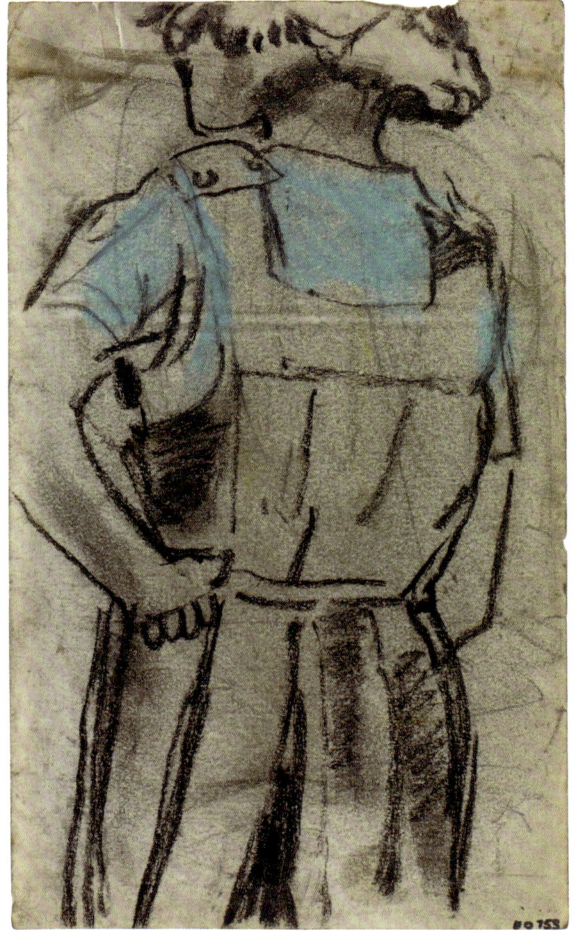

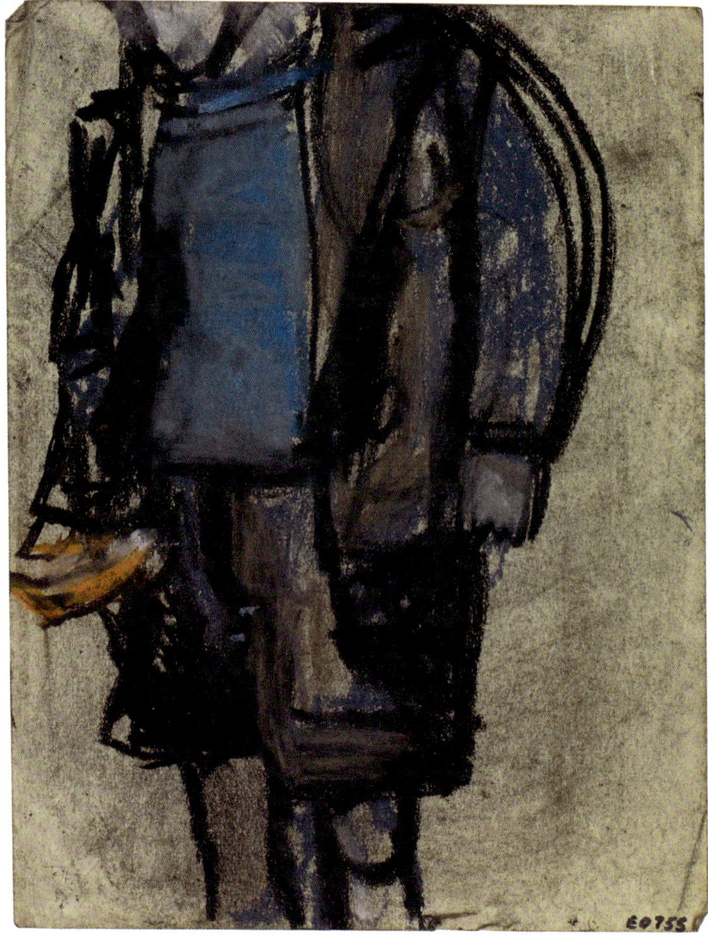

Fig.5 | Joan Eardley, *Study of a Girl in a Gymslip*, c.1955–60
Chalk on paper, 22 × 13.8 cm
Scottish National Gallery of Modern Art, Edinburgh

Fig.6 | Joan Eardley, *Study of a Boy in Blazer and Shorts*, c.1955–60
Pastel on paper, 16.3 × 12.8 cm
Scottish National Gallery of Modern Art, Edinburgh

Ministry of Works (it is now part of the Government Art Collection). This and other major Glasgow paintings that she produced during this period – such as *Back Street Bookie*, 1952 [plate 7] and *A Glasgow Lodging*, 1953 [plate 9] – depict adults. *A Glasgow Lodging* shows the artist Angus Neil in his studio at 98 Montrose Street, also in Townhead. They had met on a postgraduate year at the College of Art in Hospitalfield, Arbroath, in 1947. An idiosyncratic character, who delighted and irritated Eardley in equal parts, Neil remained a lifelong friend of hers.

These Glasgow paintings of the early 1950s were done in a measured, methodical way, which recalls some other social realist painting of the period. There is, for example, a rapport with the work of Josef Herman, whom Eardley knew, and also with the 'Kitchen Sink' school of social realists, which included John Bratby, Jack Smith and Derrick Greaves among its number. The defiantly unglamorous *A Stove* [plate 8] of about 1955 is straight out of the 'Kitchen Sink' repertoire (the term was coined by the critic David Sylvester in 1954) but Eardley never mentioned their work in her voluminous correspondence. Her family certainly had left-wing leanings, but when a critic asked her if her work was socially engaged, or should be labelled 'social realist', she replied tartly: 'I would very much dislike to have such an attitude in art.'[16]

Eardley's interest in painting children took off in the mid-1950s; this was partly serendipitous, in that

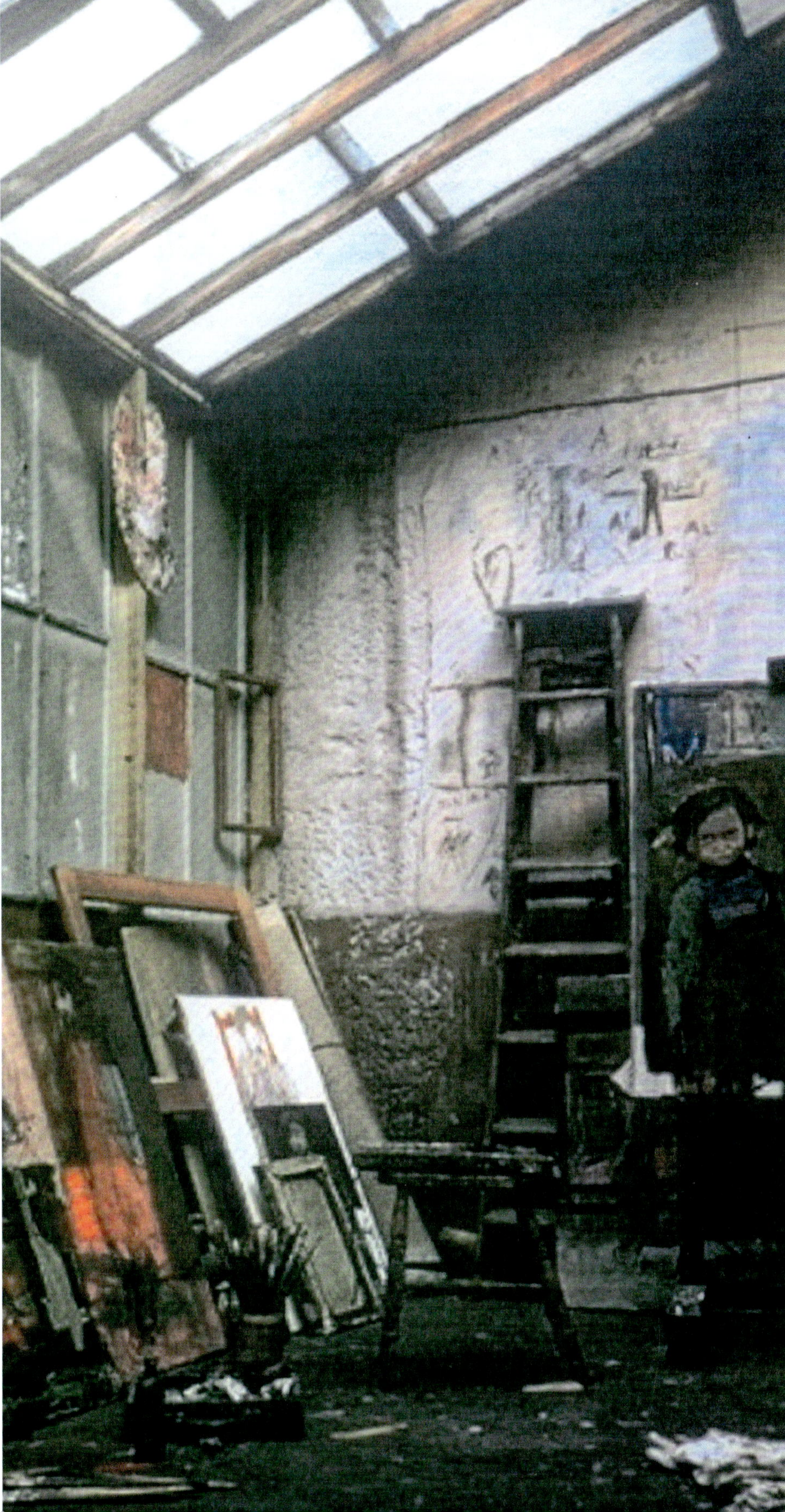

Fig.7 | Eardley's studio at 204 St James Road, *c.*1960
Photo by Audrey Walker, courtesy of The Scottish Gallery, Edinburgh

a large family who lived close by were willing models [figs 5 & 6]. The parents, Jean and Andrew Samson, lived in a two-bedroom tenement flat on the next-to-top floor at 115 Rottenrow. There were twelve children; the boys slept in one room, the girls in the other (the broad age span meant that they were never all there at once), while the parents slept in the living room.[17] Asked how she started painting the local children, Eardley was typically matter-of-fact:

> *I have a studio in Glasgow off Parliamentary Road and some of the children living in the district used to watch me at work. I thought it would be a good idea to paint them. There was only one difficulty – if they didn't sit still I couldn't paint them, and when they did sit still they tended to become rather dismal in expression.*[18]

The eldest of the children, Andrew Samson, first met Eardley in Hopetoun Place, off Rottenrow, around 1955, when he was about twelve.[19] He was intrigued by the sight of an artist pushing her easel around in a pushchair and drawing in the street. He asked to be painted and was soon posing for Eardley on a regular basis. She gave him sixpence a time, or occasionally a shilling for a long pose of up to ninety minutes. Apart from the interest of working for an artist, there was the added bonus of a mug of tea and a syrup and cheese sandwich. Andrew's brothers and sisters began posing for Eardley too: suddenly she had a ready and willing supply of girls and boys of different ages to model for her. They would go to her studio after school. Ann McKenna (née Samson) recalls:

> *To get to her studio you went up a spiral stair ... She gave us paper to draw and toys to keep us quiet. 'Sit in peace', she'd say as she was drawing us. She'd buy clothes for us*

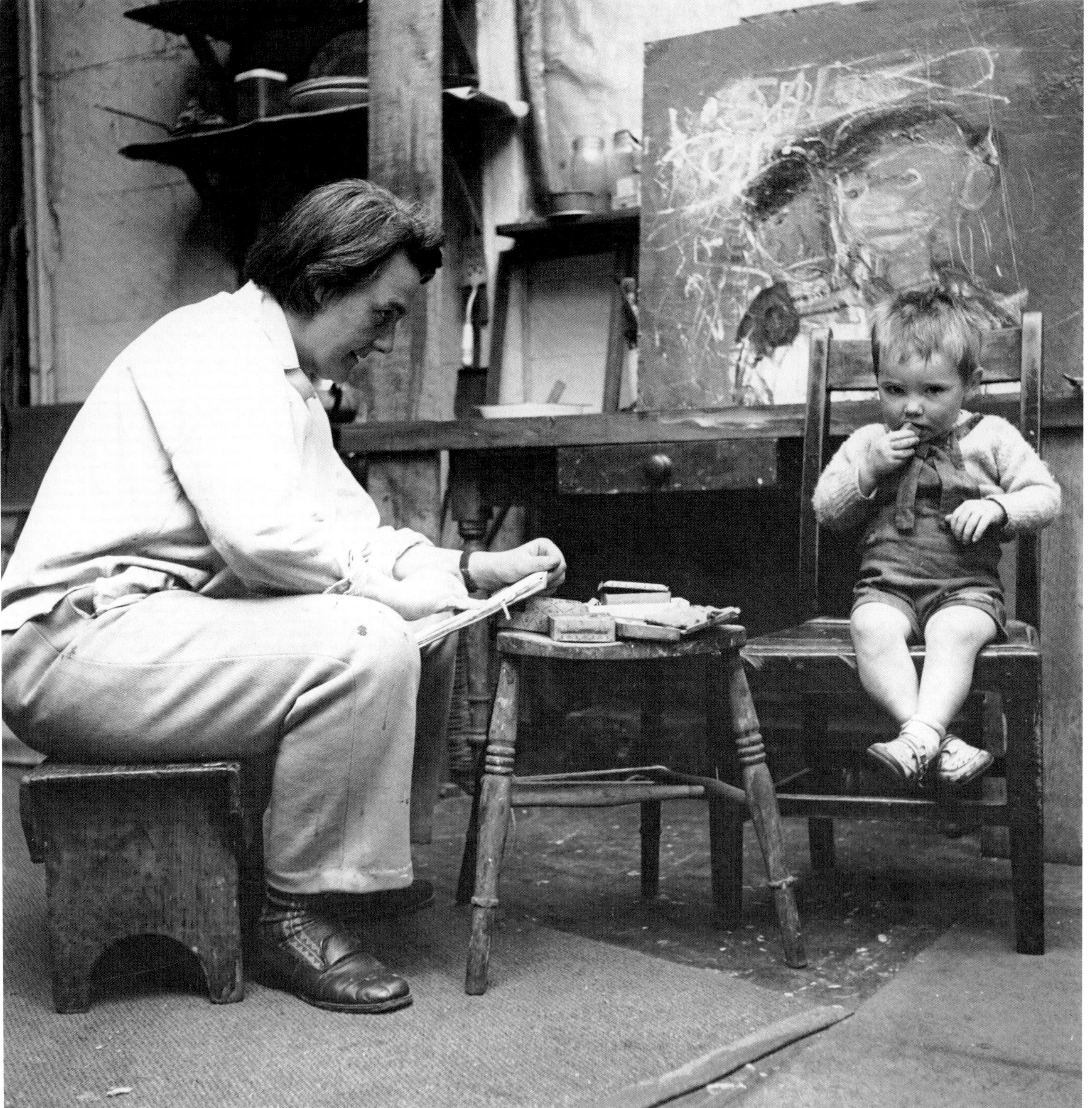

Fig.8 | Eardley sketching in her studio at 204 St James Road, *c.*1960

Joan Eardley Archive, Scottish National Gallery of Modern Art, Edinburgh
Photo by Audrey Walker

Fig.9 | Eardley sketching in the street, Glasgow, *c.*1955
Photo by Audrey Walker, courtesy of The Scottish Gallery, Edinburgh

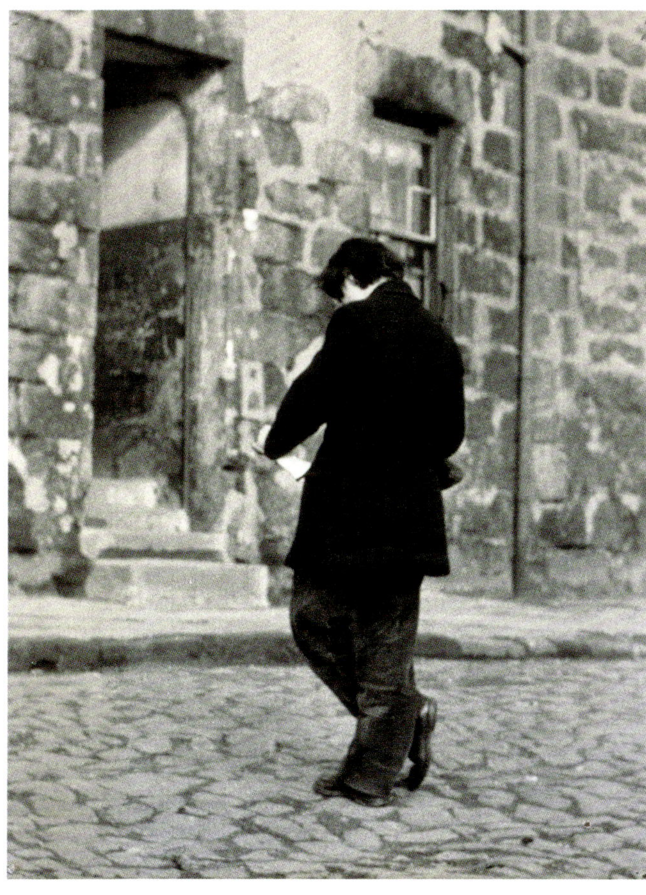

> *from second-hand shops to clothe us for the pictures. She wanted us to be in the same clothes each time. She didn't have much money. We used to get 3d off Joan for posing for her and went to Miss Bickett's to buy sweets, penny drinks and halfpenny trays and penny trays. We got Highland caramel toffees, whoppers, monkey bars and Irn Bru. It was candle lit. It didn't have electricity. She was really serious. 'Just stand at peace', she would say. She was never cheeky or angry.*[20]

After a while the floor would be littered with the children's drawings. Andrew often had the job of clearing them up and putting them on the fire, and frequently added Eardley's own drawings to the flames, at her request: 'I'm finished with them', she would say.[21] Outdoors, her favourite streets for drawing were close to the big Maternity Hospital on Rottenrow and the steep streets around Hume Street, Tarbet Street,

Fig.10 | Joan Eardley, *Yellow Sky and Gas Lamps*, *c.*1955
Pastel on four sheets of paper, 14.5 × 44.5 cm
Scottish National Gallery of Modern Art, Edinburgh

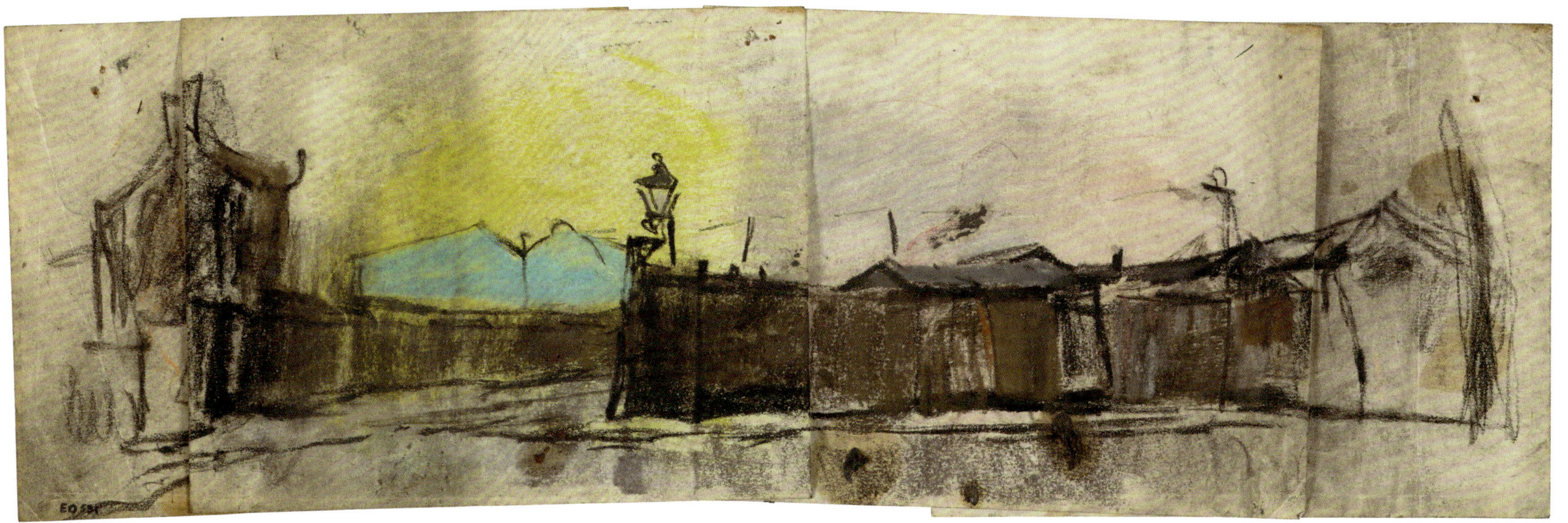

Fig.11 | Two girls, *c.*1955–60
Joan Eardley Archive, Scottish National Gallery of Modern Art, Edinburgh
Photo by Joan Eardley

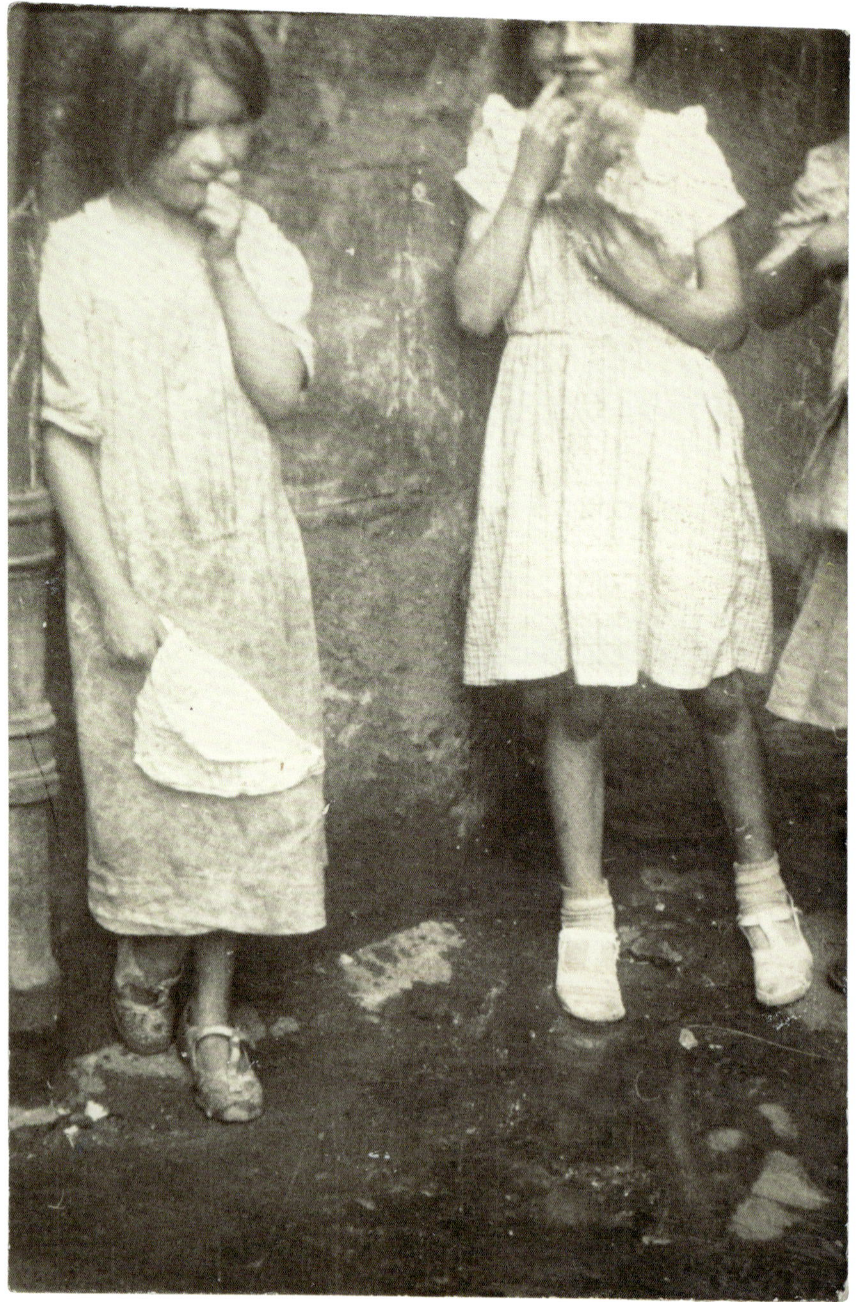

Hopetoun Place and Balmano Brae.[22] A number of the drawings, gouaches and paintings show a confectioner's shop on Rottenrow and Donald Campbell's grocery store at No.144, and between them at No.146 is the entrance to Angel Close, with a medieval sculpture of an angel above the entrance [fig.2, plates 21–24]. Both shops closed in 1954 and by the time Eardley painted them they were derelict.[23] It was evidently the dilapidated state of the shops that appealed to her. Walker took a number of photographs of the two shops, and these may have been used by Eardley in preparing her compositions.[24] Other photographs taken by Walker, possibly at Eardley's request, show graffiti on walls; segments of the same graffiti incorporating the letters 'MG' then appeared in several of Eardley's works [plates 29 & 30].

She would habitually draw standing up, and the constant and intense action of looking up at her subject and then down at the paper aggravated, or possibly caused, a slipped disc.[25] This became particularly painful in 1956 and 1957, when she often wore a surgical collar. Cordelia Oliver, one of Eardley's art-school friends and later a noted art critic, reported that the pain became so acute that Eardley drew outdoors less and less and started using a camera instead.[26] The small, mainly square-format photographs were used as study material for watercolours and paintings done in the studio [fig.11]. Several drawings and a few paintings are based on these small black-and-white photographs [plates 25–28 & 32–35].

From the late 1950s Eardley spent increasing amounts of time in Catterline, but she returned periodically to the Townhead studio. In the early 1960s she executed a series of paintings depicting two children standing against a wall – often the red wall of the scrap-metal shop below her studio, on the corner of St James Road and McAslin Street [fig.4 & plates 45–48]. The shop's advertising, specifically the word 'METAL', appears on the wall in one of the works [plate 46]. This series of paintings features the Samson children, particularly Pat and Ann – Pat is easily recognisable by her red hair and pronounced squint. Paintings from the early 1960s incorporate collage elements, especially newspaper and sweet-wrappers. Bizarrely, Gustav Delbanco, of Roland, Browse and Delbanco, her London gallery, took offence at the collage items and asked Eardley to remove them, which she declined to do. But when she showed him how they might be scraped off with a penknife, he decided to do it himself. Not surprisingly she was furious: 'Some paintings should now be signed Delbanco and Eardley. God knows what desecration will be done tomorrow as I am not going in tomorrow.'[27]

By this time the city planners were putting forward radical visions for the development of the city. The first of these post-war schemes was produced by Robert Bruce. His plan, published as The Bruce Report in 1945, proposed the destruction of the entire city centre, replacing it with an ultra-modern city in the Modernist style and a motorway interchange. The old cobbled streets that had served well for horses and carts were inadequate for modern vehicles, and the proposal was to sweep everything away. The Bruce plan was superseded by the more wide-reaching Clyde Valley Regional plan. Wide-scale demolition began in Townhead during Eardley's time, with shops – such as the confectioner's on Rottenrow – closing before being razed. Almost all of the buildings and roads in Townhead were demolished.

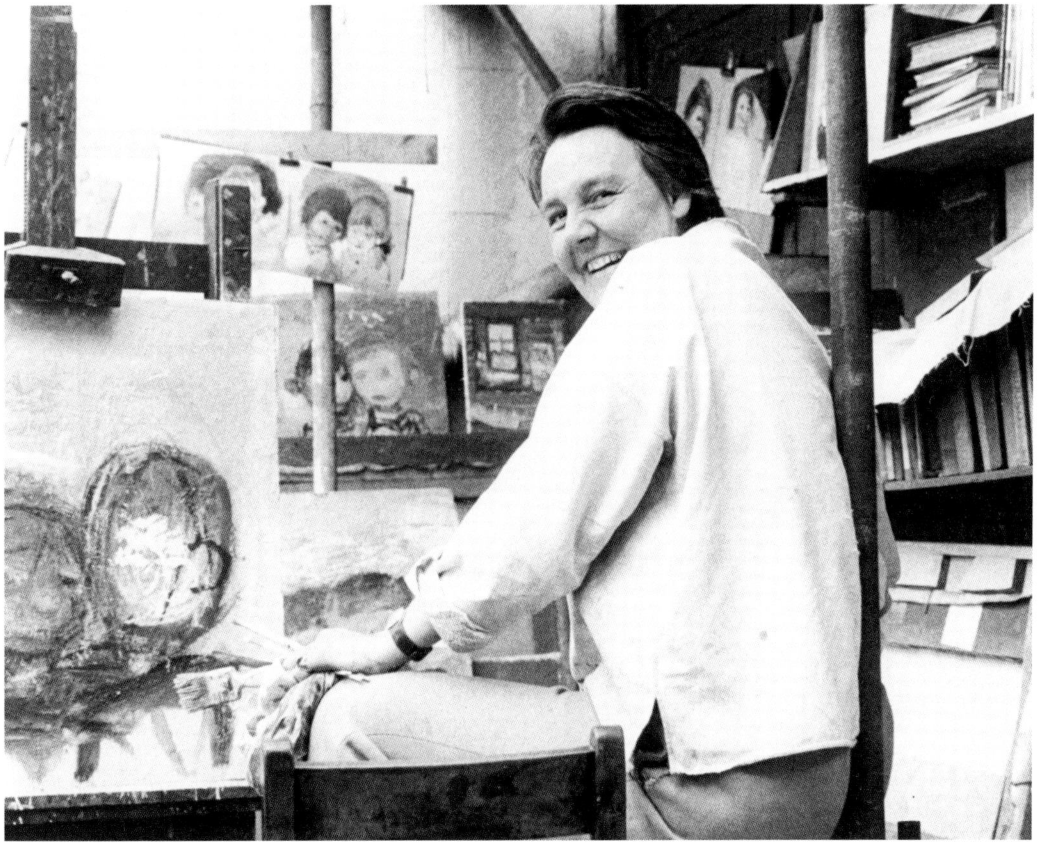

Fig.12 | Eardley in her studio, 1962
Scottish National Portrait Gallery, Edinburgh
Photo by Oscar Marzaroli

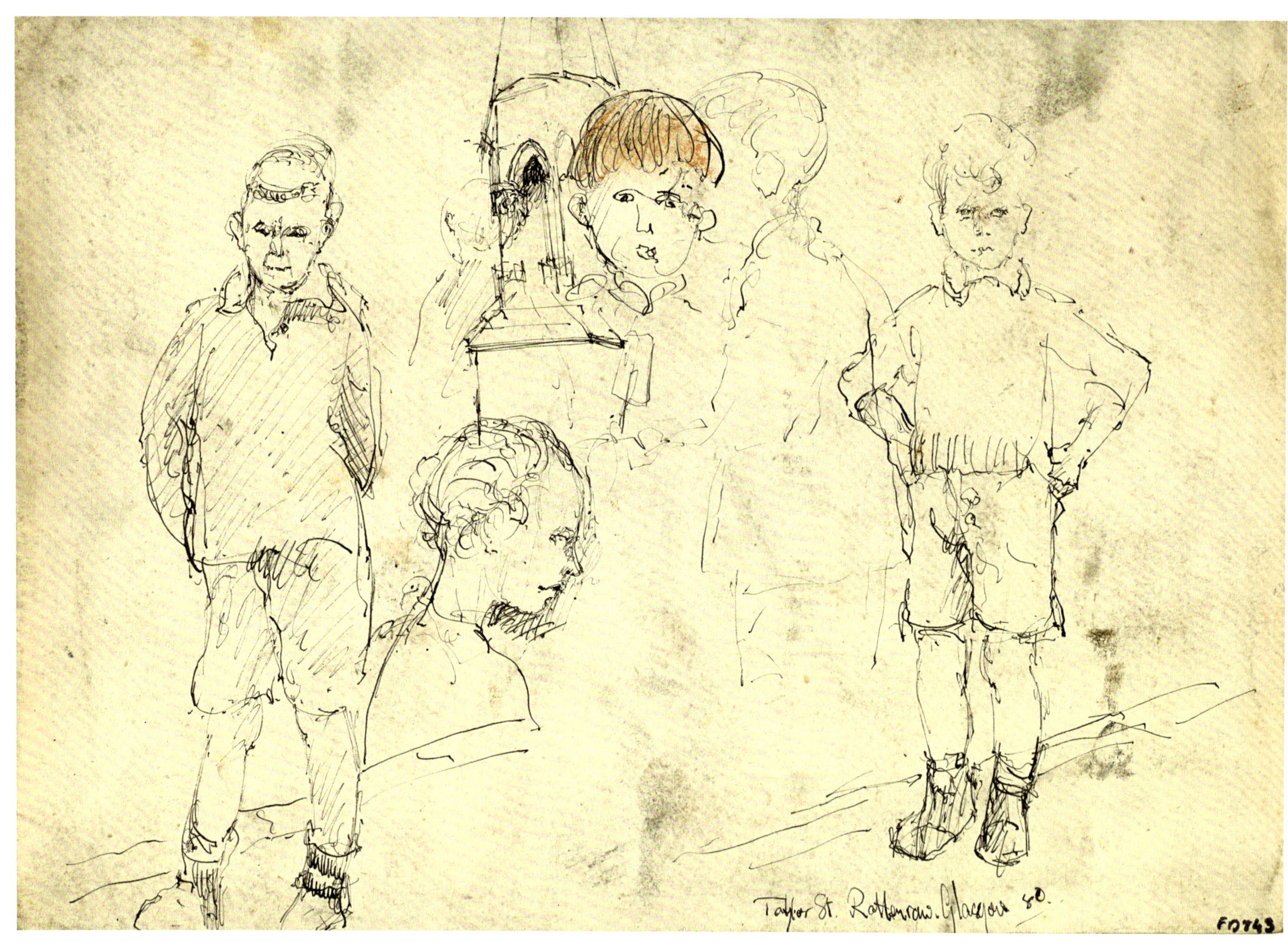

1 *Five Studies of Children, Taylor Street, Rottenrow, Glasgow*, 1940

Pen and black ink and red chalk on paper, 17.7 × 25.3 cm
Scottish National Gallery of Modern Art, Edinburgh
Presented by the artist's sister, Mrs P.M. Black, 1987

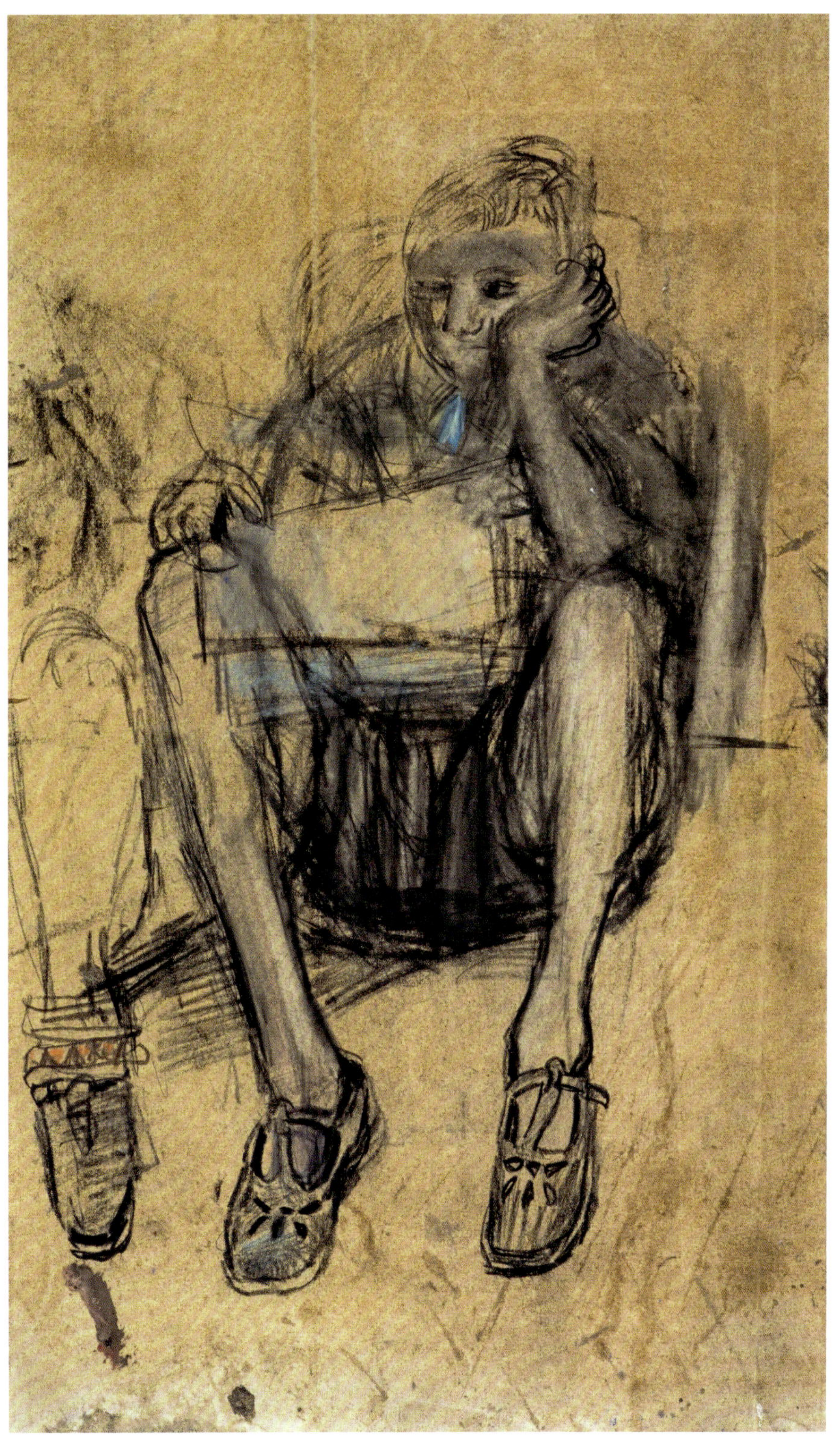

Townhead and Children

Eardley drew children right from the start of her career; her sister recalled that she did so when they lived in Blackheath in London in the 1930s, before they moved to Glasgow.[28] She drew children in Rottenrow, Townhead in 1940 when she was a student at the Glasgow School of Art [plate 1]. Paintings of children were shown in Eardley's solo exhibition at the Gaumont Cinema in Aberdeen in 1950 and she exhibited portraits of boys from Rottenrow at the Society of Scottish Artists and the Royal Scottish Academy shows in 1951. However, in the early 1950s children were just one of a number of subjects she treated, including adults, Glasgow tenements and landscape.

Children became the main focus of Eardley's Glasgow work in the mid-1950s, thanks to her rapport with the Samson children. She drew the children in the street and in her studio; they are usually shown isolated, against an indeterminate background, so it is impossible to tell whether they are inside or outside. Some of the pastel drawings were done on sandpaper, in order to catch as much of the rich pigment as possible. It is notable that few of the drawings seem to have been completed with particular paintings in mind. She made thousands of quick sketches outdoors and many resolved pastel drawings of children indoors. It seems that the former were done as exercises of a sort (often on several sheets, casually stuck or pinned together), while the more resolved drawings were destined for exhibition and sale. The oil paintings were usually done in the studio, although some of the smaller ones seem to have been completed outdoors.

2 *Boy Seated on the Ground, Reading*, *c.*1950
Black chalk and pastel on paper, 52.2 × 31.1 cm
Scottish National Gallery of Modern Art, Edinburgh
Presented by the artist's sister, Mrs P.M. Black, 1987

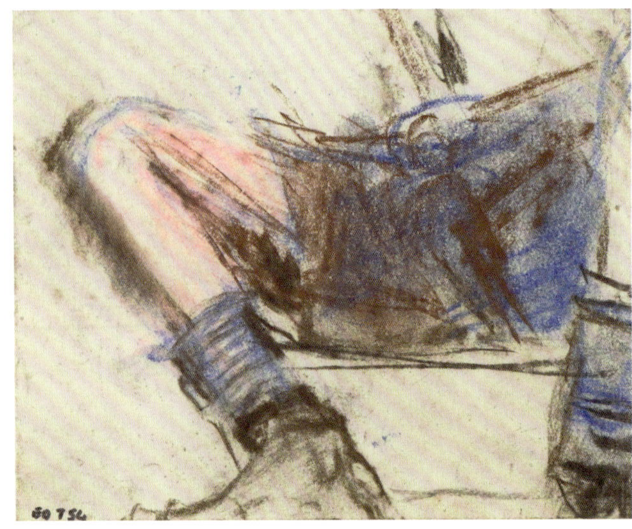

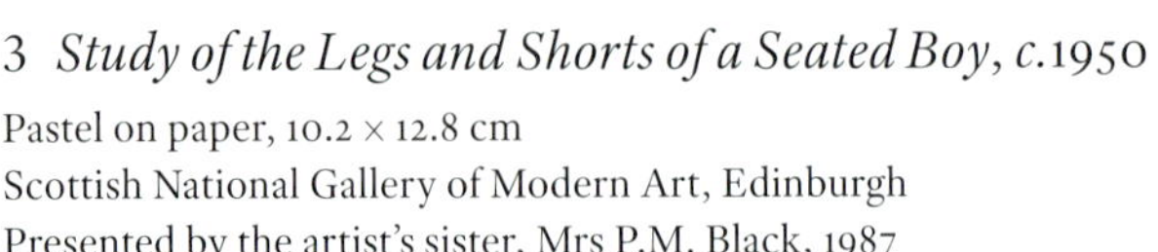

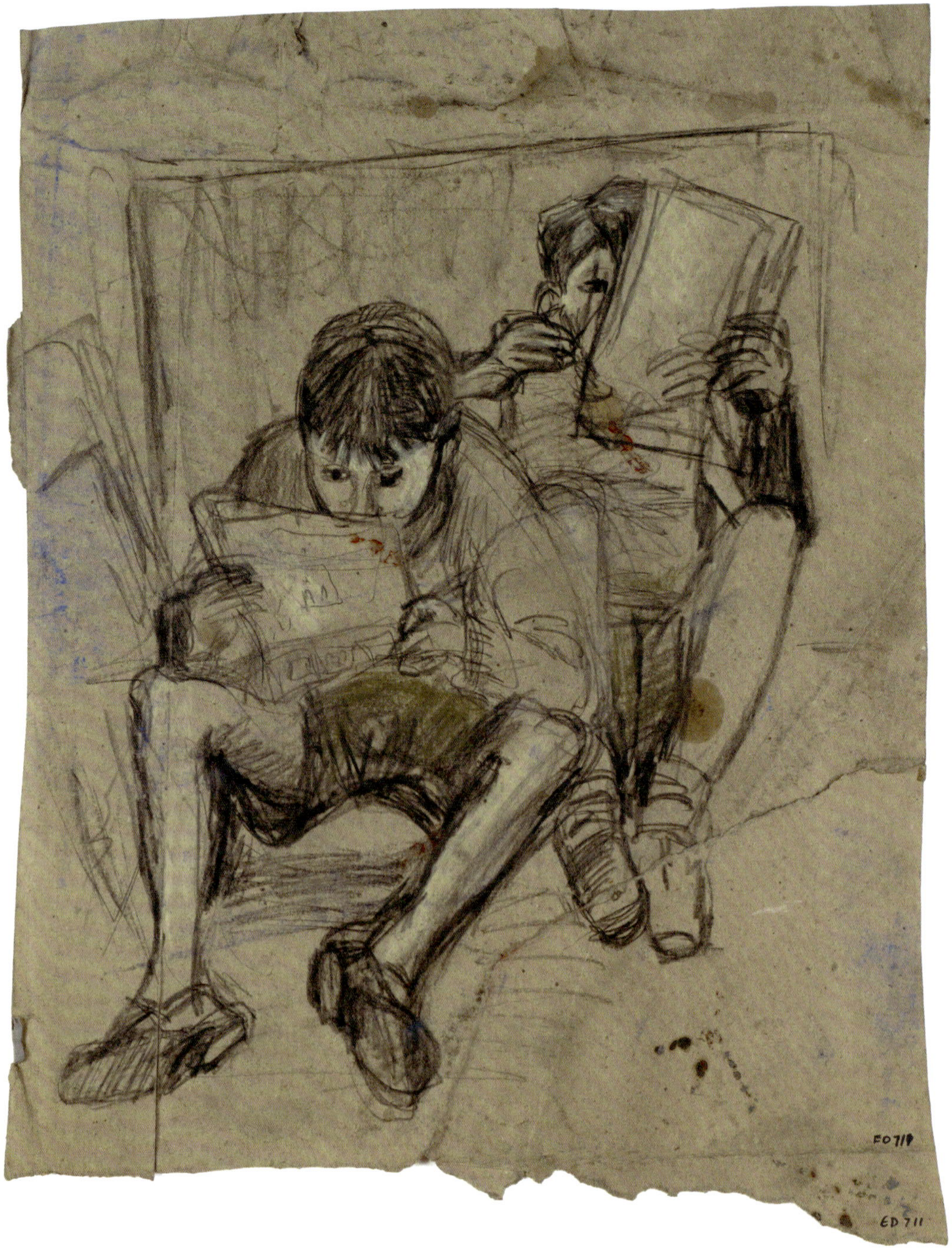

3 *Study of the Legs and Shorts of a Seated Boy*, *c.*1950

Pastel on paper, 10.2 × 12.8 cm
Scottish National Gallery of Modern Art, Edinburgh
Presented by the artist's sister, Mrs P.M. Black, 1987

4 *Two Children Seated on the Ground, Reading Comics*, *c.*1950

Black chalk and pastel on paper, 47.8 × 37.3 cm
Scottish National Gallery of Modern Art, Edinburgh
Presented by the artist's sister, Mrs P.M. Black, 1987

5 *Street Kids*, *c.*1950

Oil on canvas, laid on board, 102.9 × 73.7 cm
Scottish National Gallery of Modern Art, Edinburgh
Purchased with funds given by an anonymous donor, 1964

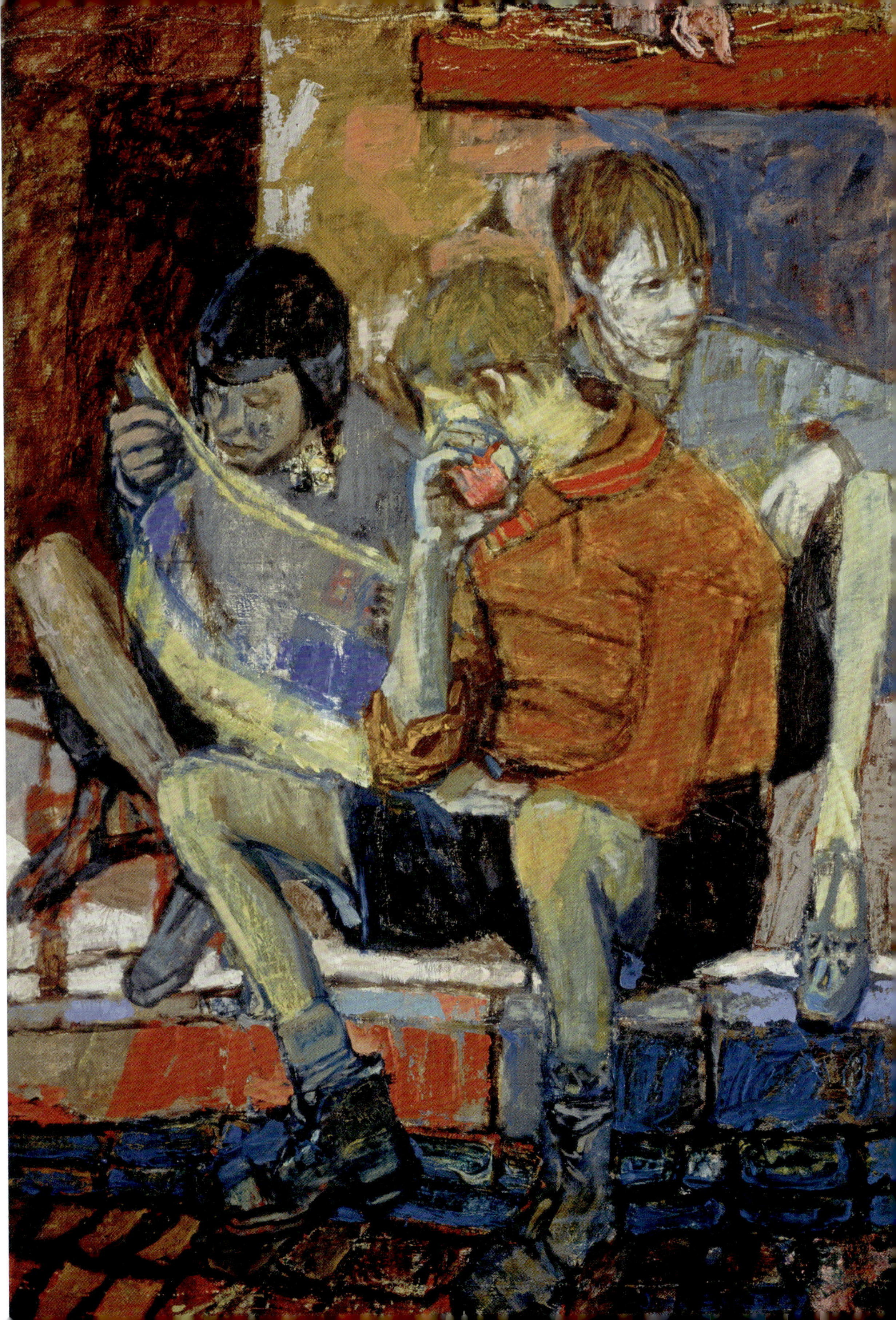

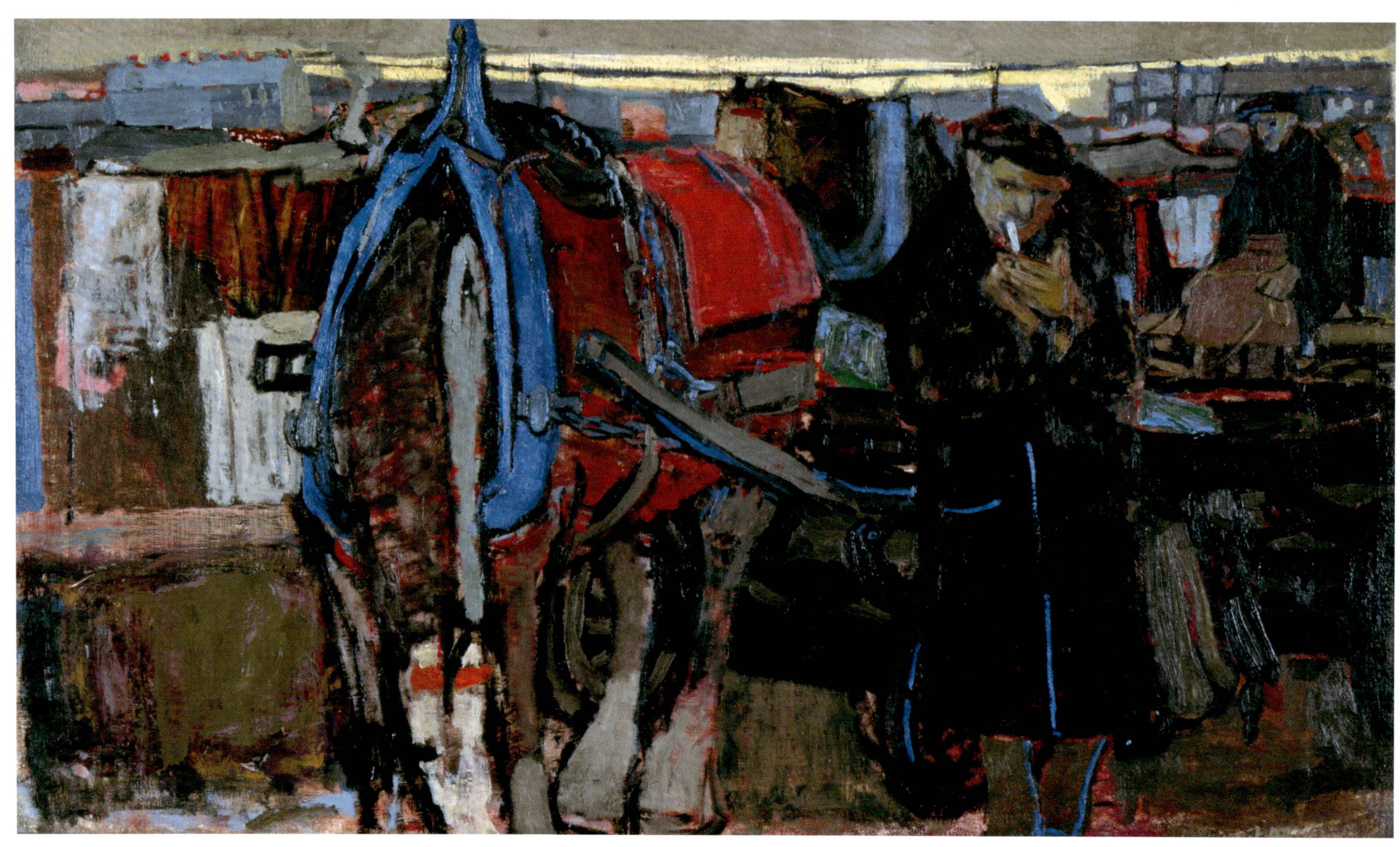

6 *A Carter and his Horse*, 1952

Oil on canvas, 70 × 119 cm
Government Art Collection

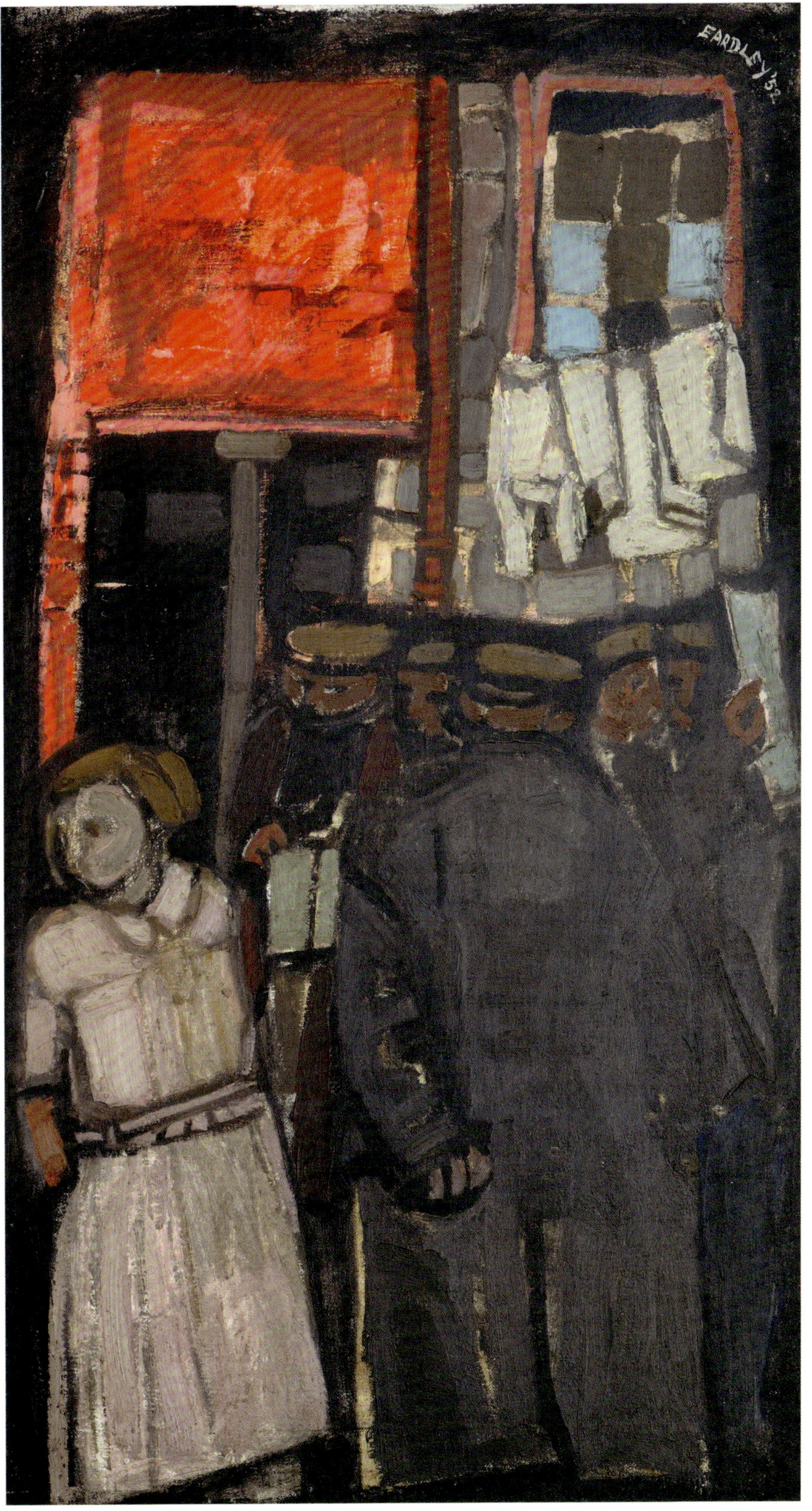

7 *Back Street Bookie*, 1952
Oil on canvas, 107.5 × 59.5 cm
The University of Edinburgh Art Collection

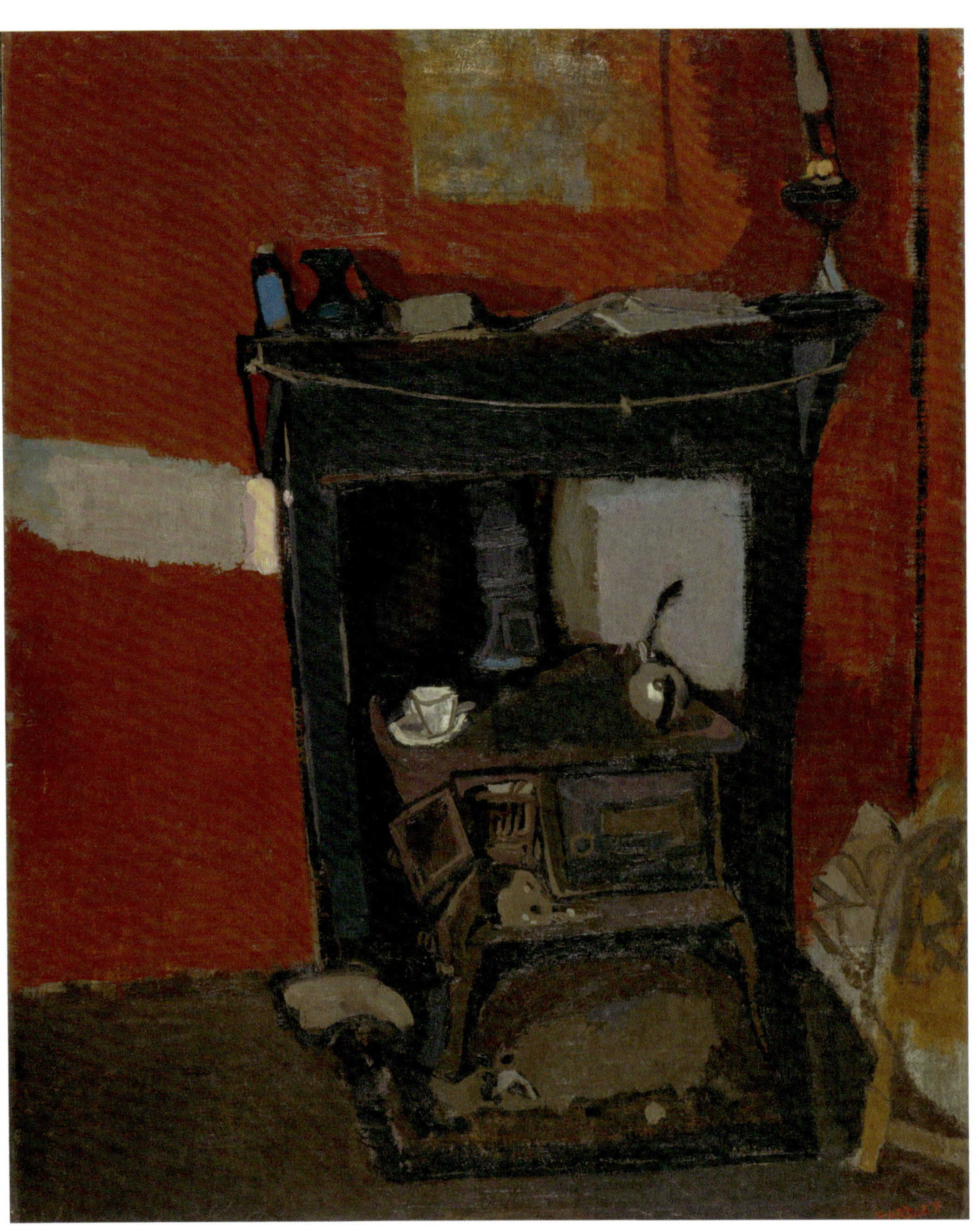

8 *A Stove*, c.1955

Oil on canvas, laid on board, 95.5 × 79 cm
Scottish National Gallery of Modern Art, Edinburgh
Purchased 1984

9 *A Glasgow Lodging*, 1953

Oil on canvas, 112.9 × 92.8 cm
Glasgow Life (Glasgow Museums) on behalf of Glasgow City Council. Presented by the Trustees of the Hamilton Bequest, 1975

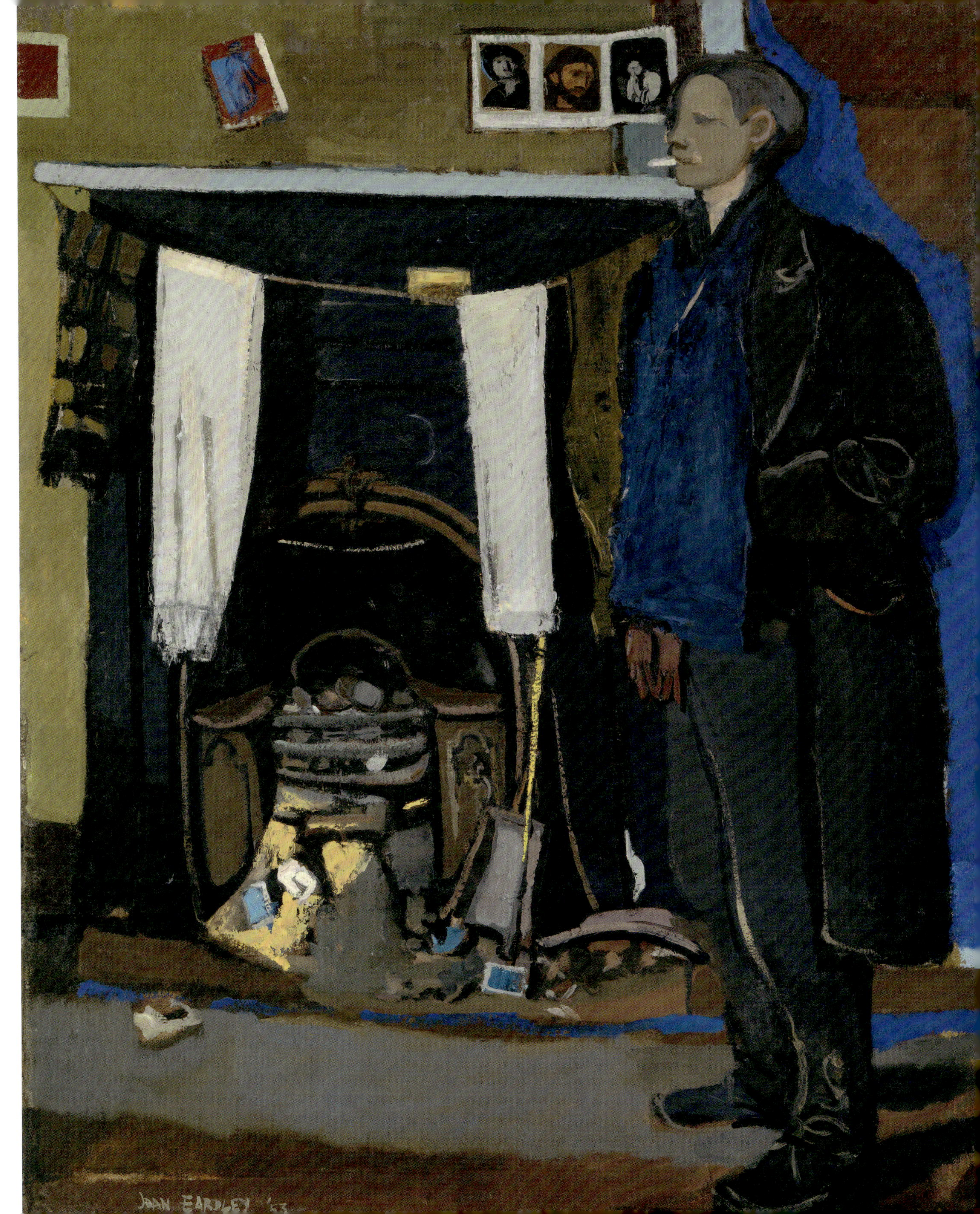
JOAN EARDLEY '53

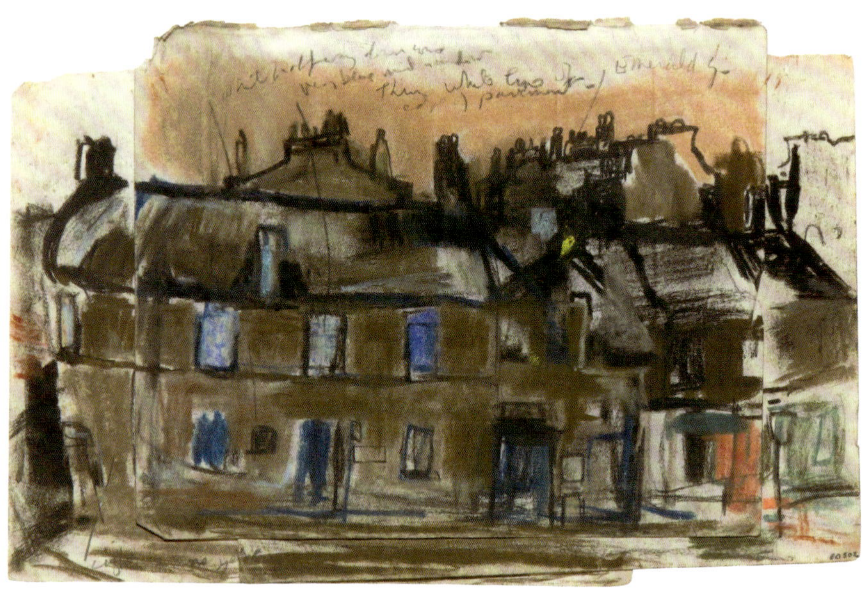

10 *Glasgow Tenements*, c.1955

Pastel on three sheets of paper, 19.5 × 31.3 cm
Cyril Gerber Fine Art, Glasgow

11 *Gable End of a Tenement and Telegraph Poles*, c.1955–60

Pastel with watercolour on paper, 25.3 × 20.3 cm
Scottish National Gallery of Modern Art, Edinburgh
Presented by the artist's sister, Mrs P.M. Black, 1987

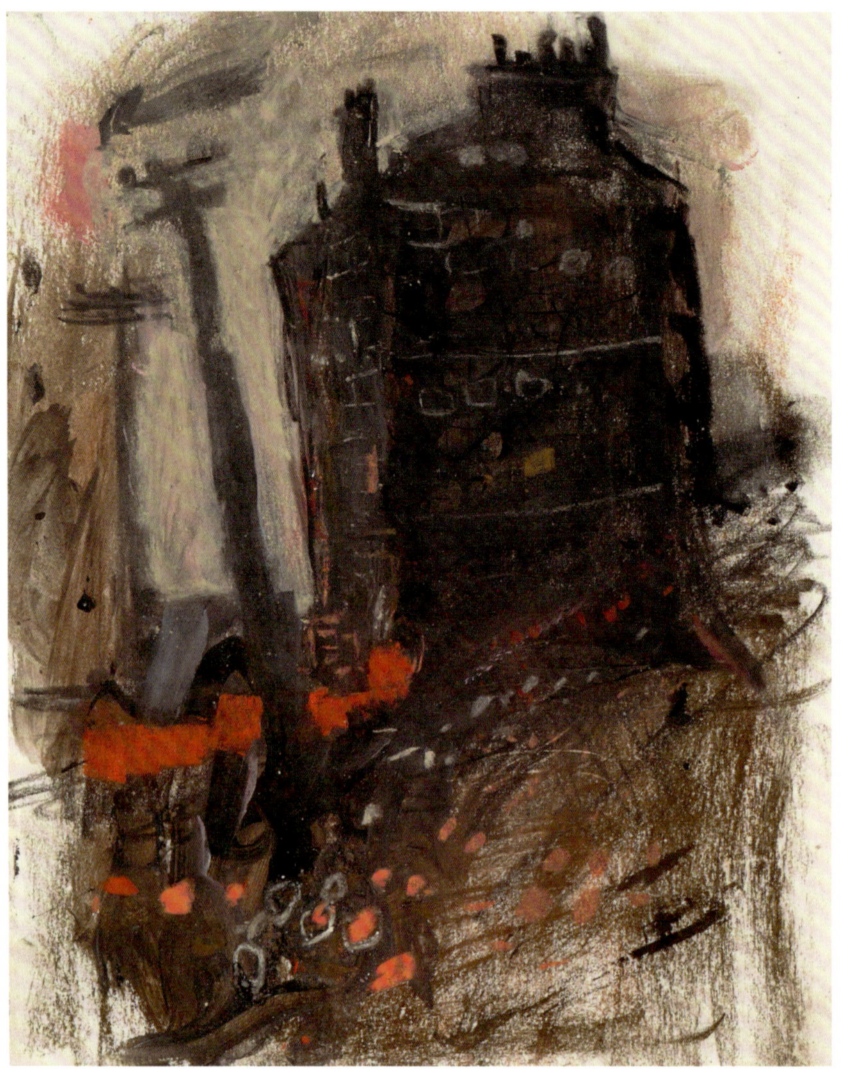

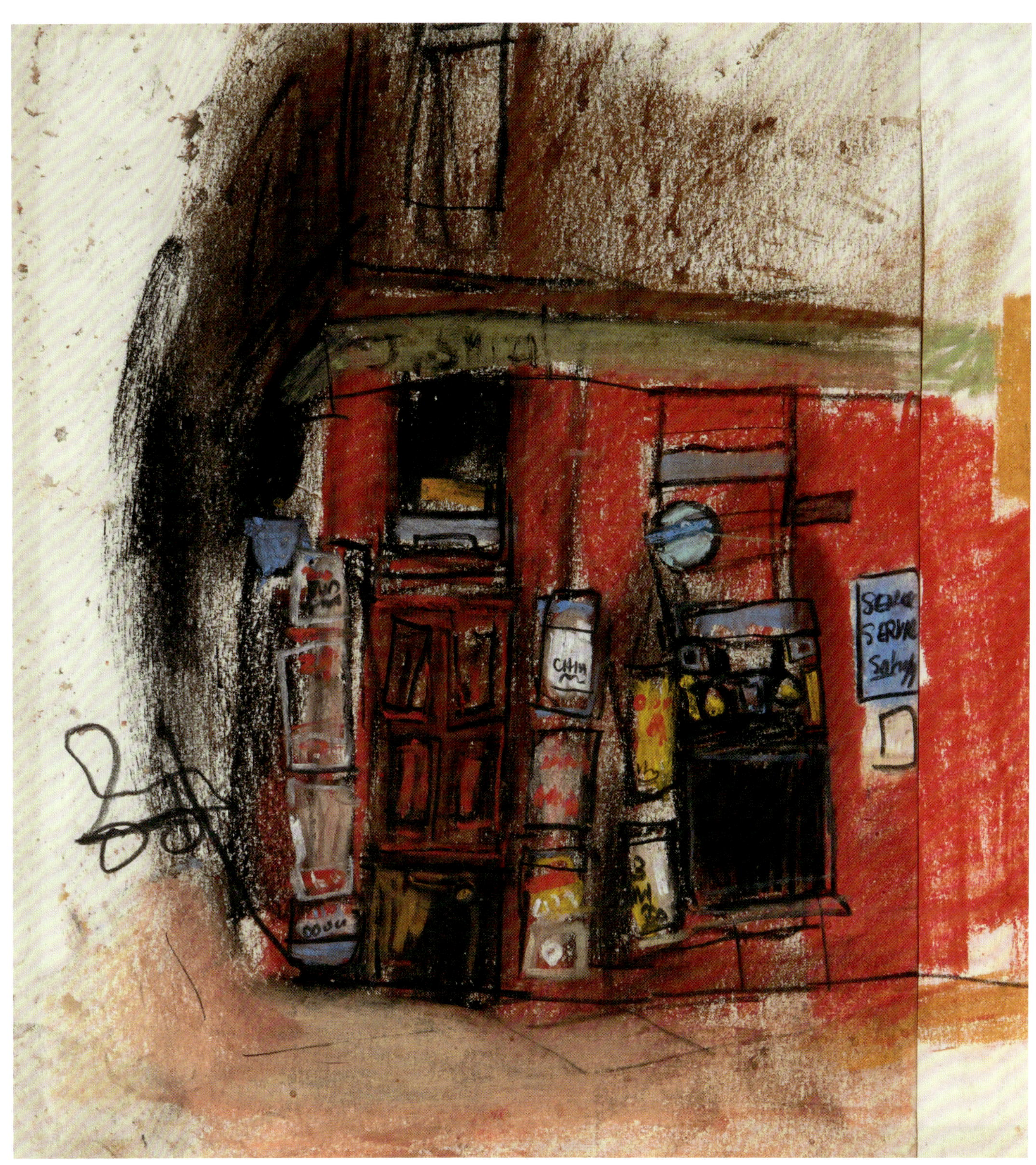

12 *Glasgow Corner Shop*, *c.*1955–60
Pastel on paper, 25.5 × 24.5 cm
Private collection

Children and the Street

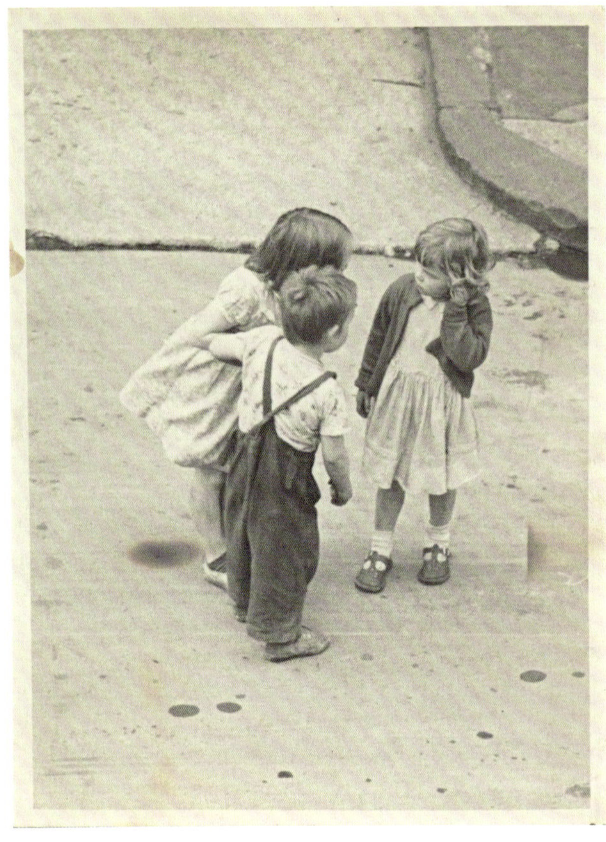

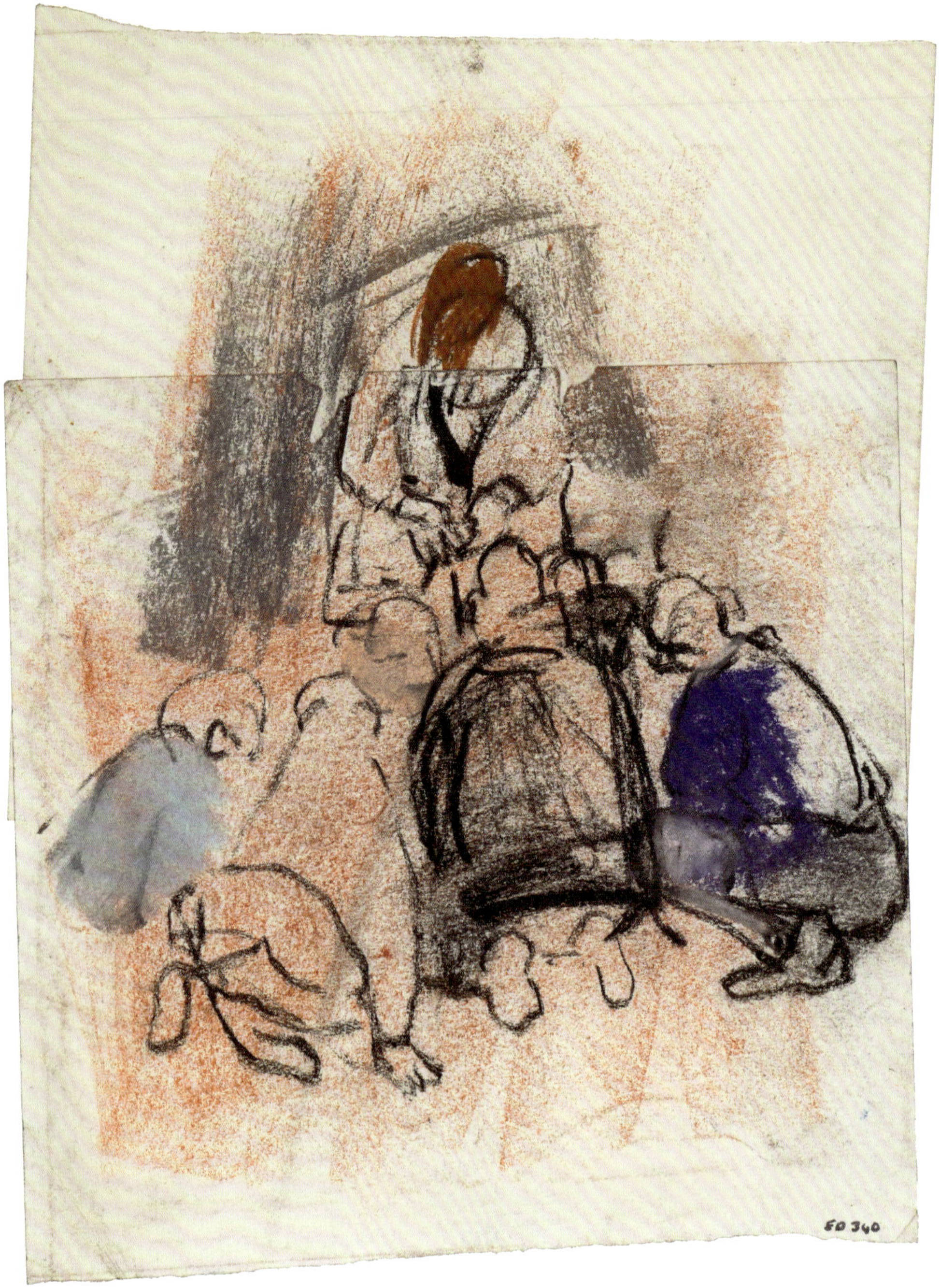

13 *Three Children in the Street*, *c.*1955–60
Silver gelatine print, 21.5 × 16.4 cm
Joan Eardley Archive, Scottish National Gallery of Modern Art, Edinburgh
Presented by the artist's sister, Mrs P.M. Black, 1987

14 *A Group of Children Playing on the Ground*, *c.*1955–60
Pastel on two sheets of paper, 24.1 × 17.4 cm
Scottish National Gallery of Modern Art, Edinburgh
Presented by the artist's sister, Mrs P.M. Black, 1987

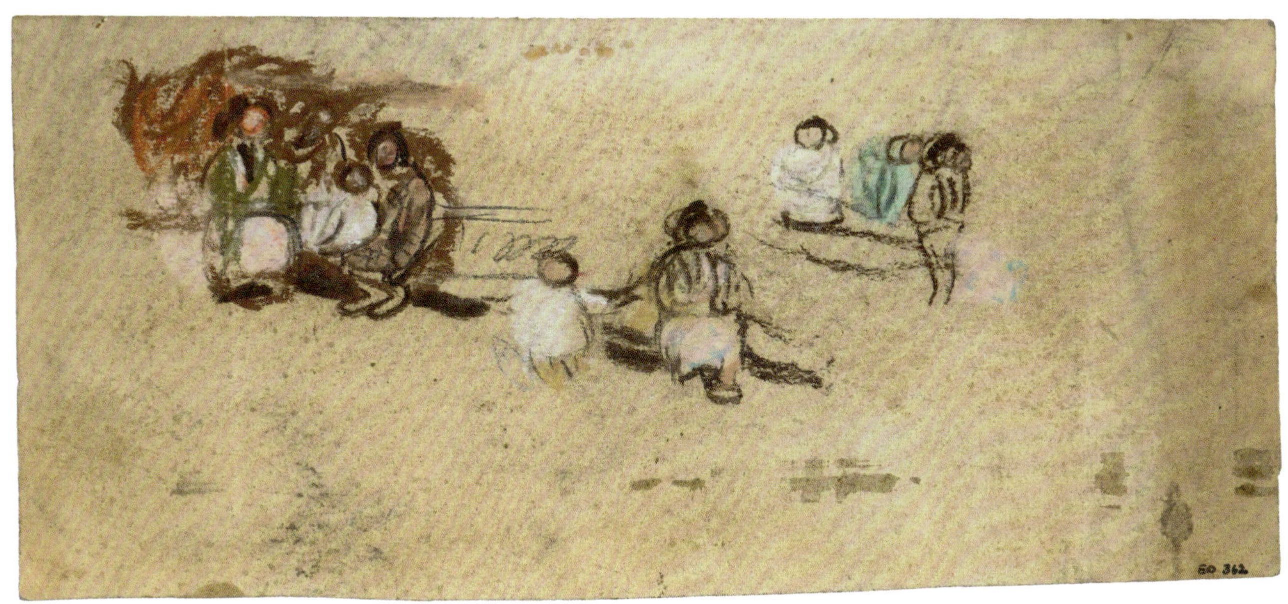

15 *Two Mothers Watching Children Playing*, *c.*1955–60

Pastel on paper, 12.1 × 27 cm
Scottish National Gallery of Modern Art, Edinburgh
Presented by the artist's sister, Mrs P.M. Black, 1987

16 *Children in the Street*, *c.*1955–60

Silver gelatine print, 13.3 × 13.9 cm
Joan Eardley Archive, Scottish National Gallery of Modern Art, Edinburgh
Presented by the artist's sister, Mrs P.M. Black, 1987

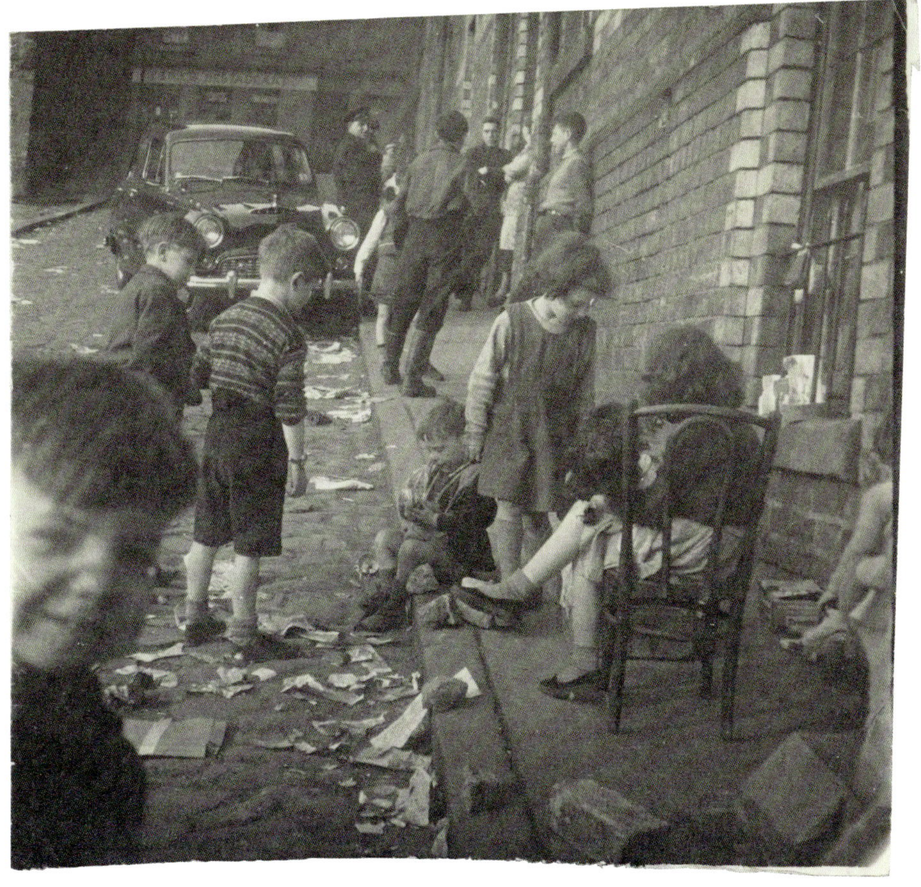

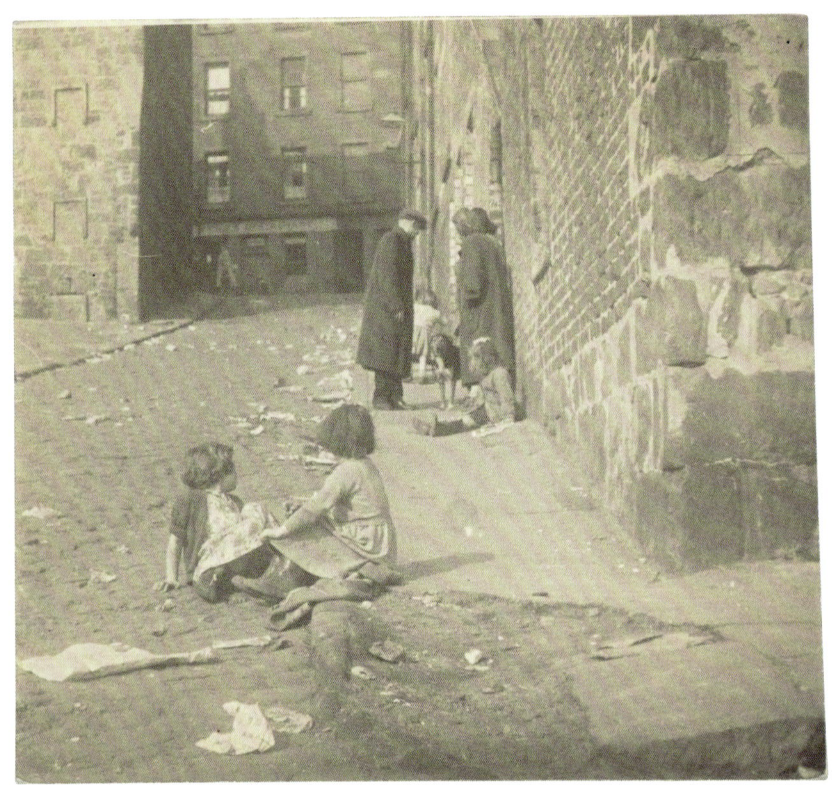

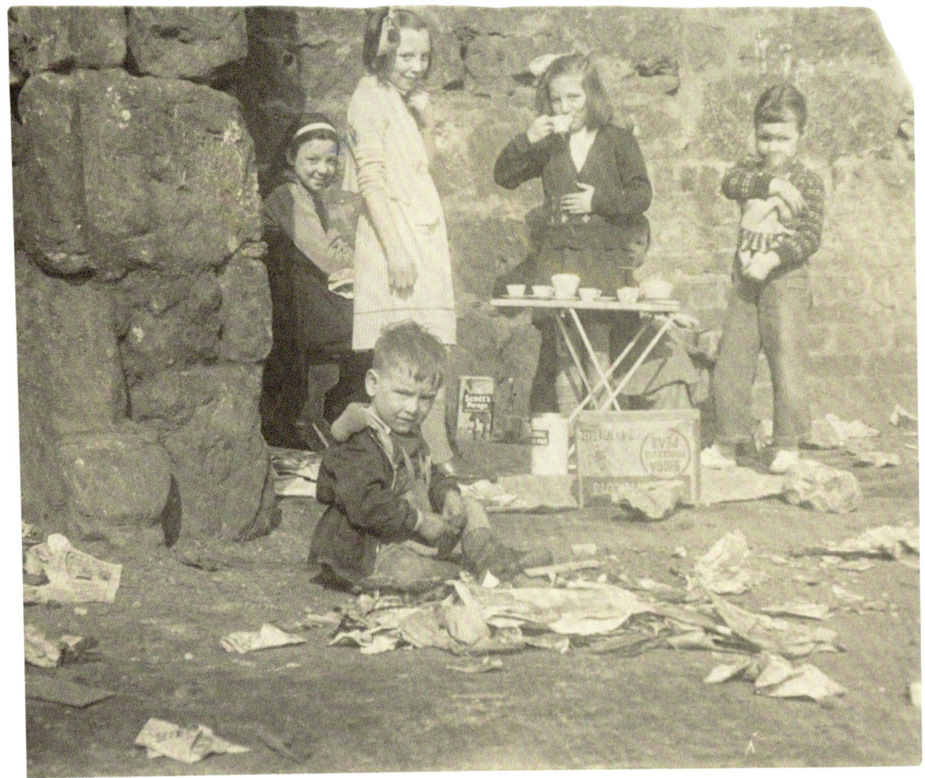

17 *Children and Adults on a Street*, c.1955–60

Silver gelatine print, 16.4 × 18 cm
Joan Eardley Archive, Scottish National Gallery of Modern Art, Edinburgh
Presented by the artist's sister, Mrs P.M. Black, 1987

18 *Children Having a Tea Party in the Street*, c.1955–60

Silver gelatine print, 16 × 19.3 cm
Joan Eardley Archive, Scottish National Gallery of Modern Art, Edinburgh
Presented by the artist's sister, Mrs P.M. Black, 1987

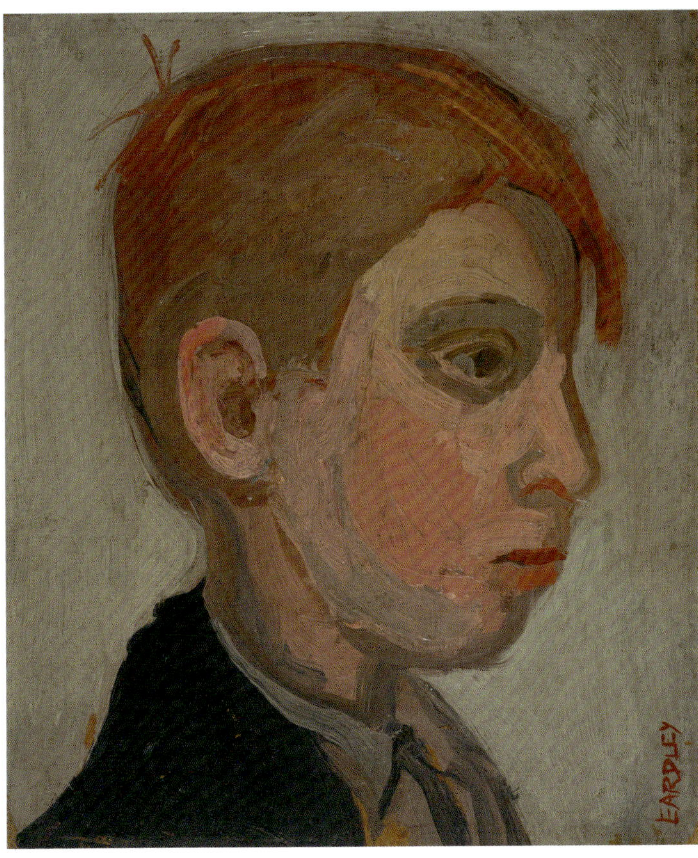

19 *Head of a Boy*, *c.*1953–55

Oil on board, 26.5 × 22.5 cm
Scottish National Gallery of Modern Art, Edinburgh
The Henry and Sula Walton Collection: bequeathed 2012

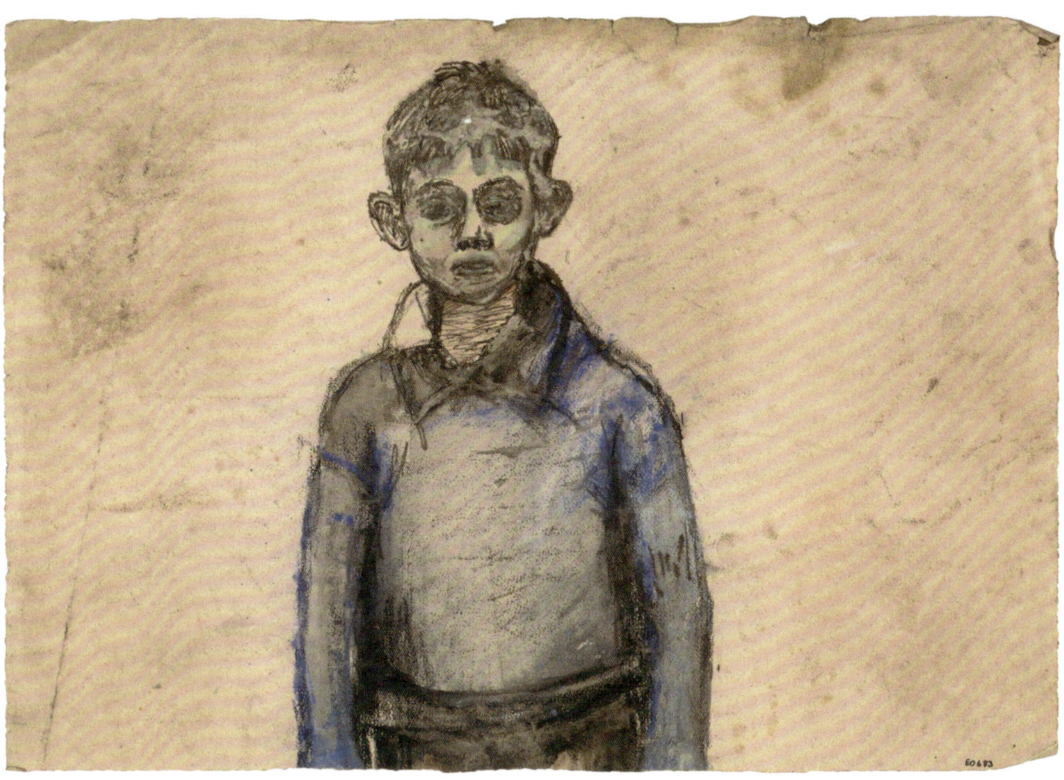

20 *Half-length Study of a Boy*, *c.*1955

Ink, pastel and watercolour on pink paper, 32.6 × 47.6 cm
Scottish National Gallery of Modern Art, Edinburgh
Presented by the artist's sister, Mrs P.M. Black, 1987

21 *Glasgow Street, Rottenrow*, *c.*1955–56
Watercolour and gouache on paper, 26 × 70 cm
Private collection

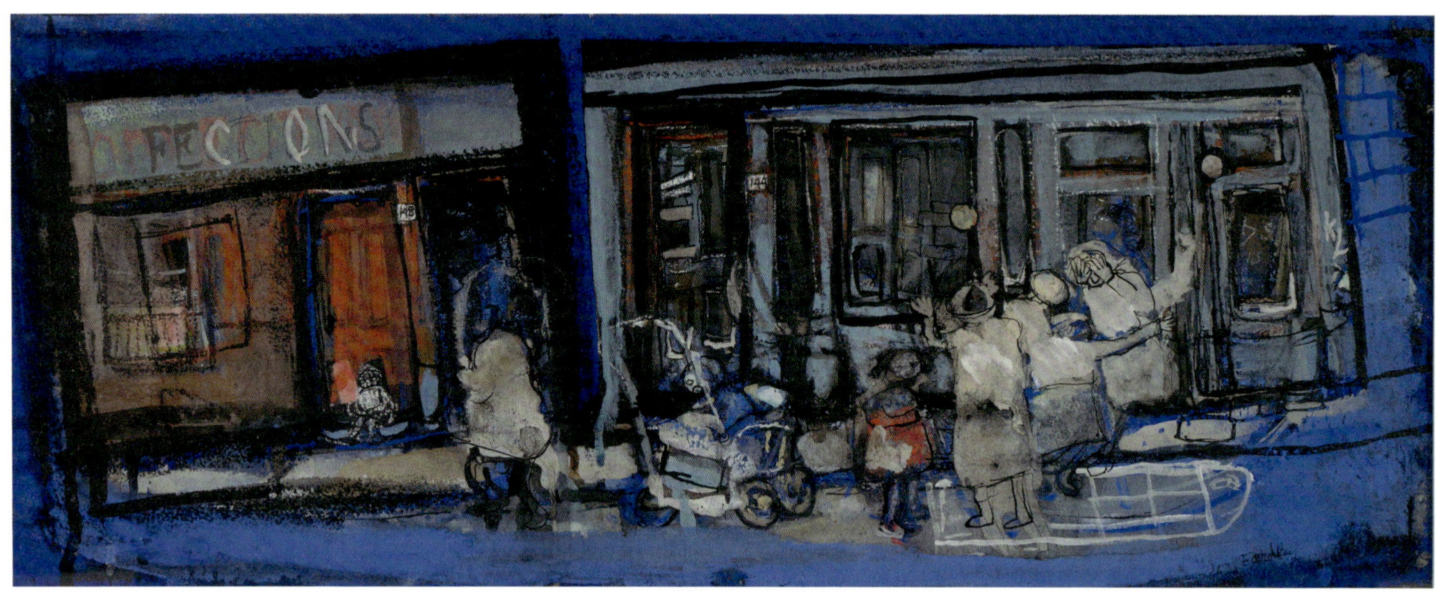

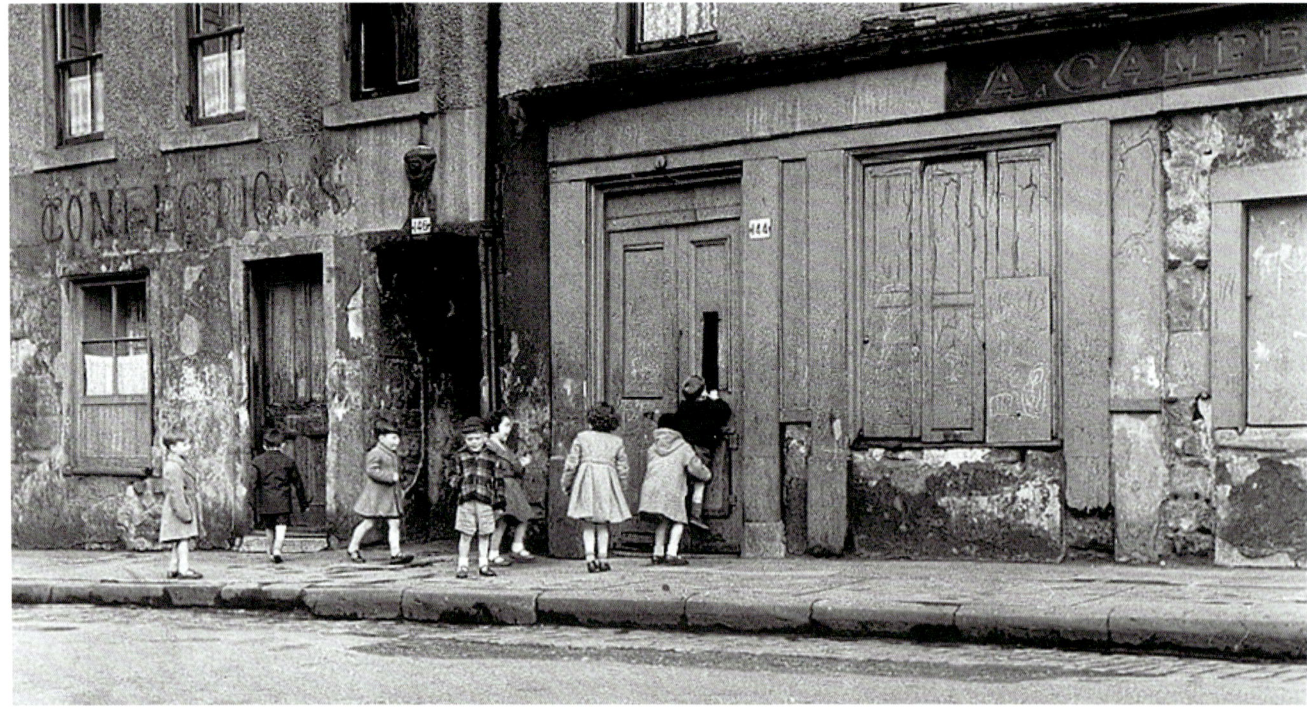

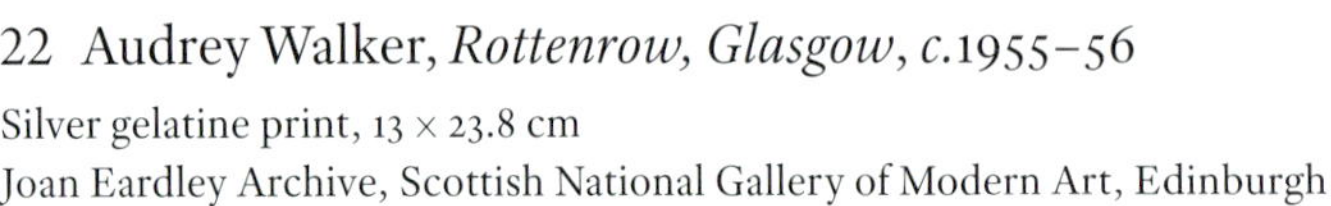

22 Audrey Walker, *Rottenrow, Glasgow*, *c.*1955–56
Silver gelatine print, 13 × 23.8 cm
Joan Eardley Archive, Scottish National Gallery of Modern Art, Edinburgh

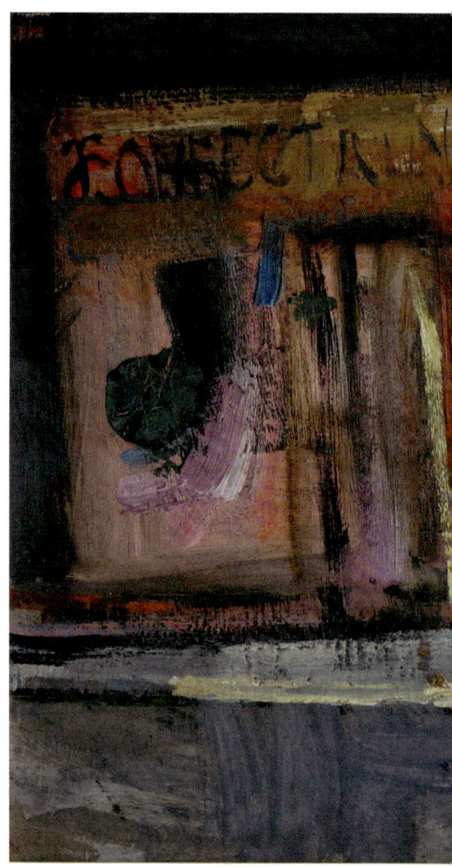

Whenever I come back [to Glasgow] I get a new feeling – chiefly the back streets – I always feel the same – I want to paint them differently – but the same thing – you can't stop observing, things are happening all the time – you are recognising them in your mind. Just now I'm using the scribbles and the word 'scrap metal' ... something I have noticed is that although the particular store I've got in mind has 'scrap metal rags & bones' written on it and some scribbles over the top I have noticed that the old writing is showing through the new writing and it has been repeated ... anyway you get bits of 'scrap' and under the 's' of the previous 'scrap' coming in and as a painter that interests me very much.

The same thing happened in a painting I did once of a confectioner's shop in Rottenrow and the word 'confection' was repeated three times in different bits of it showing through the very latest one but below that the yellow of the previous one and below that a bit of red of a previous 'c' of the 'confection' and this seemed to me very interesting – I feel it is important to know the people and the buildings ...[29]

JOAN EARDLEY
BBC radio interview, 14 January 1963

23 *Glasgow Street, Rottenrow, c.*1955–56
Oil on board, 22.3 × 64.5 cm
Private collection

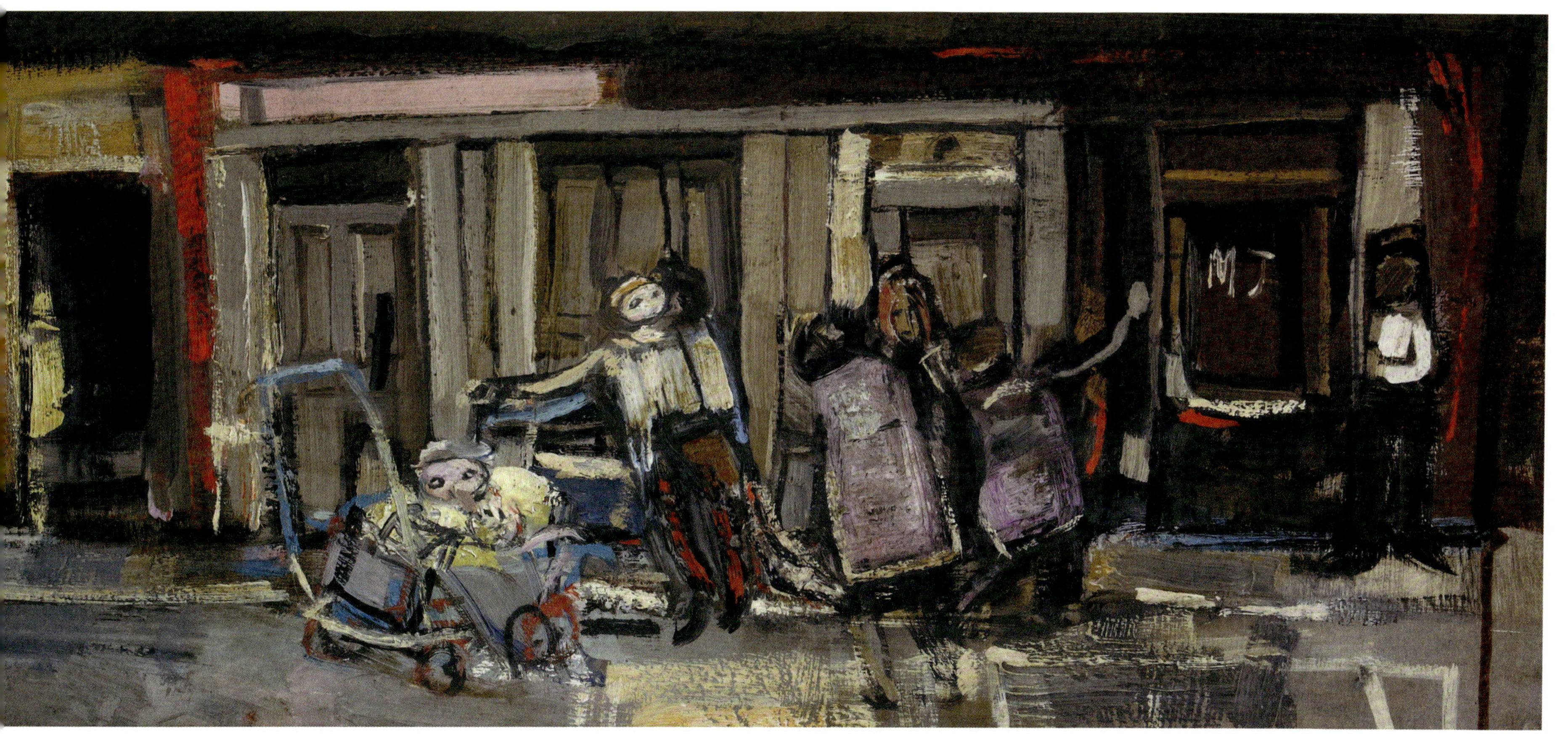

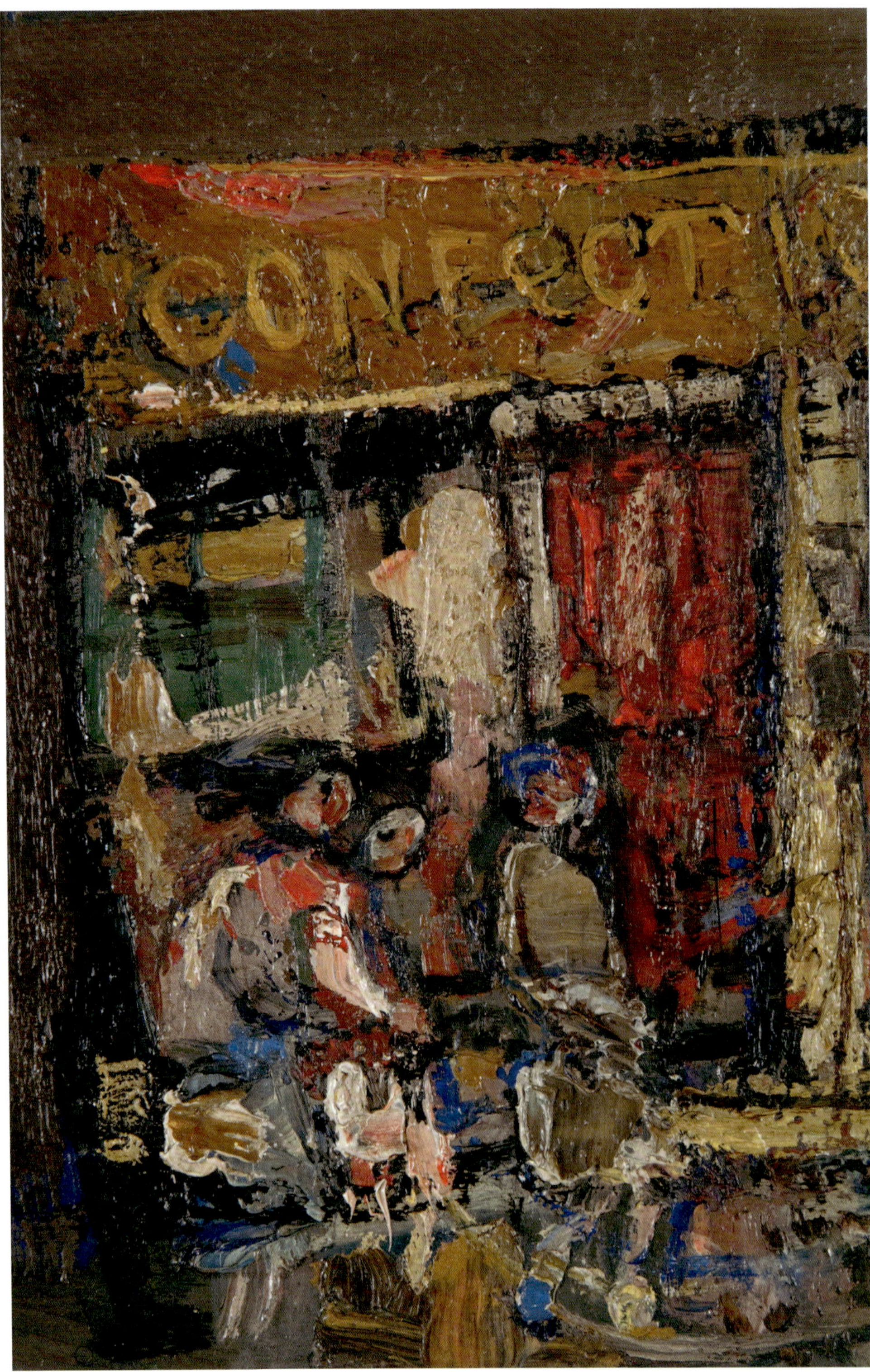

24 *Sweet Shop, Rottenrow*, *c.*1957

Oil on board, 21 × 16 cm

The Hunterian, University of Glasgow

Gift from Edwin Morgan, 2004

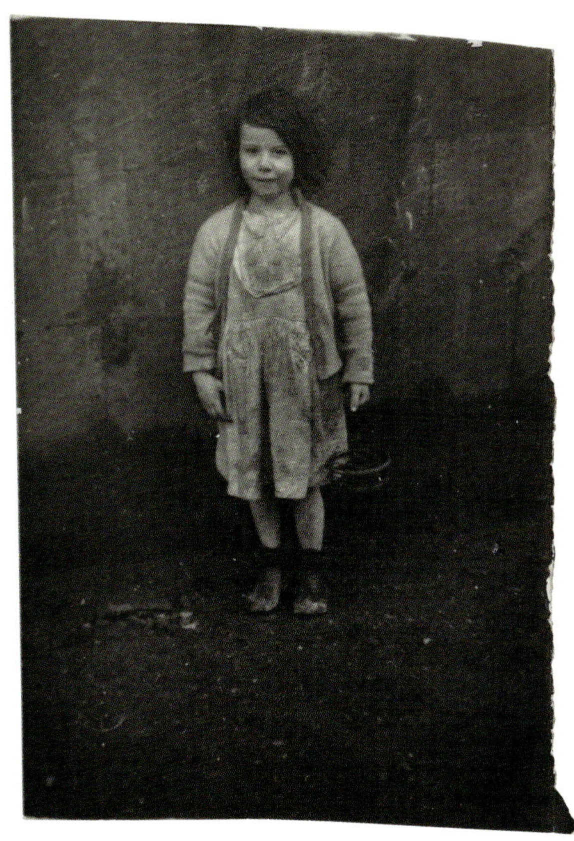

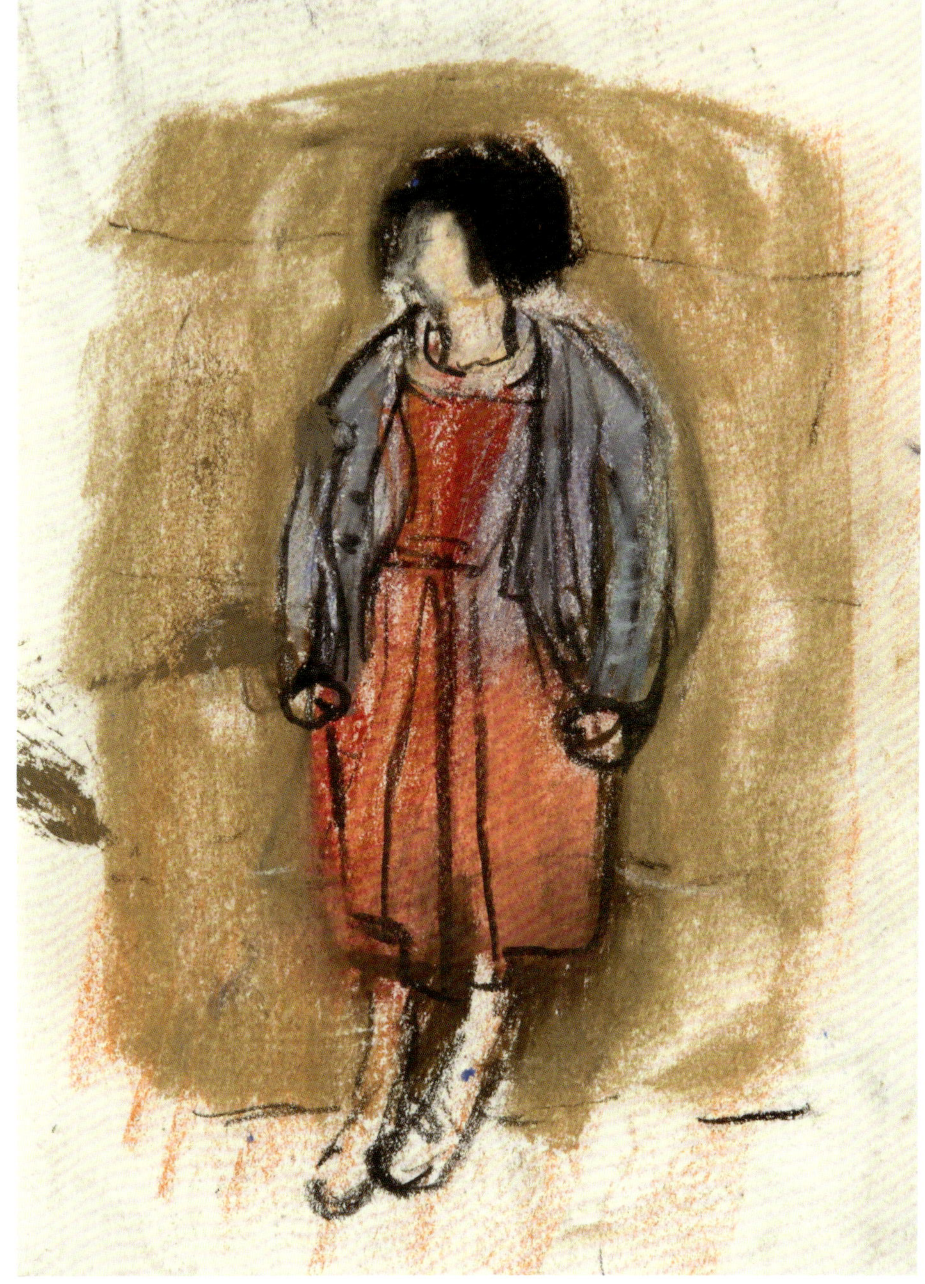

25 *Girl Standing in front of a Wall*, *c.*1955–60

Silver gelatine print, 8.6 × 6.2 cm
Joan Eardley Archive, Scottish National Gallery of Modern Art, Edinburgh
Presented by the artist's sister, Mrs P.M. Black, 1987

26 *Girl in a Red Dress*, *c.*1955–60

Pastel on paper, 17 × 12.5 cm
Cyril Gerber Fine Art, Glasgow

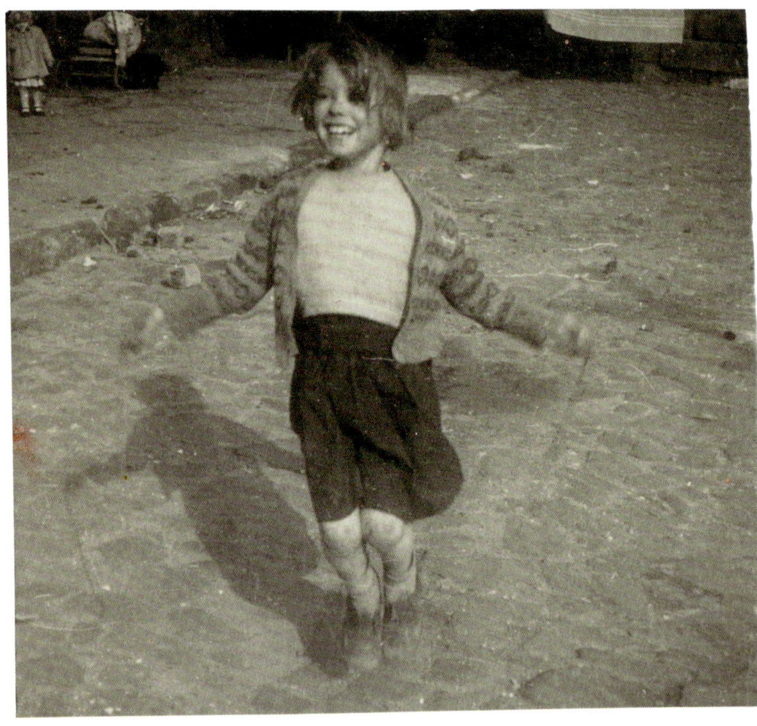

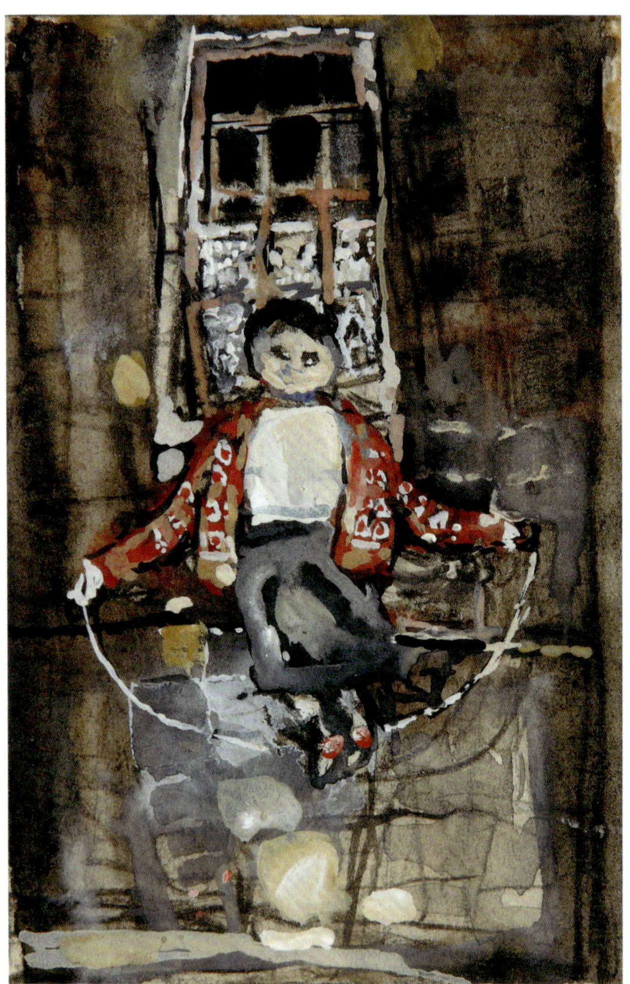

27 *Girl Skipping*, *c.*1955–60

Silver gelatine print, 12 × 16.4 cm
Joan Eardley Archive, Scottish National Gallery of Modern Art, Edinburgh
Presented by the artist's sister, Mrs P.M. Black, 1987

28 *Girl Skipping*, *c.*1955–60

Gouache on paper, 10.5 × 7 cm
Private collection

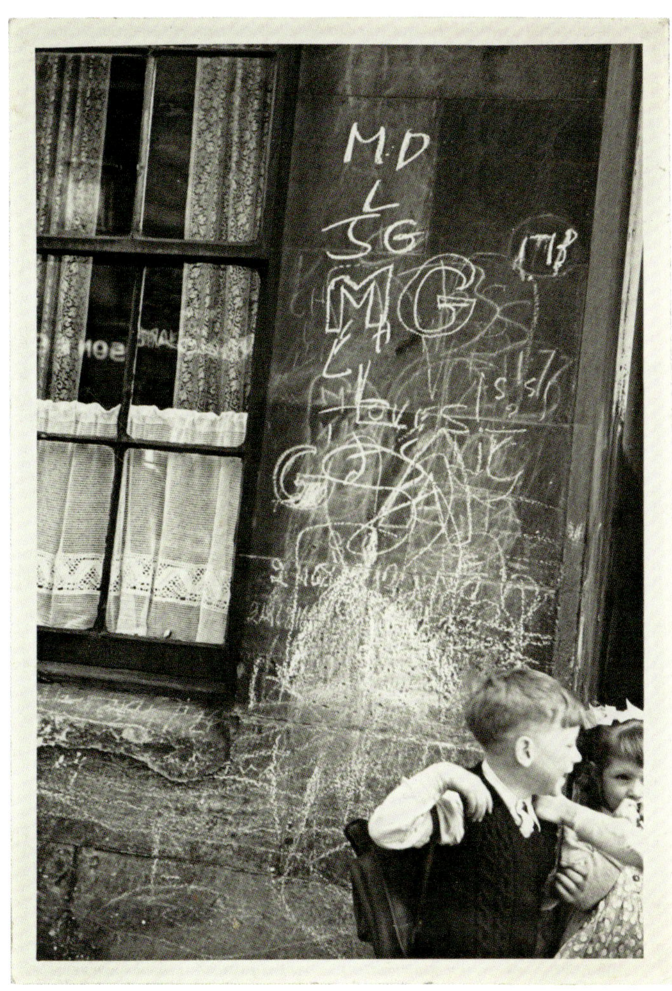

29 Audrey Walker, *Children and Graffitied Wall*, *c.*1955–60

Silver gelatine print, 21.5 × 15.1 cm
Joan Eardley Archive, Scottish National Gallery of Modern Art, Edinburgh
Presented by the artist's sister, Mrs P.M. Black, 1987

30 *Girl and Chalked Wall*, *c.*1955–60

Watercolour and gouache on paper, 47 × 28.4 cm
Private collection

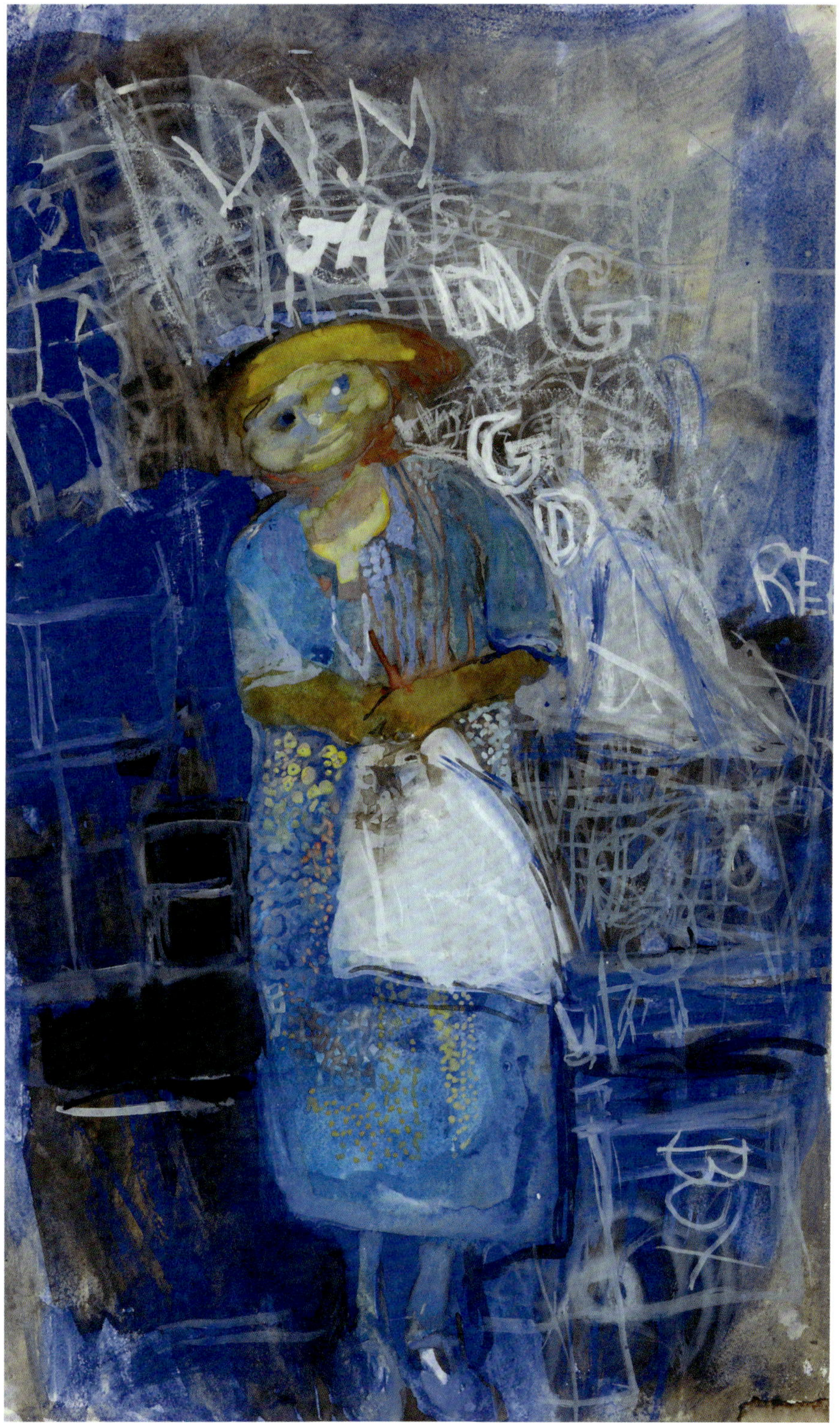

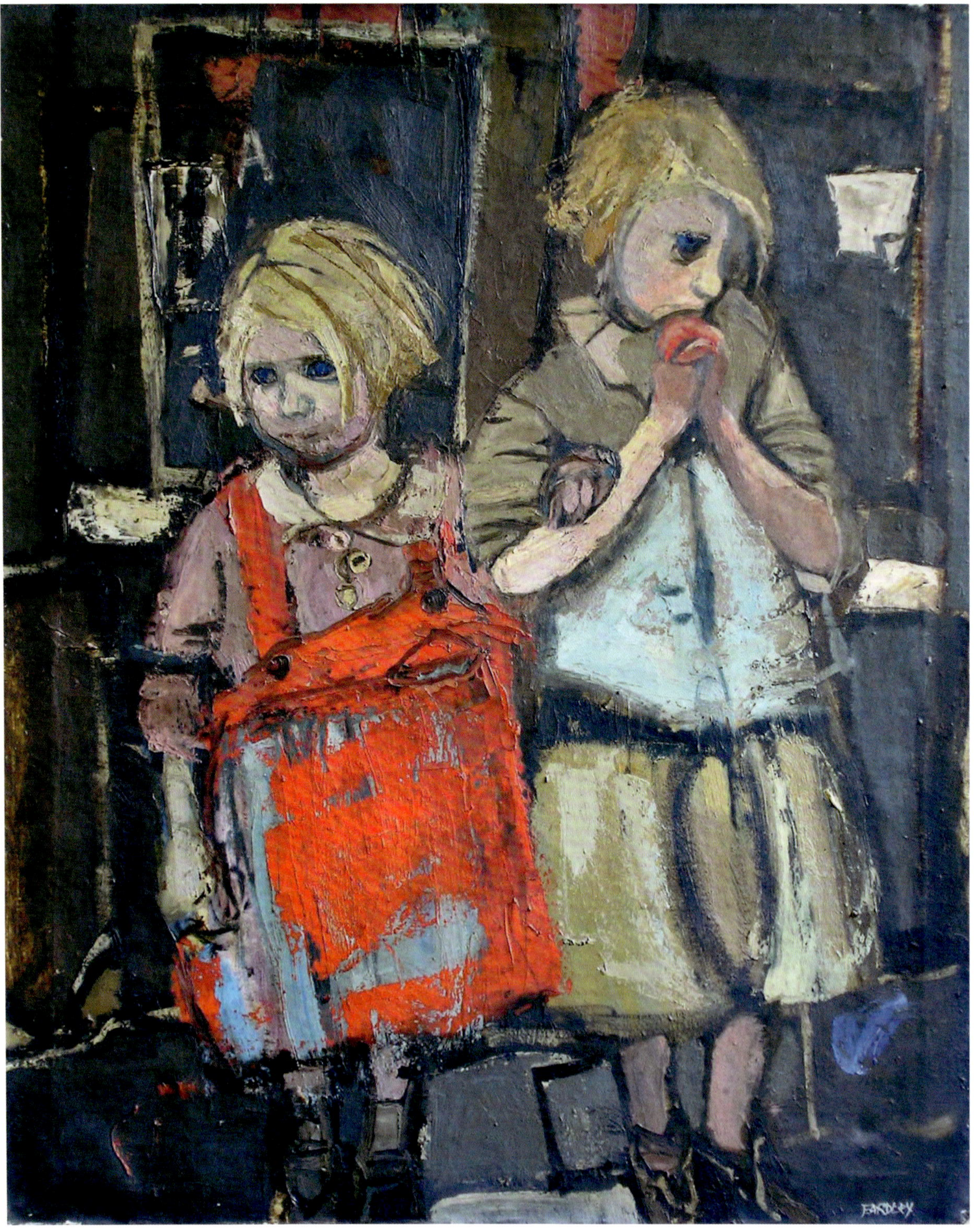

31 *Glasgow Children*, 1958
Oil on canvas, 92 × 77 cm
Private collection

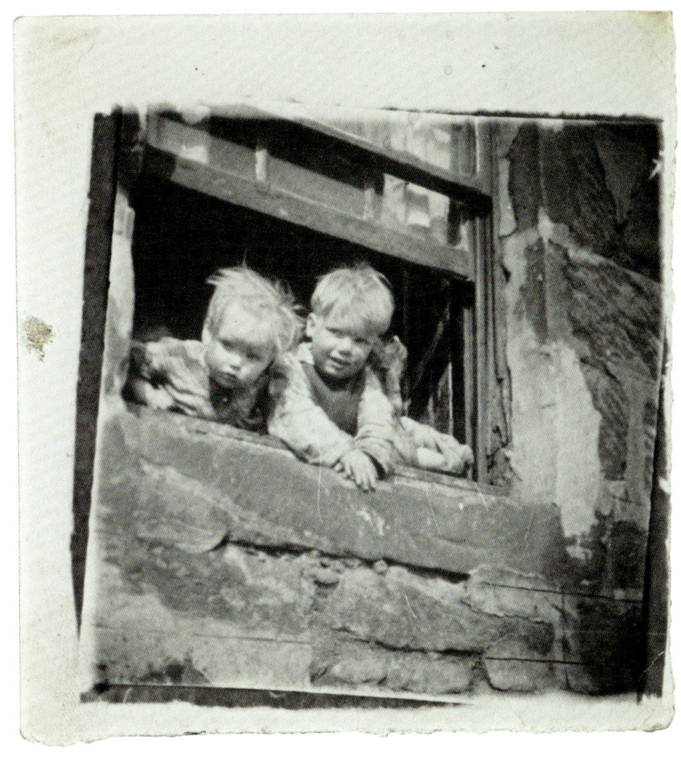

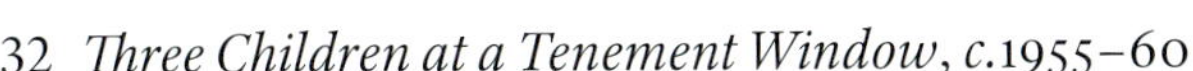

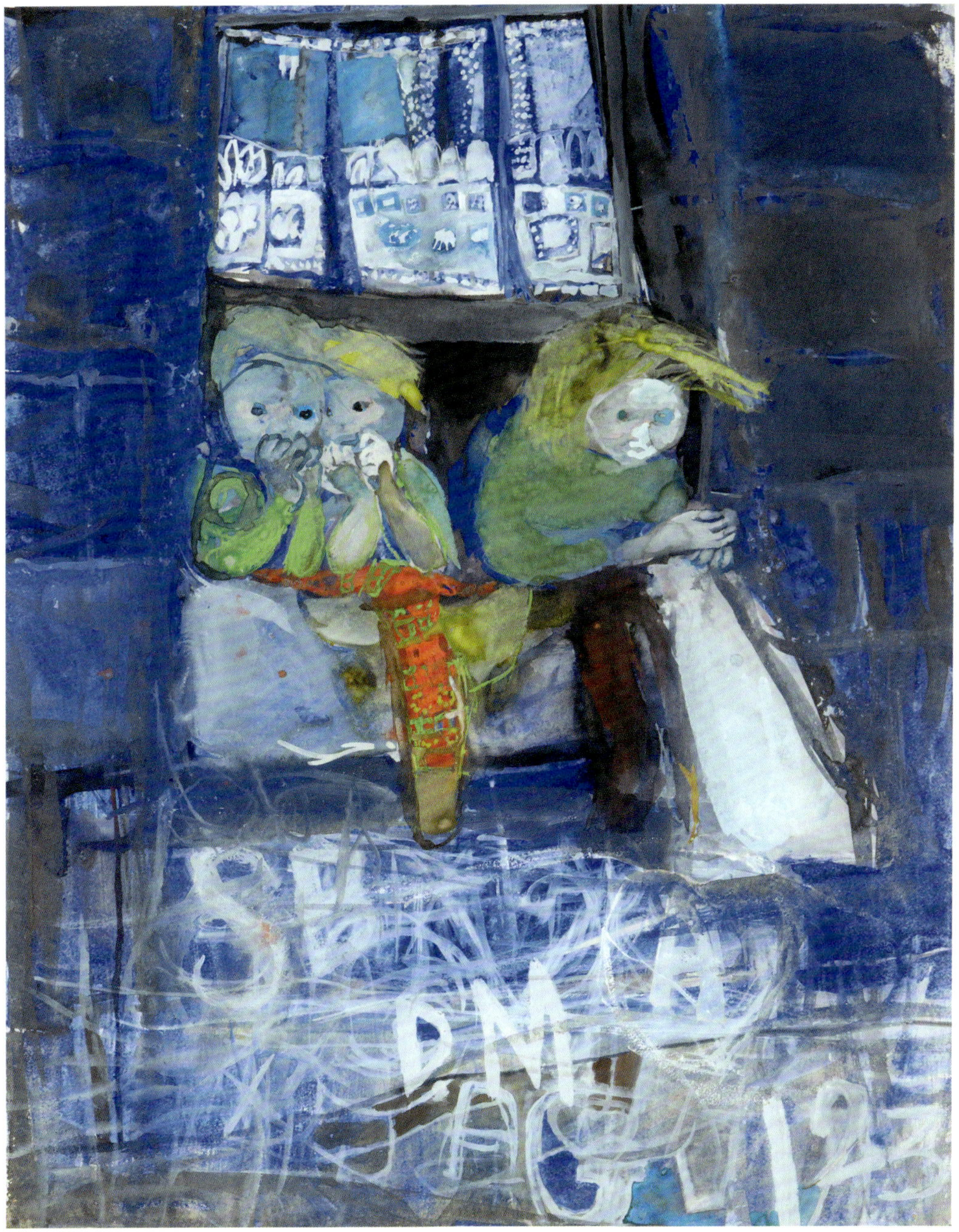

32 *Three Children at a Tenement Window*, c.1955–60

Silver gelatine print, 11 × 10 cm
Joan Eardley Archive, Scottish National Gallery of Modern Art, Edinburgh. Presented by the artist's sister, Mrs P.M. Black, 1987

33 *Three Children at a Tenement Window*, c.1961

Gouache on paper, 47 × 37.1 cm
Private collection

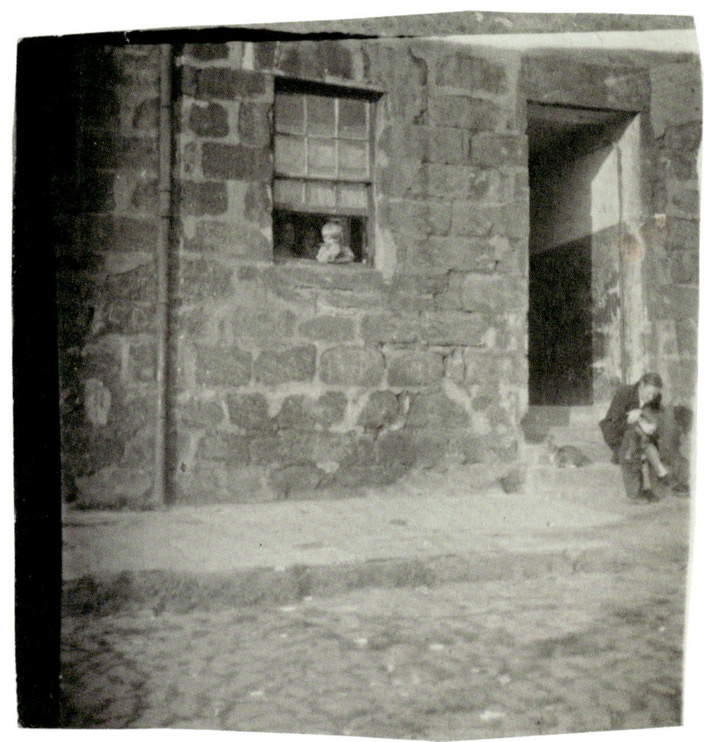

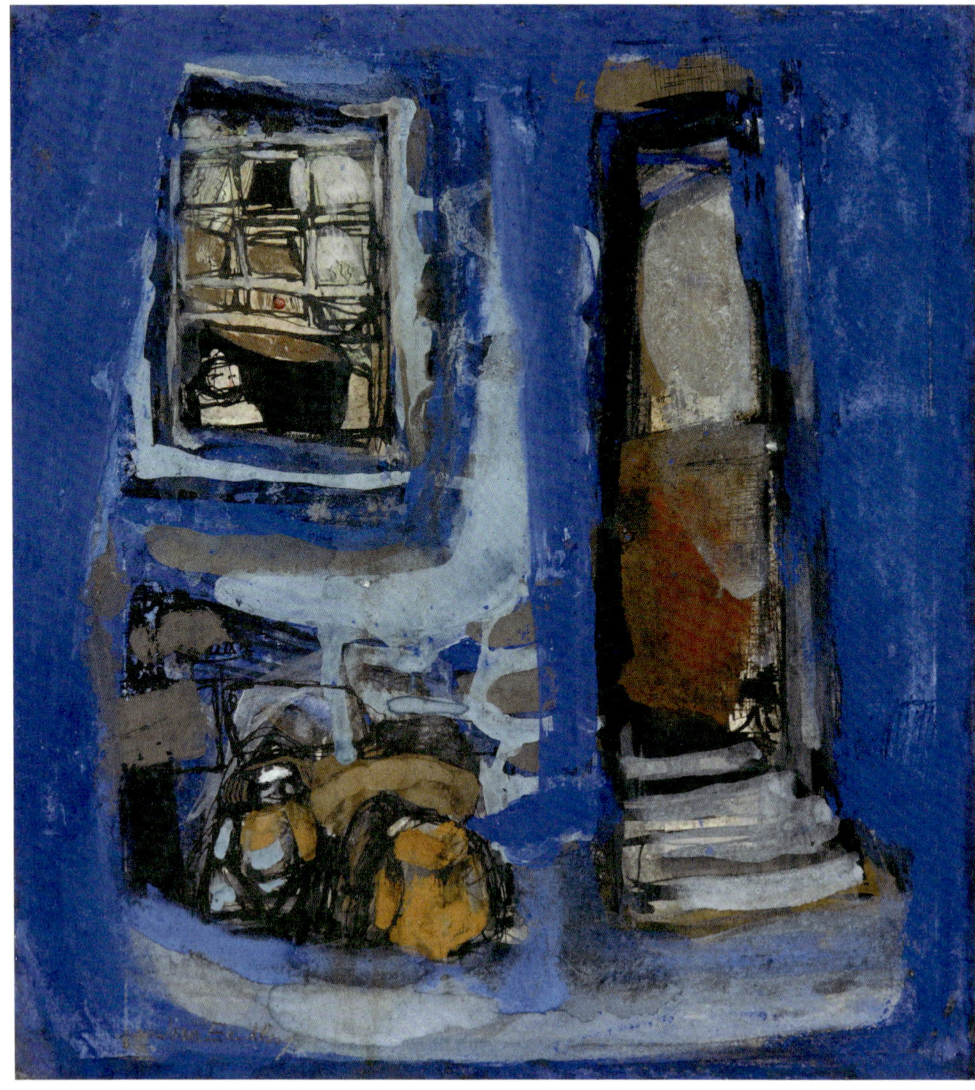

34 *The Close Mouth*, *c.*1955–57

Silver gelatine print, 9 × 8.8 cm
Joan Eardley Archive, Scottish National Gallery of Modern Art, Edinburgh. Presented by the artist's sister, Mrs P.M. Black, 1987

35 *The Close Mouth*, before 1958

Gouache on paper, 24 × 22 cm
Private collection

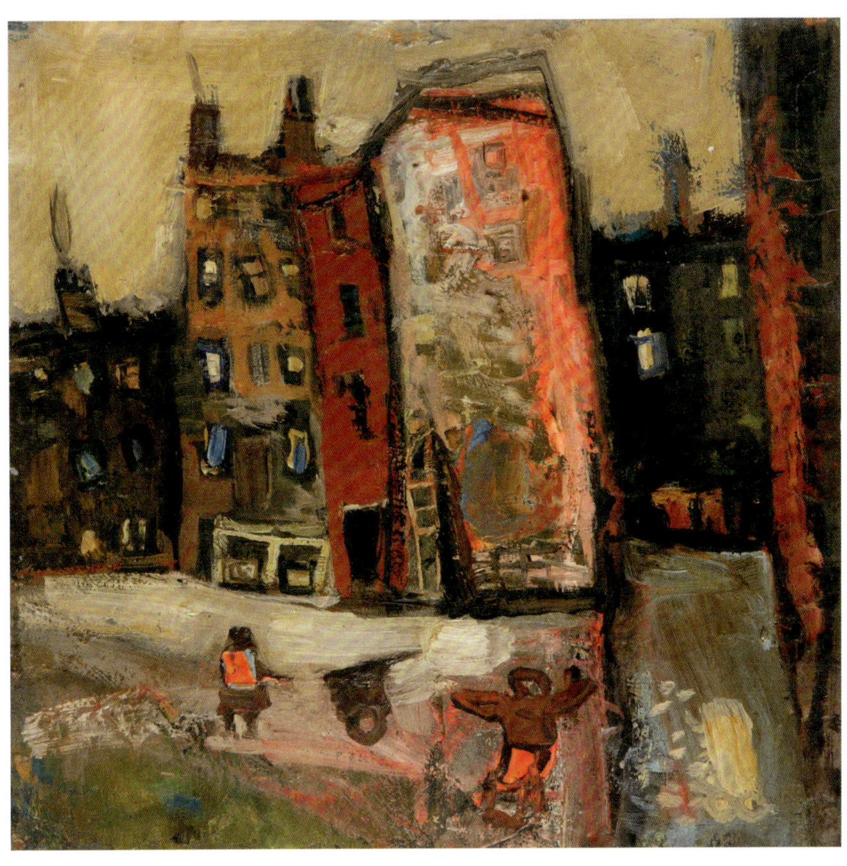

36 *Glasgow Tenement*, 1962
Oil on canvas, 28 × 28 cm
Cyril Gerber Fine Art, Glasgow

37 *Two Children with Graffiti*, *c.*1960–63
Gouache on paper, 12 × 18.5 cm
Private collection

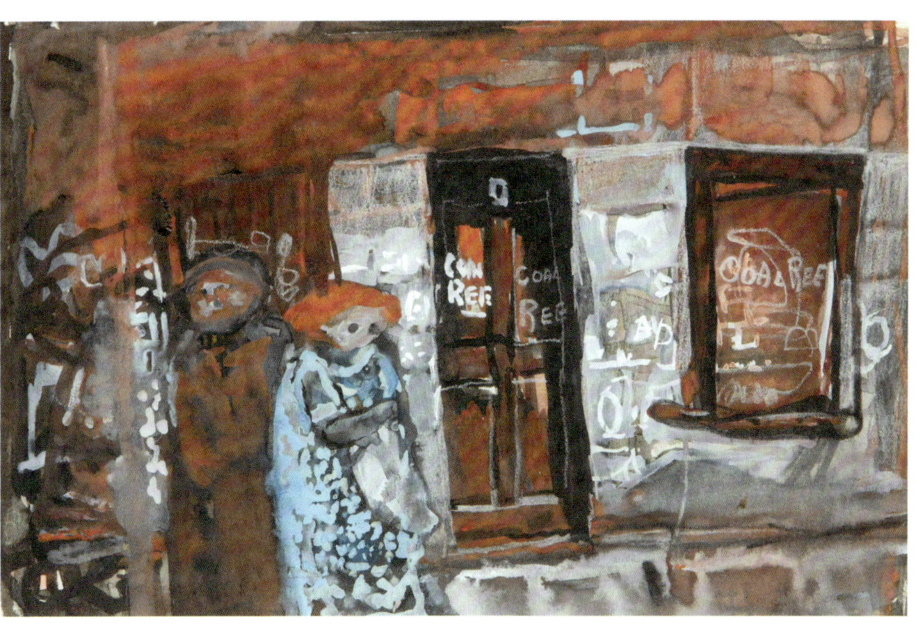

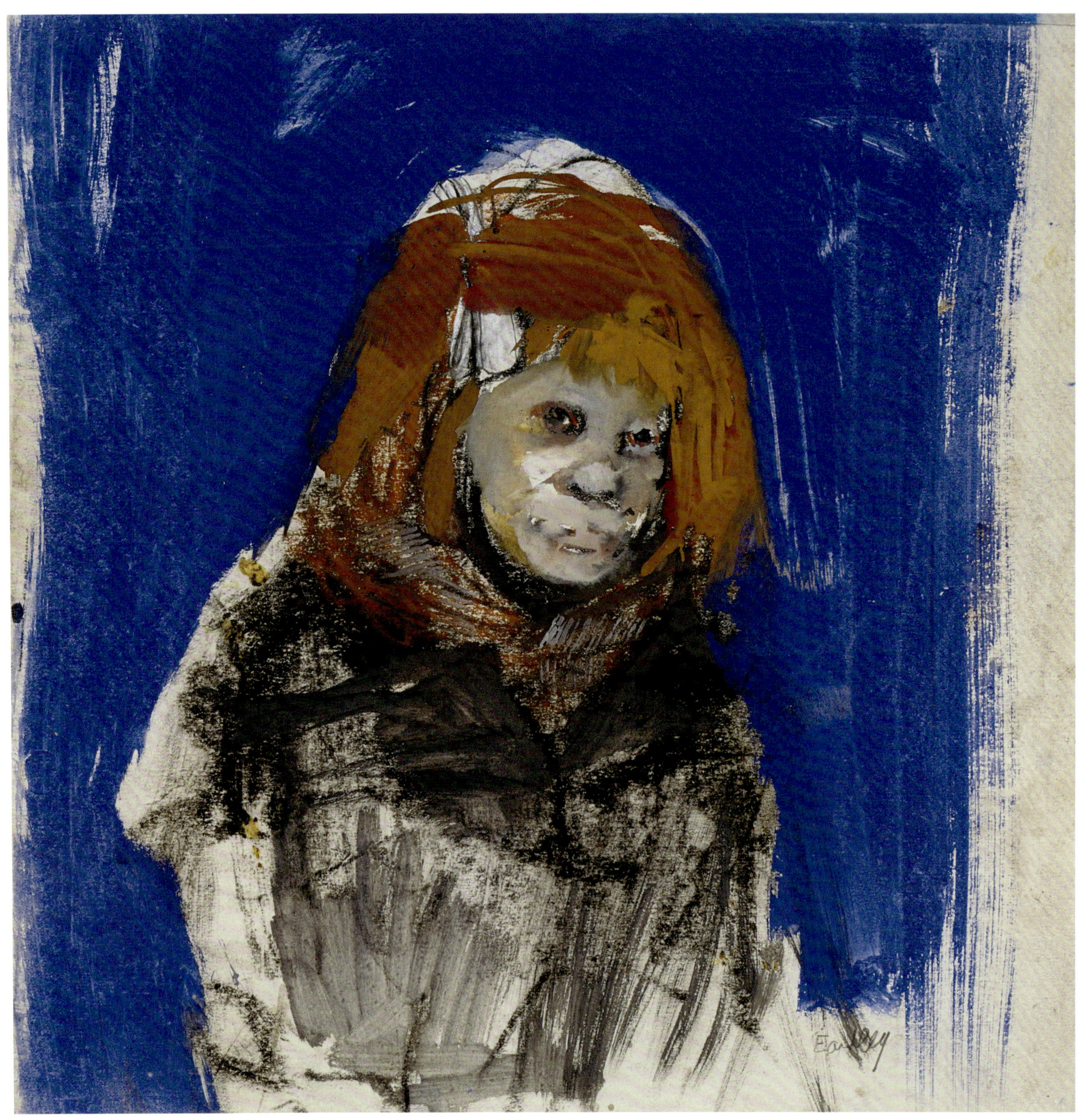

38 *Head of a Girl*, *c.*1960

Gouache and pastel on paper, laid on board, 37.6 × 37.4 cm
Scottish National Gallery of Modern Art, Edinburgh
Presented by the artist's sister, Mrs P.M. Black, 1987

39 *The Green Scarf*, *c.*1960

Watercolour and gouache on paper, 52 × 35 cm
Private collection

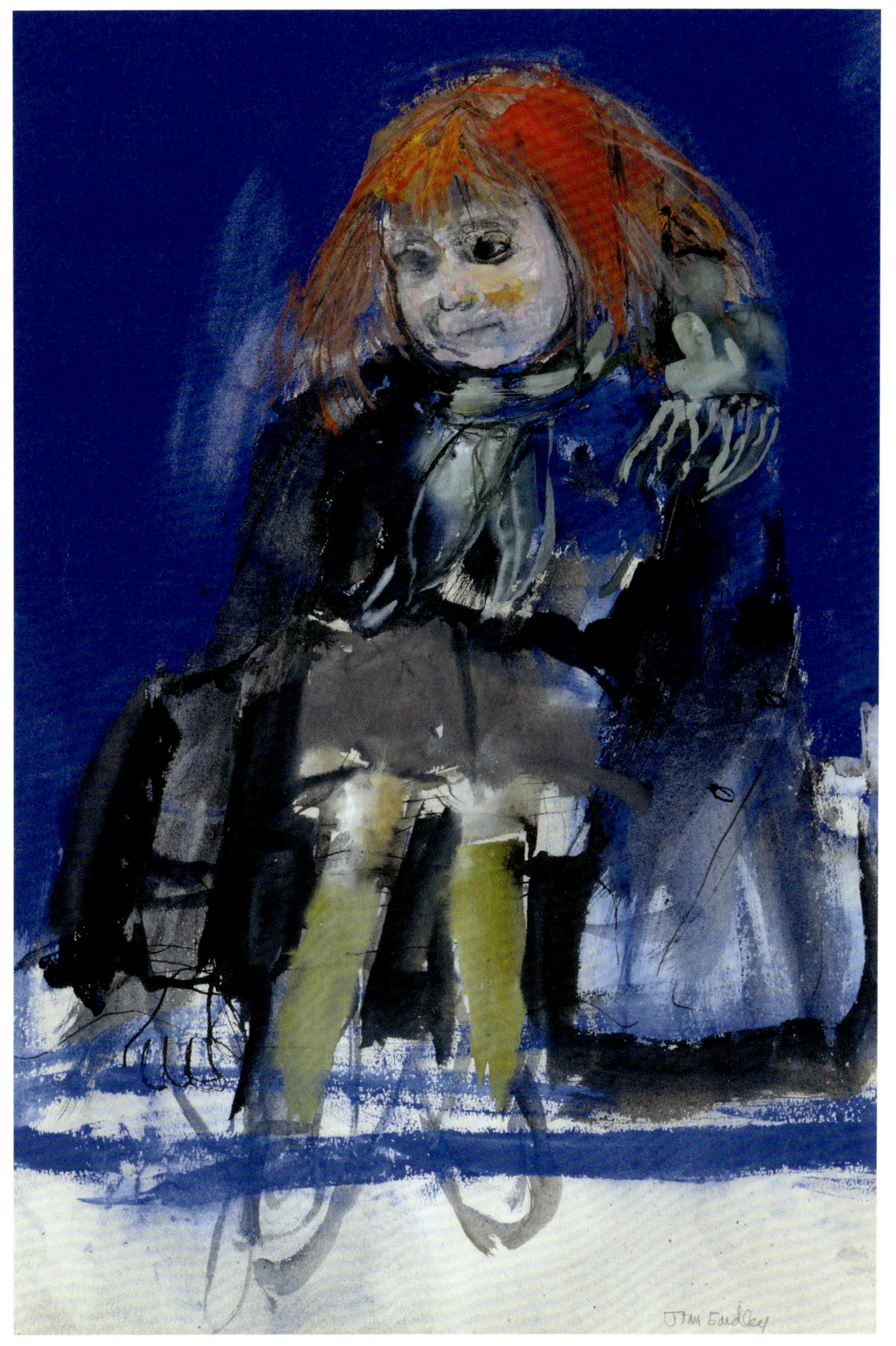

The community feeling is rapidly disappearing in Glasgow ... I do feel that there is still a little bit left. I try still to paint Glasgow so long as there is this family group quality. I've known about half a dozen families well I suppose during the period of time I've worked in Glasgow ... about ten years or more and at the present moment a family by the name of Samson. I have been painting them seven years ... There are a large number of them ... twelve ... so I've always had a certain number of children from this family of any age I choose to need ... Some children I don't like ... most of them I get on with ... some interest me much more as characters ... These ones I encourage – they don't need much encouragement: they don't pose – they come up and say 'will you paint me?' There are always knocks at the door – the ones I want – I try to get them to stand still – it's not possible to get a child to stay still ... I watch them moving about and do the best I can. ... They are completely uninhibited and they just behave as they would among themselves. They almost seem not to notice I'm there. The Samsons, they amuse me, they hardly notice me, they are full of what's gone on today: who's broken into what shop and who's flung a pie in whose face – it goes on and on. They just let out all their life and energy they haven't been able to at school and I just watch them and I do try and think about them in painterly terms as much as any other term – all the bits of red and bits of colour and they wear each other's clothes – never the same thing twice running – never the same thing next day – even that doesn't matter – it's part of the thing I feel bits and pieces and well I feel they are for me – they are Glasgow – this richness that Glasgow has – I hope it will always have – a living thing, intense quality – you can't ever know what you are going to do but as long as Glasgow has this I'll always want to paint.[30]

JOAN EARDLEY
BBC radio interview, 14 January 1963

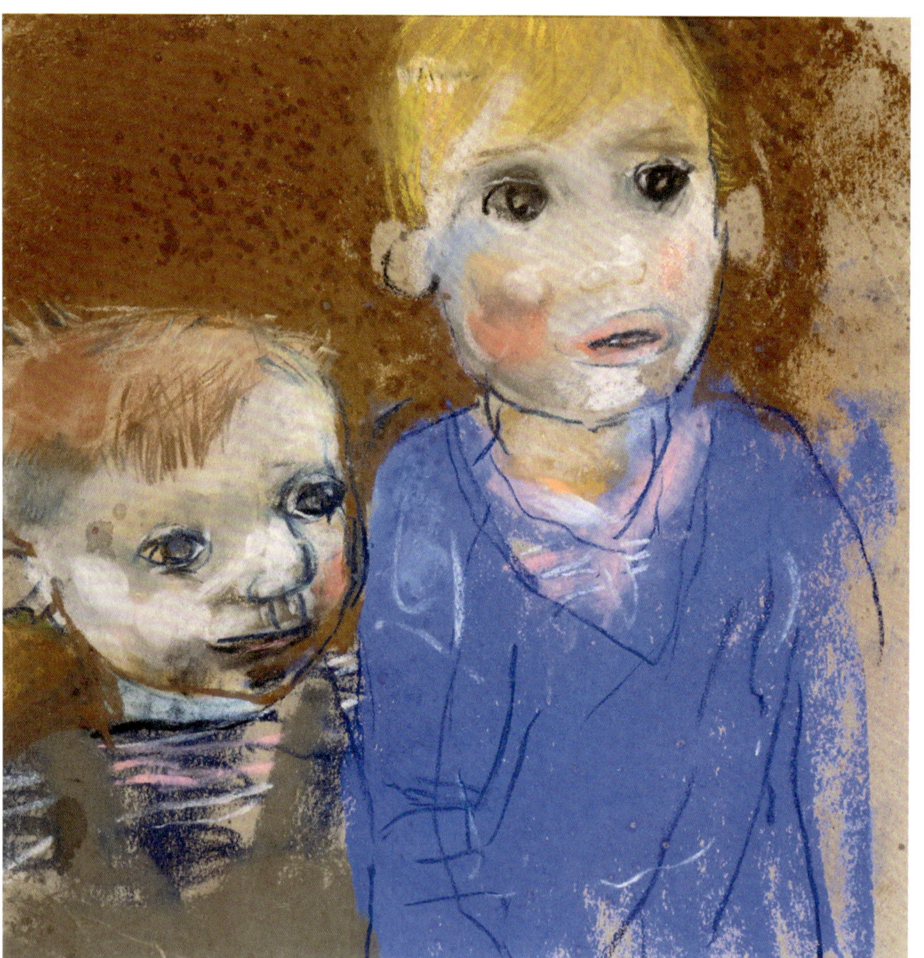

40 *Two Boys*, c.1960
Pastel and gouache on sandpaper, 21 × 20.5 cm
Scottish National Gallery of Modern Art, Edinburgh
The Henry and Sula Walton Collection: bequeathed 2012

41 *Two Glasgow Lassies*, c.1962–63
Pastel on sandpaper, 29 × 24.5 cm
Private collection

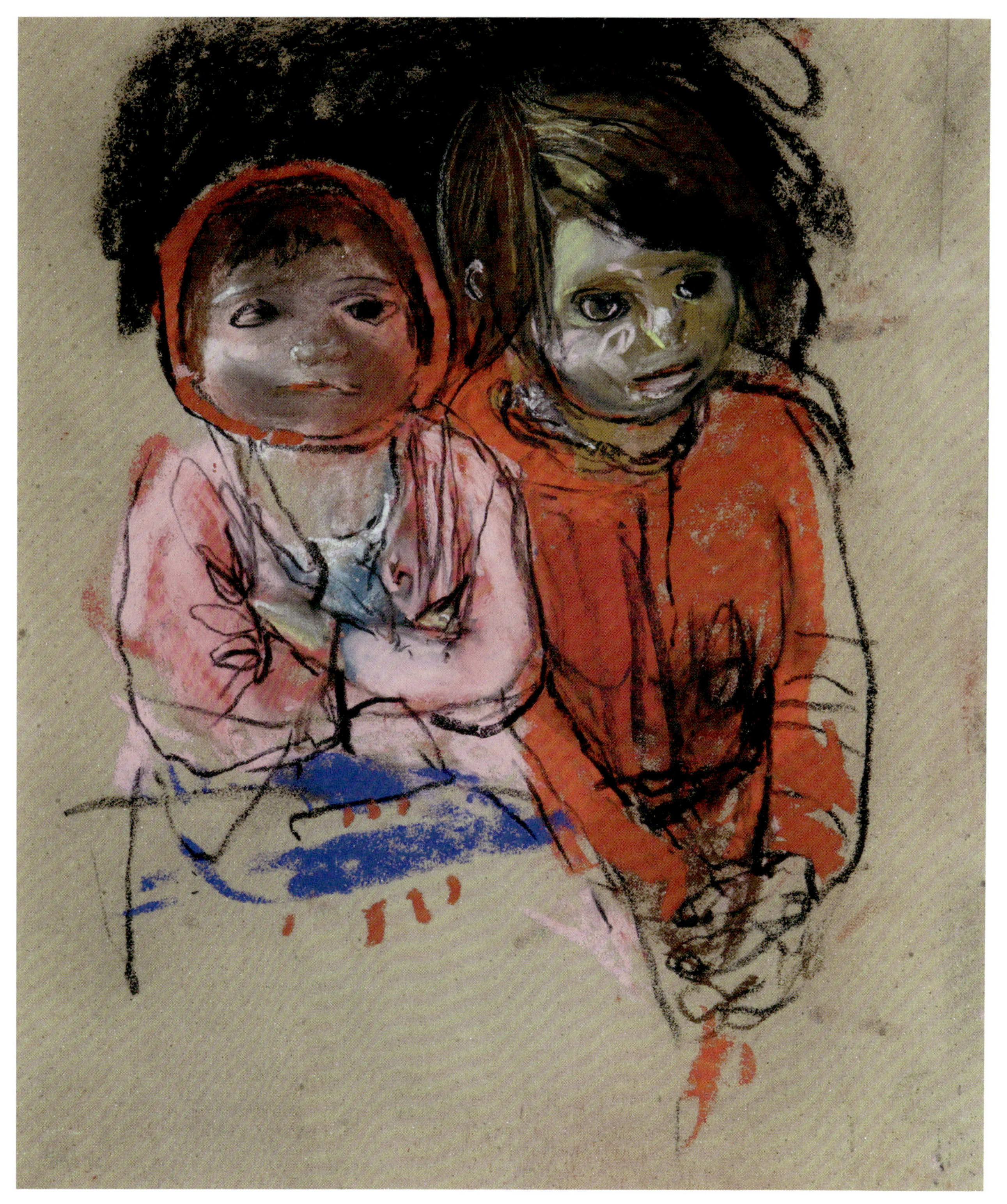

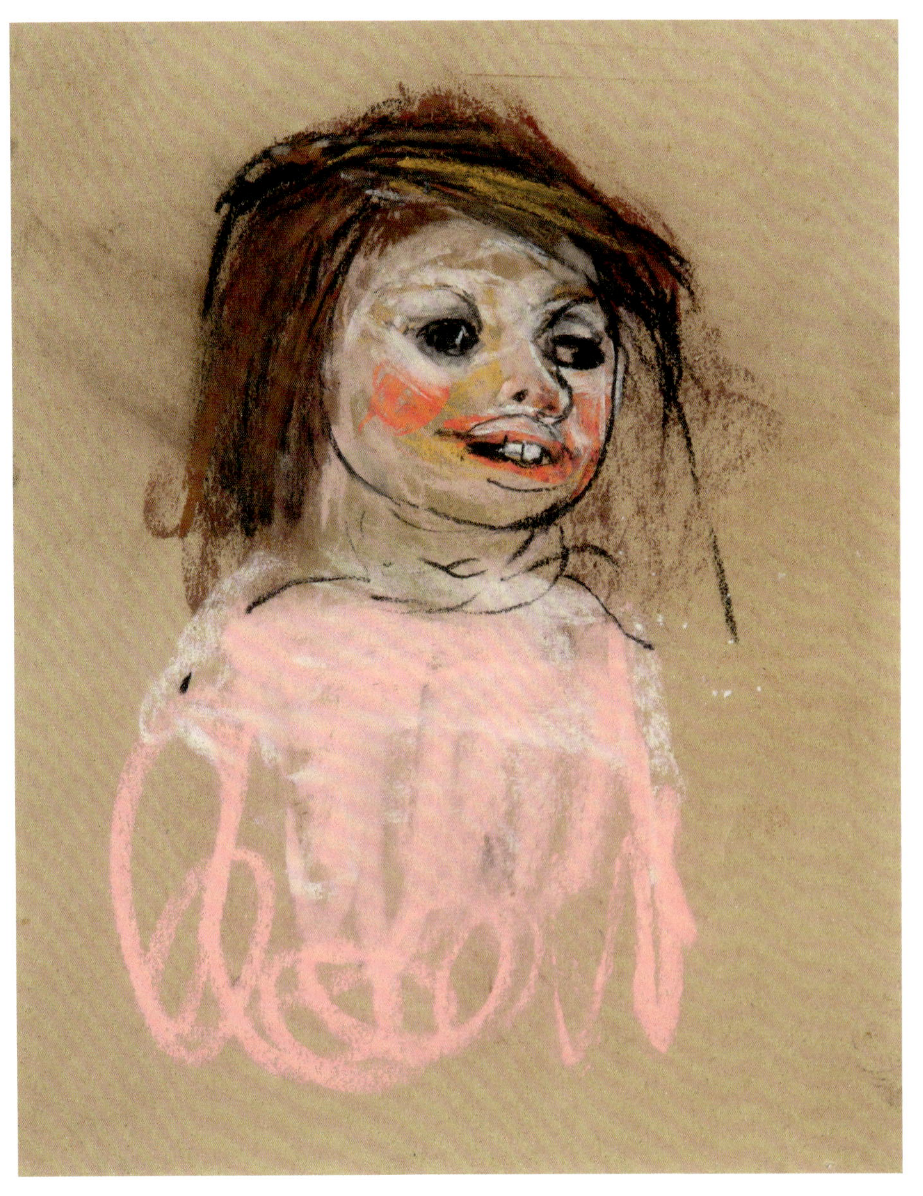

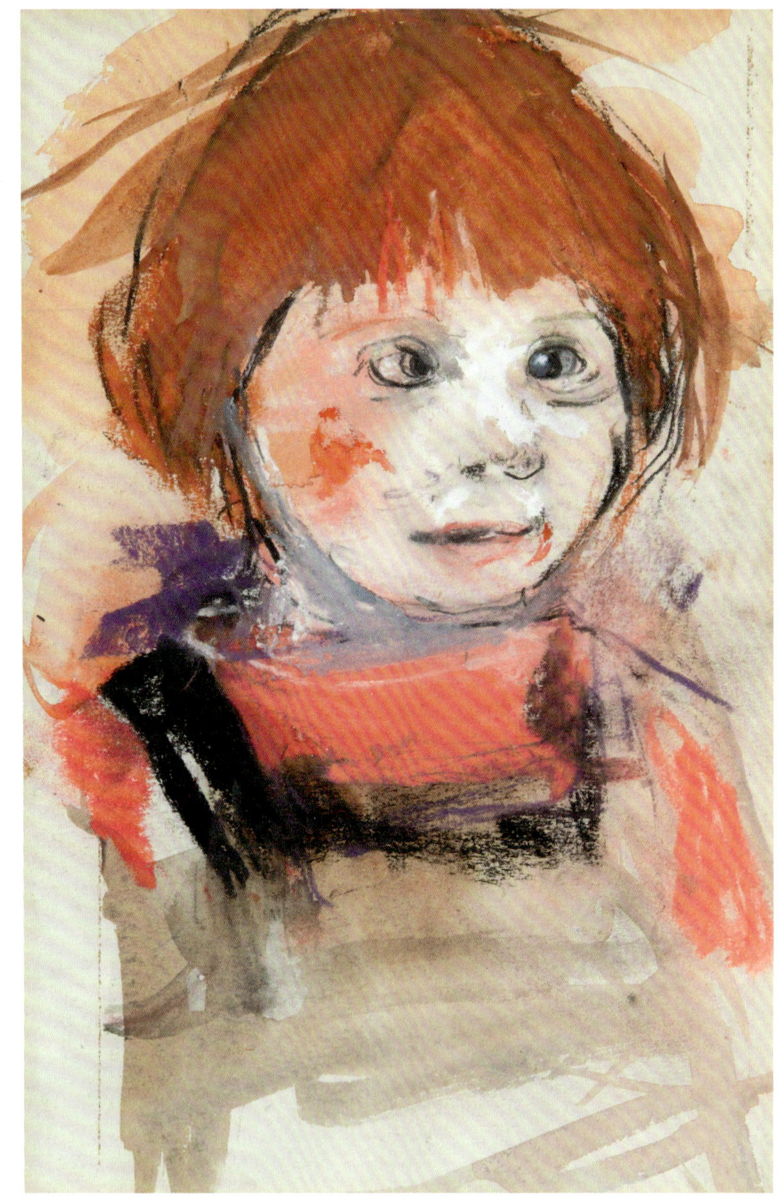

42 *Pink Jumper*, *c*.1960

Pastel on paper, 21 × 19 cm
Private collection

43 *Red Haired Girl*, *c*.1960

Gouache and pastel on paper, 22 × 14.5 cm
Private collection

44 *Child before Tenement Window*, *c.*1958–60

Oil on canvas, 34 × 24 cm

Private collection

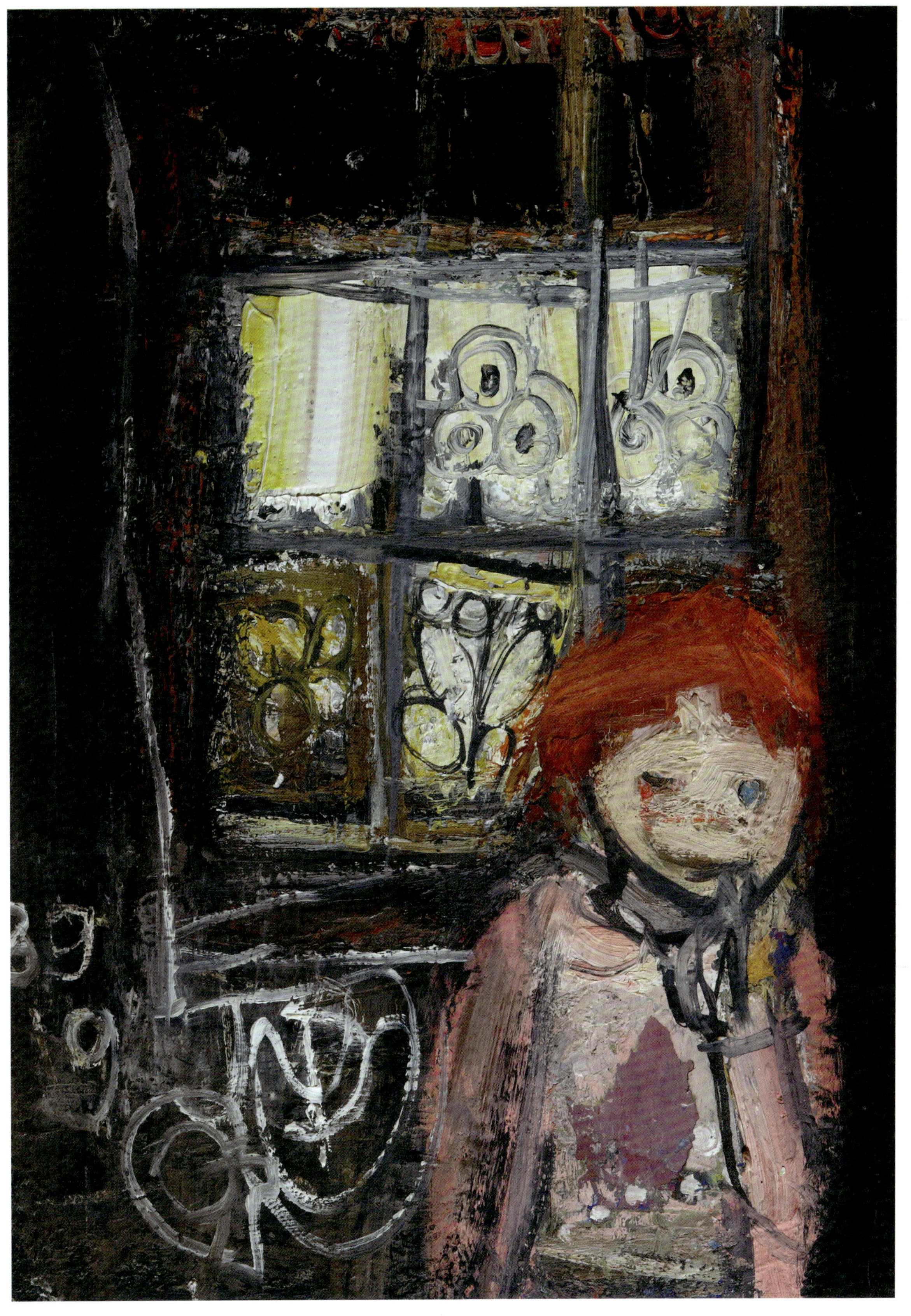

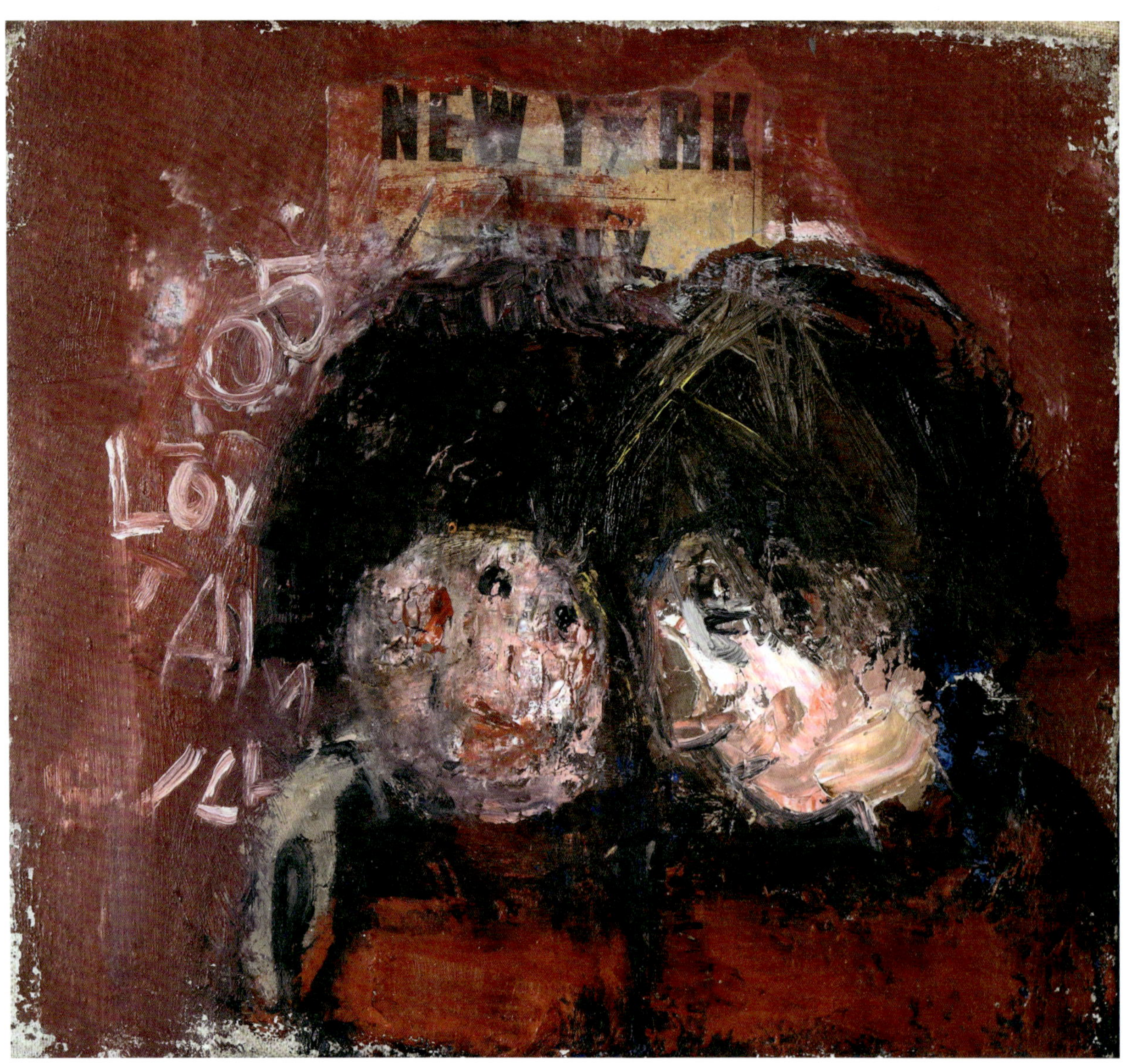

45 *Two Children*, *c.*1962

Oil and collage on canvas, 26 × 29.5 cm
Cyril Gerber Fine Art, Glasgow

46 *Two Children before Lettered Wall*, 1963

Oil and collage on board, 69 × 70 cm
Private collection

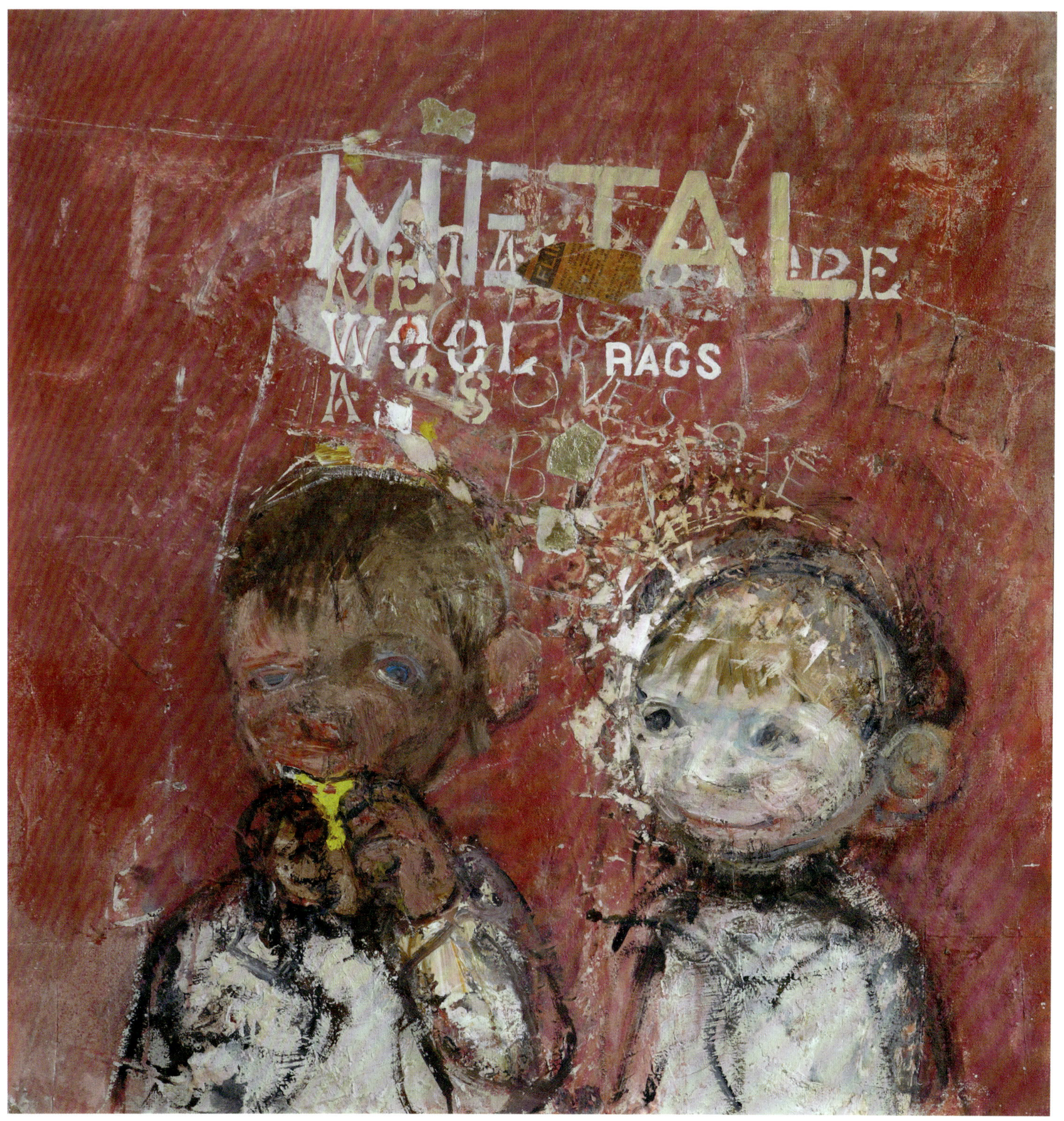
METAL
WOOL
RAGS

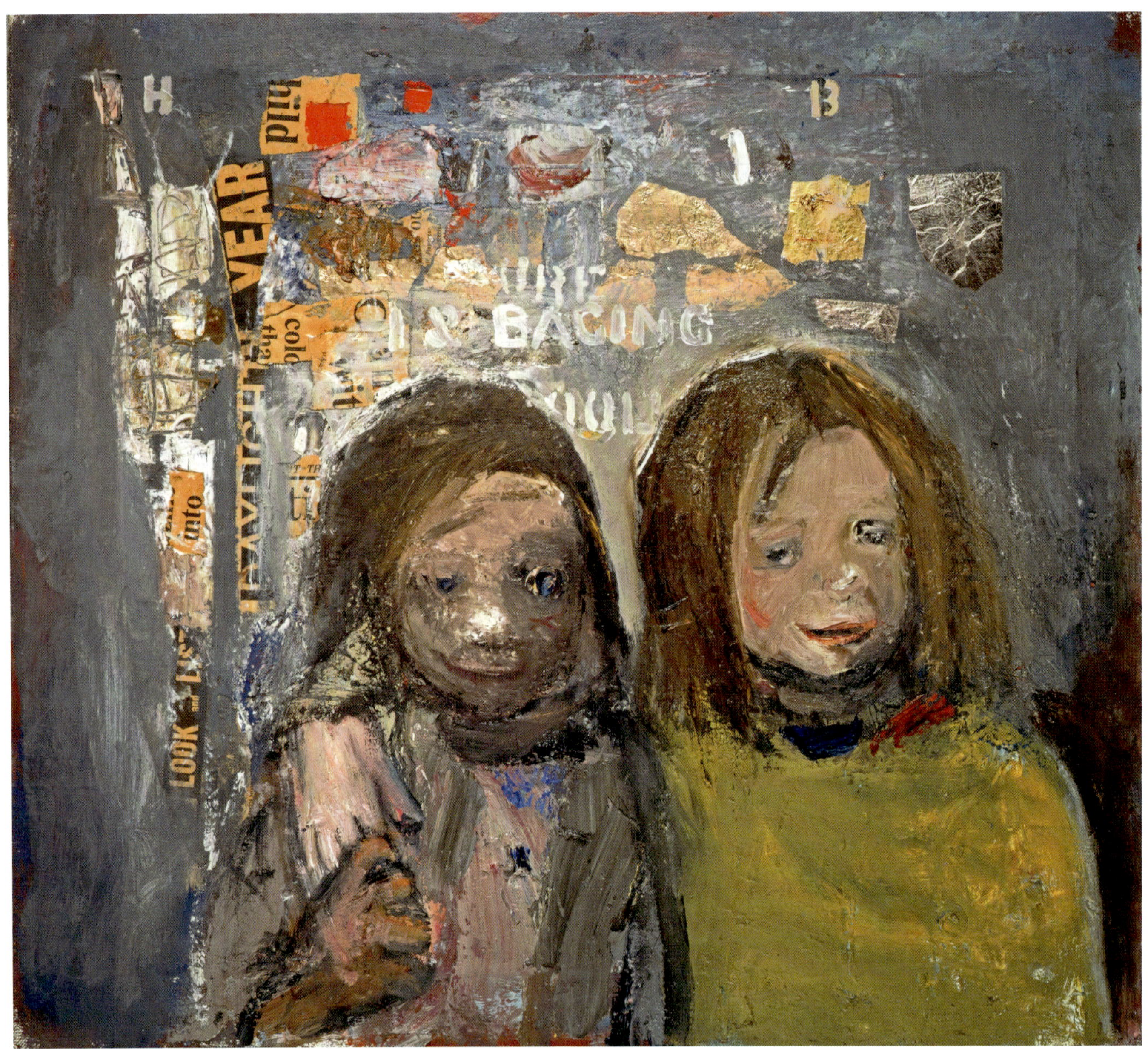

47 *Children and Chalked Wall 3*, 1962–63

Oil, newspaper and metal foil on canvas, 61 × 68.6 cm
Scottish National Gallery of Modern Art, Edinburgh, purchased 1963

48 *Children and Chalked Wall 2*, 1963

Oil on canvas, 80.5 × 86 cm
Abbot Hall Art Gallery, Kendal

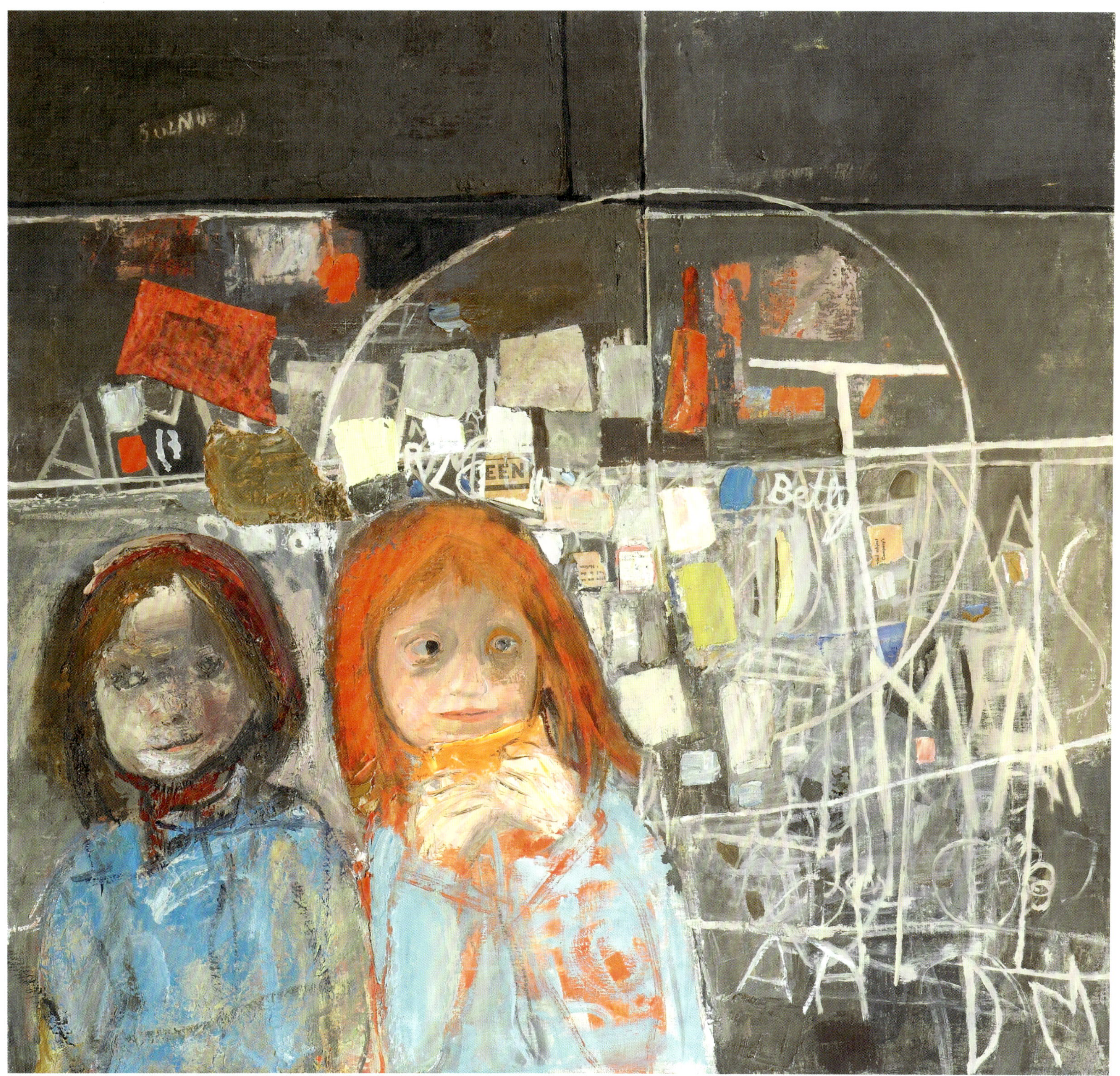

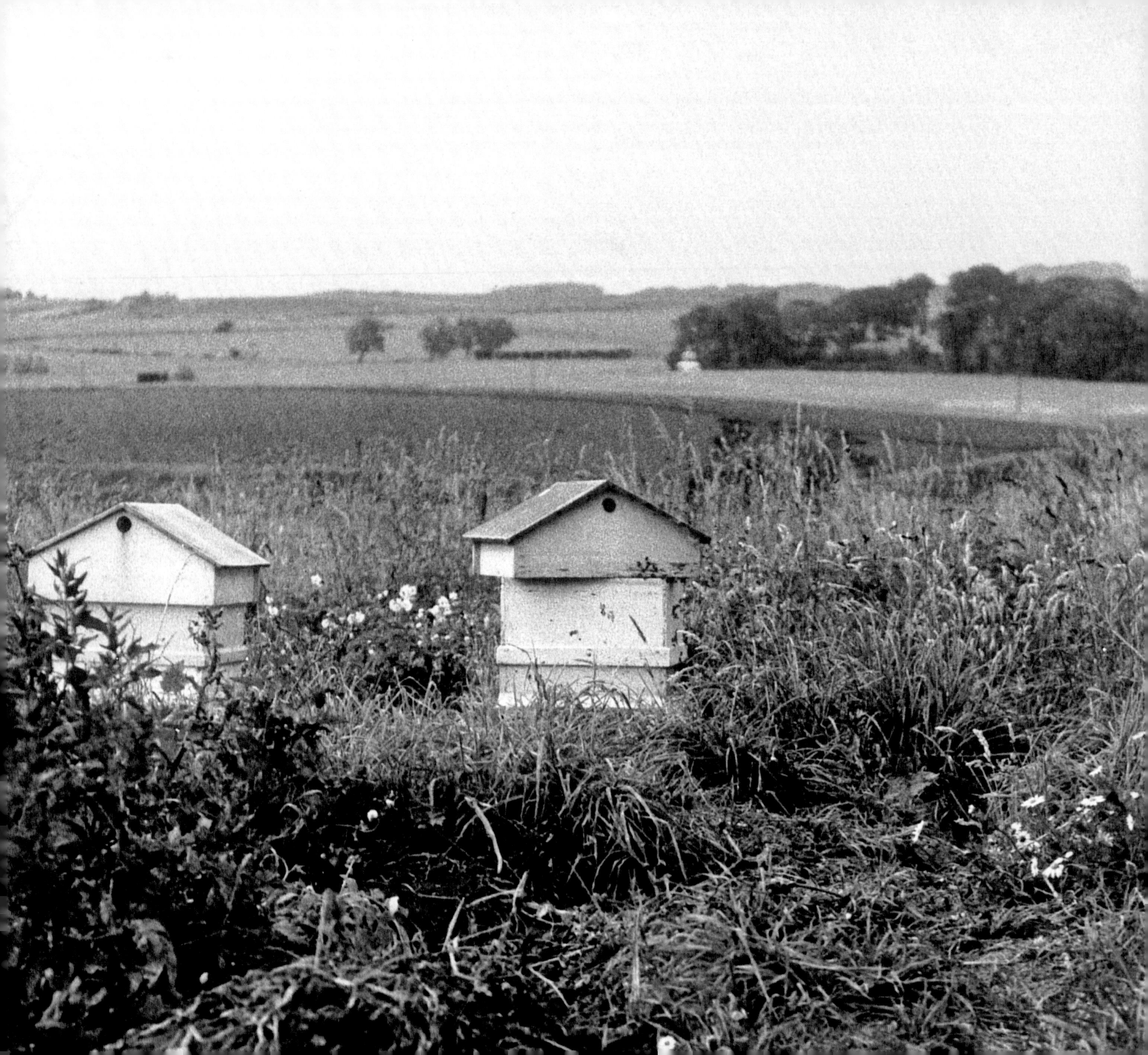

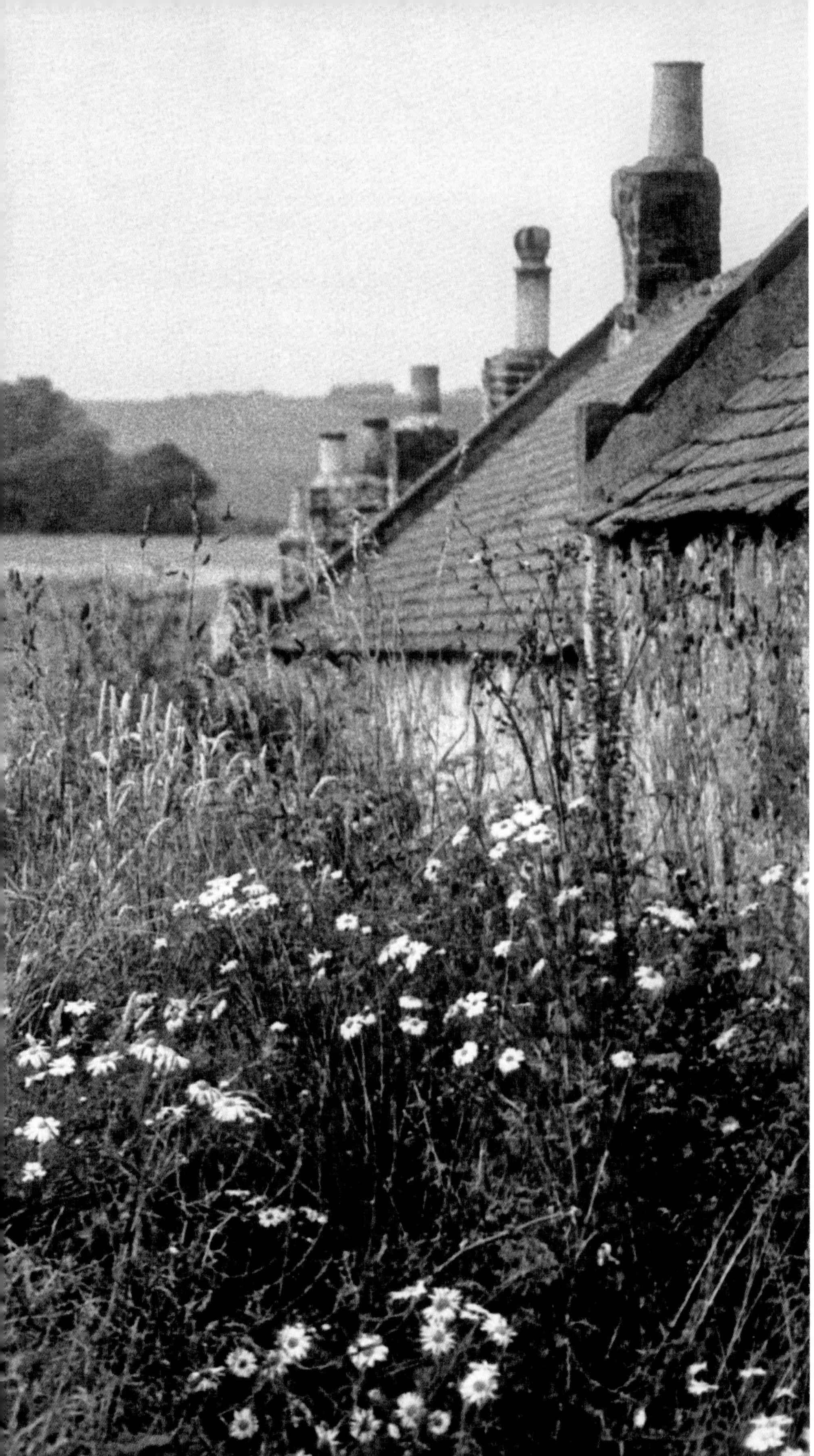

II CATTERLINE

In April 1950 Eardley, who had not yet turned thirty, held a solo exhibition at the Gaumont Gallery, which was part of the Gaumont Cinema in Aberdeen.[31] It had come about thanks to a local schoolteacher, Annette Soper, who had read a review of Eardley's postgraduate exhibition at the Glasgow School of Art. Eardley stayed with the Soper family, who lived in Stonehaven, fifteen miles south of Aberdeen. She evidently did some serious work there: when the Arts Council bought a drawing from the exhibition and took it away, she replaced it with another done in Stonehaven.[32] In a letter to her mother, penned while she was invigilating the exhibition, Eardley wrote:

> *The schoolteacher whom I am staying with is very nice. Margot* [Sandeman] *and I thought she was terribly schoolteachery. Which she is but one can get over that. And it is her family actually who are all so nice. An old mother and father, both quite characters and 3 sisters ... They live in an enormous house. And everything kind of higgledy piggelty – the way I like it! ...*
>
> *I go out drawing mostly in the mornings, so I am able to relieve my feelings a bit then. It is really very lovely country, I have quite fallen for it, both the sea and the country behind. One of the sisters, who is on holiday at the moment, a gym teacher, took me out in her little car this morning with 2 of the boys to collect peat. Not very far, just about 7 or 8 miles behind where they live, back up the glen, where there are lovely moors, and new forests and rushing burns, quite different from the west, more rolling and lovely reddish earth – much nicer to me. On the way back she dropped me at a place where I wanted to draw – where there were sheep in an*

Fig.13 | The beehives behind No.1 Catterline, July 1959
Photo by Audrey Walker, courtesy of The Scottish Gallery, Edinburgh

Fig.14 | South Row, Catterline, *c.*1900
Private collection, courtesy of Ron Stephen

Fig.15 | The Watch House ('the Watchie'), Catterline, 1955
Photo by Audrey Walker, courtesy of The Scottish Gallery, Edinburgh

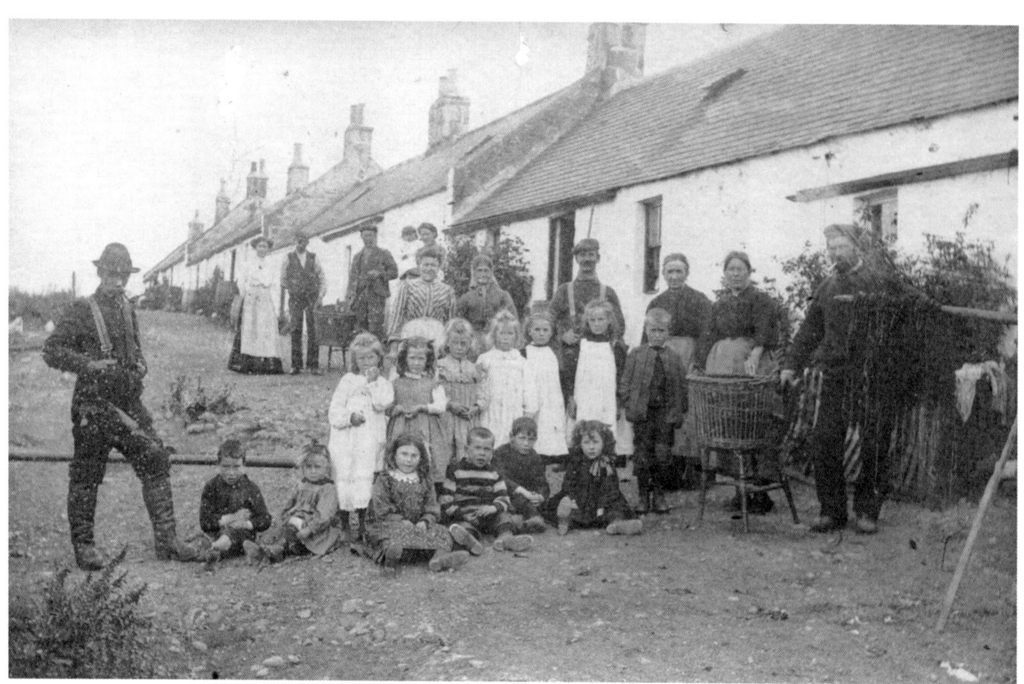

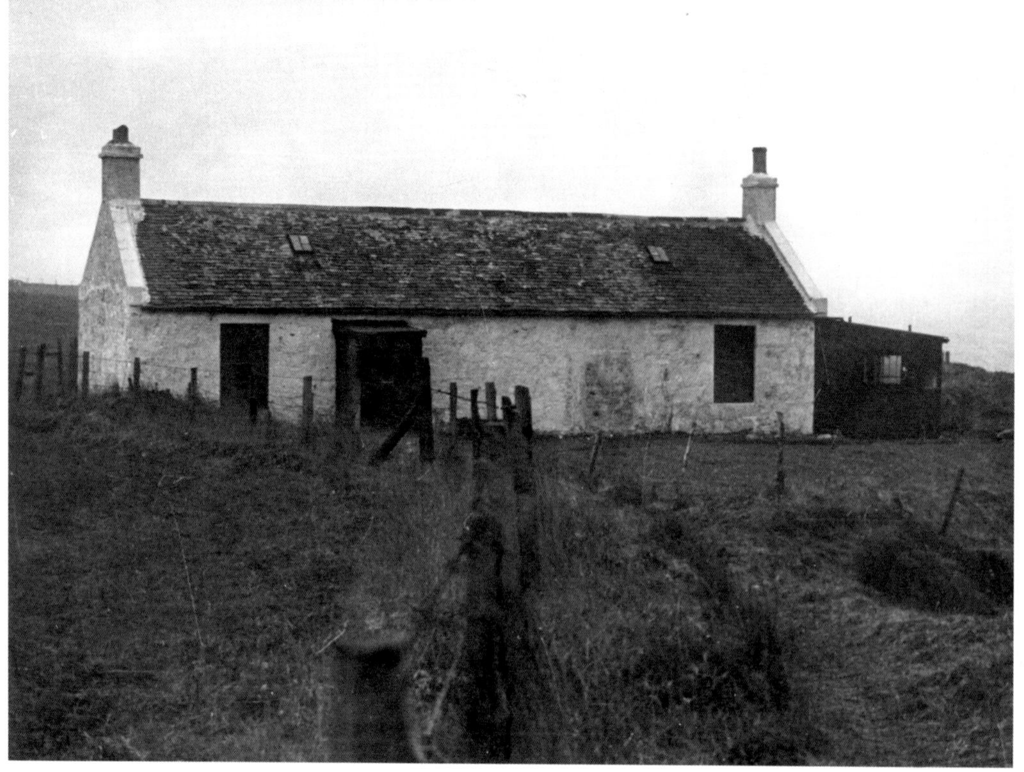

> *enclosed turnip field next to a little croft, and when I had finished I walked the 2 miles back …*
> *I think I shall probably stay on next week. So long as the Sopers don't mind my being with them, I think they expect me to stay all the time actually, so it will be all right I expect …*[33]

As it turned out, Eardley contracted mumps while the show was on. She recovered at her mother's house in Bearsden and then returned to Stonehaven soon after, when she seems to have visited Catterline for the first time with Annette Soper [fig.14].[34] Rudimentary rural life was not new to her: in the 1940s she and Margot Sandeman had often stayed in a little bothy in Corrie on the Isle of Arran. Eardley probably returned to Catterline on several occasions over the next year or two, staying with Soper or at the Masson's Inn. In 1952 Eardley and Soper heard that the Watch House – known locally as the Watchie – was for sale. The most northerly home in the village, and somewhat isolated from the other houses, it was built for Customs & Excise to keep a watch-out for smugglers, and accordingly had magnificent views right down into the crescent-shaped bay, facing south. It had since been decommissioned and sold as a single cottage [fig.15]. Like many other cottages in the village, it had been uninhabited for some while and was used mainly for storage. It transpired that the owner, Charles Wilson Smith, the water bailiff, was prepared to sell it for £40 and so Annette bought it on 25 August 1952.[35] Eardley was invited to stay there whenever she liked.

Eardley came almost straight away, probably in the autumn or early winter of 1952. Andrew Stephen, who as well as being a fisherman was also the local taxi driver and delivery man, was asked to meet her at Stonehaven train station, and he went in his Austin lorry along with his young son, Ron. Instructed to pick up a 'young lassie', Mr Stephen declared that there was no such lassie at the station, but his son pointed to a figure in a tweed jacket and corduroy trousers with two suitcases and a box, and this was indeed Joan Eardley.[36] Mr Stephen's other son delivered coal to her at the Watchie the next day. Seeing two mice on the kitchen table, he was on the point of dispatching them when Eardley intervened; she liked them there.[37]

Catterline was predominantly a fishing village, although villagers also took agricultural work when need be. There were about thirty cottages, the oldest ones numbered from 1 to 24 Catterline, plus the Coastguard Buildings and the Station Officer's House (see map p.125). Many of the dwellings and the pier were built by Viscount Arbuthnott, who originally owned the village. A Scottish Episcopal church, St Philip's, and an adjoining school were about half a mile to the north of the village. Three farms, a mill, a garage and a few other buildings were scattered about nearby. Provisions could be bought at Duncan's Shop near the main road, a good mile away to the west, which also housed a Post Office. By the time Eardley first visited the village, the fishing industry was in steep decline: a report produced in 1928 recorded that only thirty people lived there, while about 100 had been resident twenty years earlier.[38] By 1928 only eleven fishermen remained, and almost all of them were over fifty years of age. The report added that the future of fishing in the 'quaint' village was under threat partly because of the cost of getting the fish to market, since the village was off the main road and had no train station. The young were leaving Catterline for the bigger fishing ports where the offshore trawlers operated. Many of the little cottages had been abandoned and used for storage; some had bare earth floors. There was no mains electricity, gas or water in the village until about 1954–55, when the council built three cottages (the Burnside Cottages) and a new school. The cottages in the northern part of the village acquired mains services at that time, but the strip of ten cottages (Nos 1–10) at the southern end did not.

From 1952 to 1954 Eardley made regular trips by train from Glasgow to Catterline, always staying at the Watchie. Soper, Eardley, Angus Neil and Soper's nephew helped make the cottage habitable, converting it from two small, separate dwellings (to permit two customs officials to keep a twenty-four-hour watch) into one. Eardley's earliest and most ambitious paintings done in Catterline continued the style, approach and format of the paintings she was then doing in Glasgow. *Catterline Coastguard Cottages* [plate 49] is probably Eardley's first large Catterline painting. It dates from 1951, before Soper had bought the Watchie; Eardley presumably stayed at the Masson's Inn.[39] The paintwork and colouring are comparable to the contemporary Townhead painting of *Street Kids* [plate 5]. Executed with deliberation, the early Catterline paintings are solidly constructed, like the buildings themselves [plates 49–53]. They are done on canvas, as the Townhead paintings are, whereas Eardley's later Catterline paintings were usually on board. At this time, she concentrated her attention on the cottages in the northern part of the village, not far from the Watchie: all her major paintings of the time were done just a short walk away from her front door and within a radius of a few hundred metres. What is striking, and in a way surprising, is that in these early Catterline paintings there is no indication of the sea being anywhere nearby.

It was in fact right next to her, or just beyond the buildings she was painting, but she chose to ignore it.

With Soper's nephews using the Watchie more and more, Eardley kept her eye out for a place of her own in the village. In 1954 she rented No.1 Catterline (now known as No.1 South Row), the most southerly of the houses in the village.[40] It belonged to a Mrs Peacock from Aberdeen, who owned a couple of other cottages on the same row. It had been uninhabited for a while, indeed only two of the cottages in the row seem to have had permanent residents at the time: Mrs Taylor at No.7 and her brother at No.8. The cottages were basic two-room dwellings, with wooden ladders leading up to attic storage. They each had a chemical toilet housed in little sheds at the front (except No.1, where the toilet was at the back). No.1 was probably the most basic of all the cottages, having, when Eardley moved in, a bare earth floor and no ceiling. Standing at the far end of the row, it was also the most exposed. It suited Eardley perfectly.

During the first couple of years at No.1, Eardley and her friend Angus Neil spent time repairing the building and installing a makeshift ceiling, using old canvases and boards that had been painted but rejected. She used an old canvas sail to divide the room in half. Eardley had plenty of experience in this type of maintenance work, having served as a joiner's apprentice during the Second World War. They also installed a rough wooden floor in one half of the cottage. In 1957 the toilet shed was remodelled, to include a new door – sufficiently important news for it to merit photographing and mentioning in a letter to Walker: 'It's got a WINDOW and it's going to have a curtain, so as those folks what is shy can pull that wee lace curtain – and feel right soft and cosy'.[41] Soon after moving in, Eardley wrote to Walker:

> *It is a great wee house. The floor is all levels at once. And the table three tarry boards nailed together. There's a great big bed, half wood and half spring. A Grannies' pot, a bucket, a basin, and that's about all, except for three lovely wee chairs ... I think I shall paint here. This is a strange, strange place. It always excites me.*[42]

Eardley's range of subject matter expanded in the mid-1950s, once she had settled into No.1. The cottage featured regularly in her work, sometimes depicted in the distance from the other side of the bay, outside the Coastguard Buildings [plates 54–59], or from the vegetable gardens behind the cottages, or with the beehives [fig.13; plates 61–63]. Sometimes she painted her cottage from the edge of the field to the south, so that we see only its gable end [plates 60 & 67]. Often, she painted the fields behind, and especially the edge of the field, to the south of the house, where the hedgerow flowers grew [fig.16; plates 66–76]; or the vista behind, looking over the fields called The Reath, which were part of the nearest farm, the Mains of Catterline [plates 64 & 65].

From 1960 Eardley collaged actual grasses onto the surface, making them stick with wet oil paint (*Seeded Grasses and Daisies, September,* 1960, plate 76; and *Summer Fields, c.*1961, plate 69). This collage approach seems to precede the collage of newspaper and sweet-wrappers seen in her late Townhead paintings. A few of the landscapes and seascapes have collaged newspaper (*January Flow Tide*, by 1960, plate 91). The later works, from about 1960, often feature splattered or dripping paint.

When her cottage is not the subject of the picture, it is often the place from which she paints. Many of the views of the bay are painted from right in front of the cottage, but looking away to the north-east, over the bay

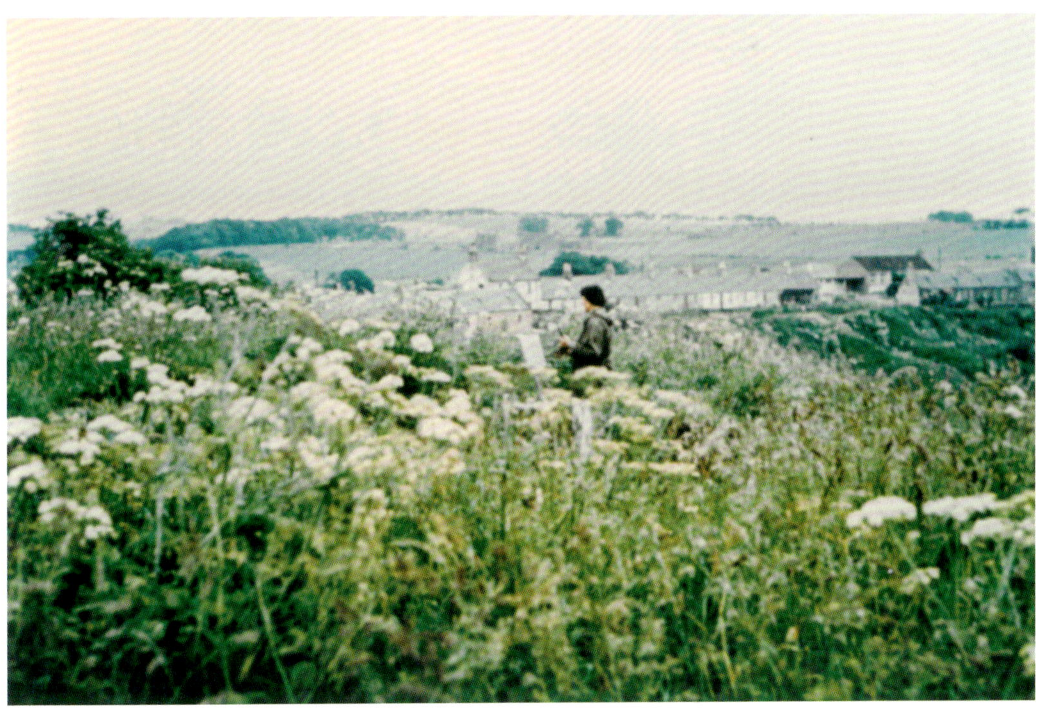

Fig.16 | Painting in Catterline, *c.*1960
Photo by Audrey Walker, courtesy of The Scottish Gallery, Edinburgh

[plates 95–97]. Certain motifs recur in these pictures: the oddly shaped pier, built in the late 1830s, which gets broader at the tip in order to withstand storms [fig.17]; the Watchie, shown perched on top of the promontory; the boat shed and the salmon bothy, just to the right of the pier; a tall rock feature known as the Kale Tap, where villagers once grew kale on the grassy top; and to the right of that, a longer, lower rock formation known as Dunnie Woof (according to some sources, it was so named because it looked like a recumbent dog if approached from the north, but did not bark, hence, in dialect, 'Does not woof').[43] Later on in her time at Catterline, Eardley painted from that shore, looking south, directly at the sea.

All of these subjects – which lie within a short walk of each other – were painted in varying weather conditions, and on boards of different sizes and formats. Eardley painted mainly on canvas in Glasgow, and on board in Catterline. Cost and availability may have played a part, but more importantly she painted mostly indoors in her Townhead studio, and outdoors in Catterline, where big, robust boards could more easily be carried in the wind and rain. Her boards were procured from a joiner in Stonehaven; her paints came from Glasgow or, if need be, she would travel into Aberdeen by train. She also made her own paints: photographs by Walker show her grinding pigments. She tended to use square boards for paintings of fields and long boards up to six feet (1.8 metres) across for seascapes. She sometimes used a large pram to ferry her materials about or otherwise put them on her motor scooter [fig.18]. Her struggles in getting her painting gear down to the shore during heavy gales, and then keeping the easel moored, are legendary. On occasions she even used an anchor to hold the easel down. She described the method as 'Certainly effective – in fact I have left the easel outside anchored and half buried in the snow.'[44] If you look at the edges of her paintings, you can sometimes see circular marks about the size of a two-pence coin: this is where she attached a G-clamp to fix the board onto the easel. One report noted that 'The immense and heavy hardboards are carried to and from her cottage by friendly muscular fishermen.'[45]

It is not clear exactly how she divided her time between Glasgow and Catterline, or how long she spent in each place. The trips seem to have been irregular and random, stays in Catterline lasting perhaps a few weeks at first, and then, as the years passed, she remained there for longer periods. She always took the train between Glasgow and Stonehaven (she never learned to drive a car, although it was an ambition she regularly mentioned in letters). She had the scooter and while it is sometimes said that she took it on the train from Glasgow, it is more likely that she simply parked it at Soper's parents' house at Stonehaven, which was close to the railway station, and used it only in the Catterline area. Andrew Samson recalls that he saw the scooter only once in

Fig.17 | Catterline, from South Cliff outside No.1, showing the pier, boat shed, salmon bothy and, above, the Watchie, late 1950s
Photo by Audrey Walker, courtesy of The Scottish Gallery, Edinburgh

Glasgow, when he accompanied Eardley to Catterline for a fortnight, around 1956. They boarded the train at Glasgow's Buchanan Street Station, where Eardley put the scooter in the guard's van, and they alighted at Stonehaven and drove to Catterline.[46] She occasionally took the scooter out into the country around Catterline, but the great majority of her paintings were done in and around the village.

Eardley evidently painted quickly and worked on many paintings at a time – partly out of necessity, owing to changing light and weather. In August 1955, in a letter to Walker, she reported that she was 'bashing on' with work: 'I've got at the moment about 14 paintings on the go – hardly any of them will ever get finished.'[47] A month later, she was telling Walker: 'I painted all day today. One painting in the morning, one in the afternoon, and one at night. It's a great place for skies here ... And clouds grow out of the sea. I think I am thinking a lot about clouds and sky in relation to painting.'[48] When she initially settled in Catterline, Eardley said that she had wanted to paint the landscape, not the sea, and that was reflected in the work she did in the first few years in the village.[49] Around 1956 she began to take an interest in the stony beach, and particularly the salmon nets, which were hung up to dry on tall larch poles just to the east of the salmon bothy, in an area known as the Makin Green (see pp.102–7). The nets were the subject of numerous photographs, pastels and paintings over the next few years. She also began to depict the fishing boats. By the 1950s, fishing in Catterline was reduced to just four or five of the smaller, in-shore boats; they can be seen in many of her paintings and drawings. These boats, which unlike the salmon coble were owned by the Catterline fishermen themselves, had two main catches: lobsters and crabs, caught in creels (which can often be seen in the foreground in Eardley's paintings); and haddock and cod, caught on long lines baited with mussels.

The crabs, known locally as 'Partans', were abundant off Catterline and on a good day a boat could net over 300 kilograms of them. The crabs and lobsters were put into separate wooden barrels; the village children packed the tops with grass grabbed by the fistful from the brae. The barrels were taken to Stonehaven and would then go by train to Billingsgate in London. The salmon went to

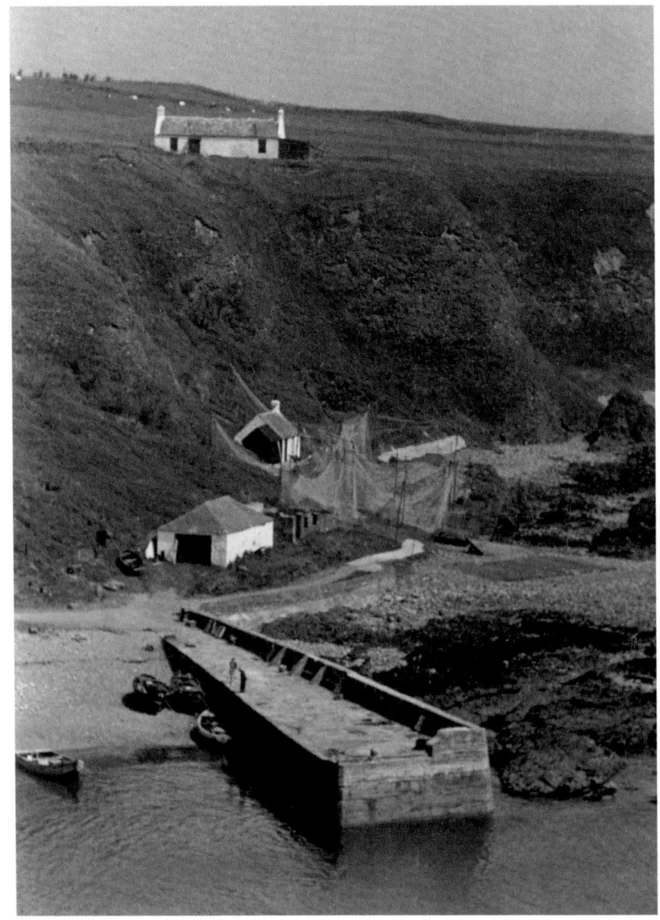

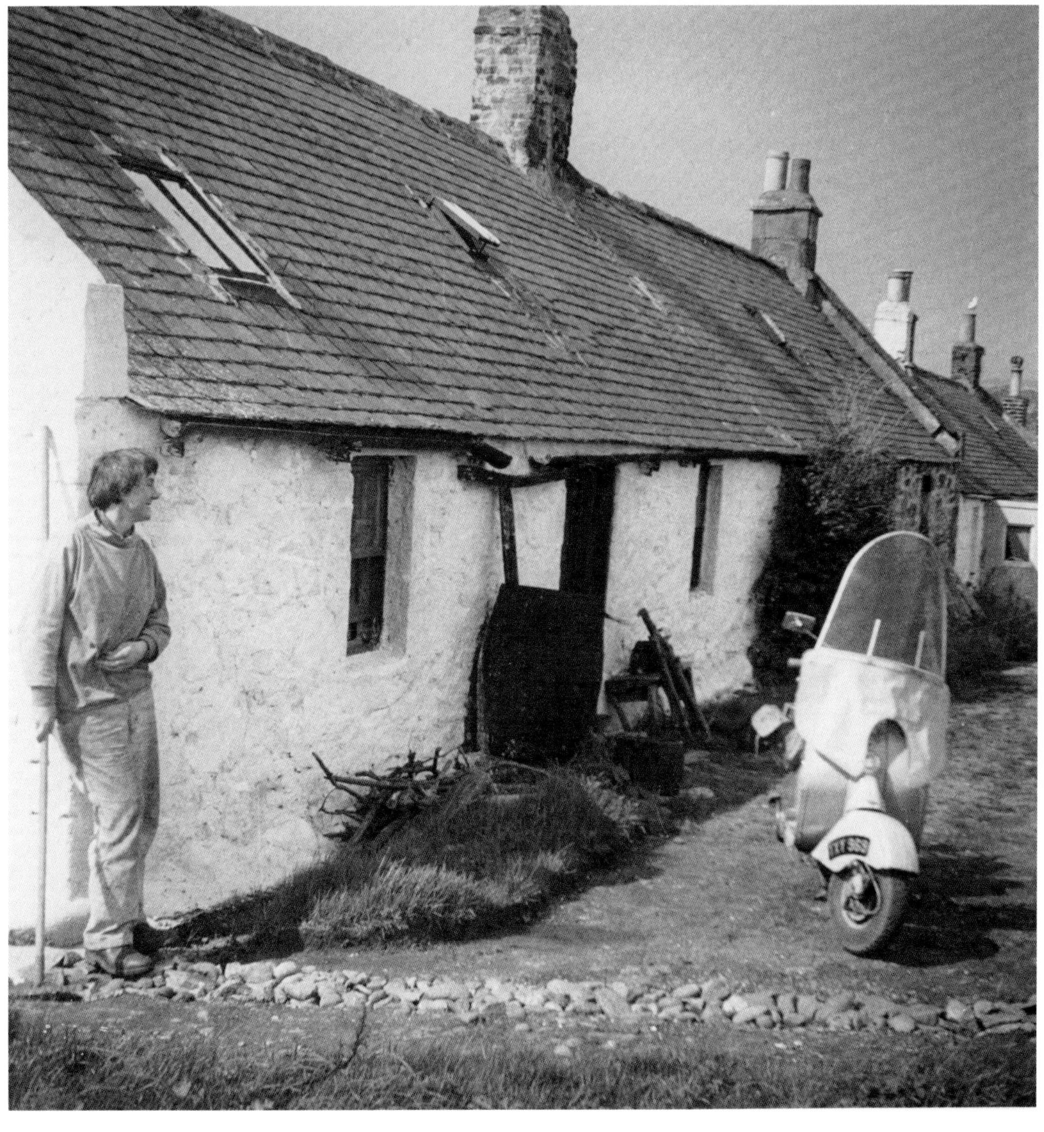

Fig.18 | Eardley outside No.1 Catterline, probably late 1950s
Joan Eardley Archive, Scottish National Gallery of Modern Art, Edinburgh

Montrose by road. It is telling that Eardley never painted any of this human activity in Catterline, whereas the interaction of people with their surroundings was her main focus in Townhead.

The village children found Eardley fascinating. She was a strange new arrival who, unlike everyone else, neither fished nor farmed, but painted. As Ron Stephen recalls:

> *In the 1950s it was a village and this strange person doing something different was exciting. 'Where's the artist today?' we'd say. We didn't know her as Joan. And we'd find out where she was. She'd be painting often at night-time; there was no routine. We would go up to her, two, three or four of us. It was better in a smaller number because she always had a bag of sweets on her easel. She'd chat away and would tolerate us, then she'd produce the bag of sweeties and it was almost like a signal to say goodbye, without actually saying so. We knew our place.*[50]

Thanks in particular to letters she sent to Walker, we get a good sense of Eardley's thoughts and routine in Catterline. If there is one sentiment that recurs, it is self-doubt: Eardley was never satisfied with her work. Apart from that, a frequent observation is that, if she has not finished a painting, she has to wait for near-identical conditions to return before she can continue with a work. This meant that the sun, the tide and so on had to be in the same position. In one letter she notes:

> *Today has been a perfect day – warm sunshine. I was working on the shore. Have now got thoroughly interested in these shore paintings – Oh dear. Because due to all the reasons which you know so well by now – these things take so long to work out. So much dependent on so much – type of day, place of sun, place of tide – (this more than anything determining what can be worked at and what not). The case particularly brought home today – because everything was perfect for a particular painting – lighting, type of day, sun, which went down red as I wanted – but the tide instead of being full in was full out and therefore where there should have been a whole foreground full of sea lighted by the sun there was a whole foreground full of rock and no sea at all. So no good.*[51]

Fig.19 | Eardley painting the pier and bay from in front of her house at No.1 Catterline; the painting may be *Winter Sea* [plate 97], *c.*1958
Photo by Audrey Walker, courtesy of The Scottish Gallery, Edinburgh

Sunny days sometimes bored her, and were deemed unsuitable for painting.[52] She liked extreme weather conditions. In February 1958 she reported that:

> *In between blizzards it has been so much just what I wanted for my painting – that stupidly I imagined that I could rush out and in with my canvas. You know what a job it was setting up that canvas at the back of the house. Well I've had it 3 or 4 times to do and undo in the teeth of the gale … You really need to be tough for this game.*[53]

Whereas Eardley's early work in Catterline had focused on buildings, and been almost documentary, even 'social realist' in character, by 1957 her work had become more liberated, more personal, more expressive of her interior life, and this happened through the process of painting the landscape. It was partly a matter of needing particular weather conditions in order to finish a picture, and by necessity embarking upon new works in the meantime. Again, she wrote of this in a letter to Walker:

> *It is awful that there are always as you say other paintings – so that one is never really able to finish off. This is particularly so in landscape. For the very simple reason that one can't sit and wait – perhaps for a week or as in the case of my waves much more – for the particular situation to recur. There must be other paintings to fill in the time – and these paintings lead to other ideas and so on and so on – an awful chain.*
>
> *But I do feel that the notion of landscape inside me is becoming satisfied. And therefore there won't be I hope too much wastage – when I'm forced to stop. There's bound to be some feeling of having left bits of myself behind. But I'll try and not be too complainy, when I do eventually have to contend again with that nasty place Glasgow. I know I feel most thankful and grateful to providence and you – too – for having had this long time of continuous thought upon landscape.*[54]

Eardley mixed well with the villagers. If anyone realised that she was lesbian, nobody said anything or seemed to mind: 'There were no inappropriate remarks', said Ron Stephen, 'there was certainly none of that in Catterline, no way.'[55] Although it may have remained secret, Eardley enjoyed a full and passionate private life and this continued in Catterline. In the late 1940s she began a relationship with Dorothy Steel, a student from the Glasgow School of Art.[56] Eardley and Steel spent three months together in Catterline, probably in the summer of 1953.[57] Eardley also had strong feelings for Margot Sandeman, who was married. She was caught in a difficult triangular situation, which fed into, frustrated and probably enriched her work. This may have contributed to her need to stay in Catterline, where she had few other distractions and could focus on her painting. It is probably no coincidence that the two cottages she liked best in the village – No.1 and the Watchie – were at the extreme ends of the village, where she had no next-door neighbours and could enjoy some privacy.

Her relationships with the villagers were easy and straightforward. Mrs Taylor at No.7 was her main support [fig.20]. When Eardley was ill, Mrs Taylor brought round food and tea; Eardley in turn would collect Mrs Taylor's pension from the Post Office in Duncan's Shop, on the main road. Bad weather could cut off deliveries to the villagers, and then everyone would rally round and lend or give each other what they needed. Apart from the cottages, there was only one building in the centre of the village where they could gather: the Inn, which was two houses (Nos 13 and 14) knocked together.

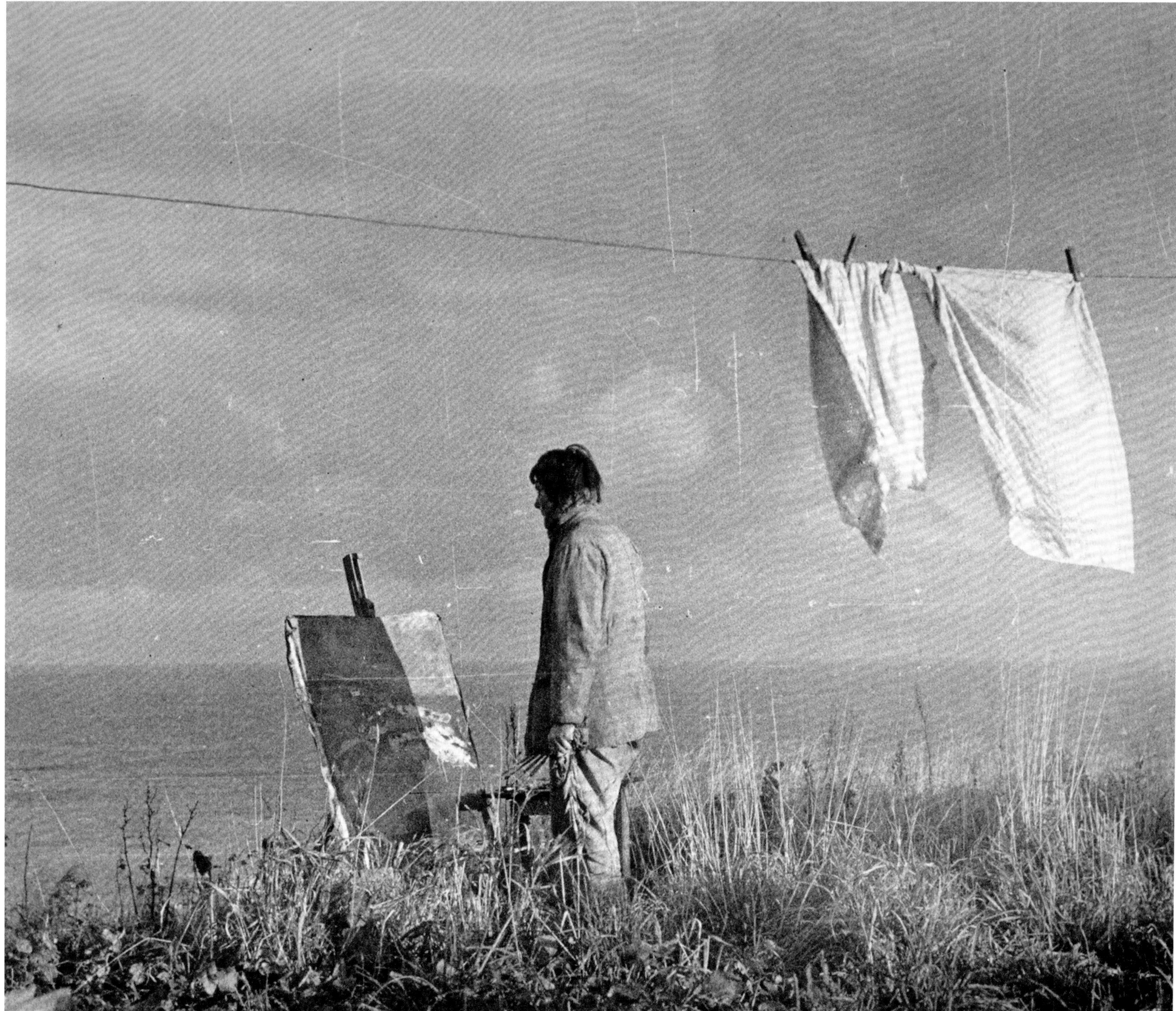

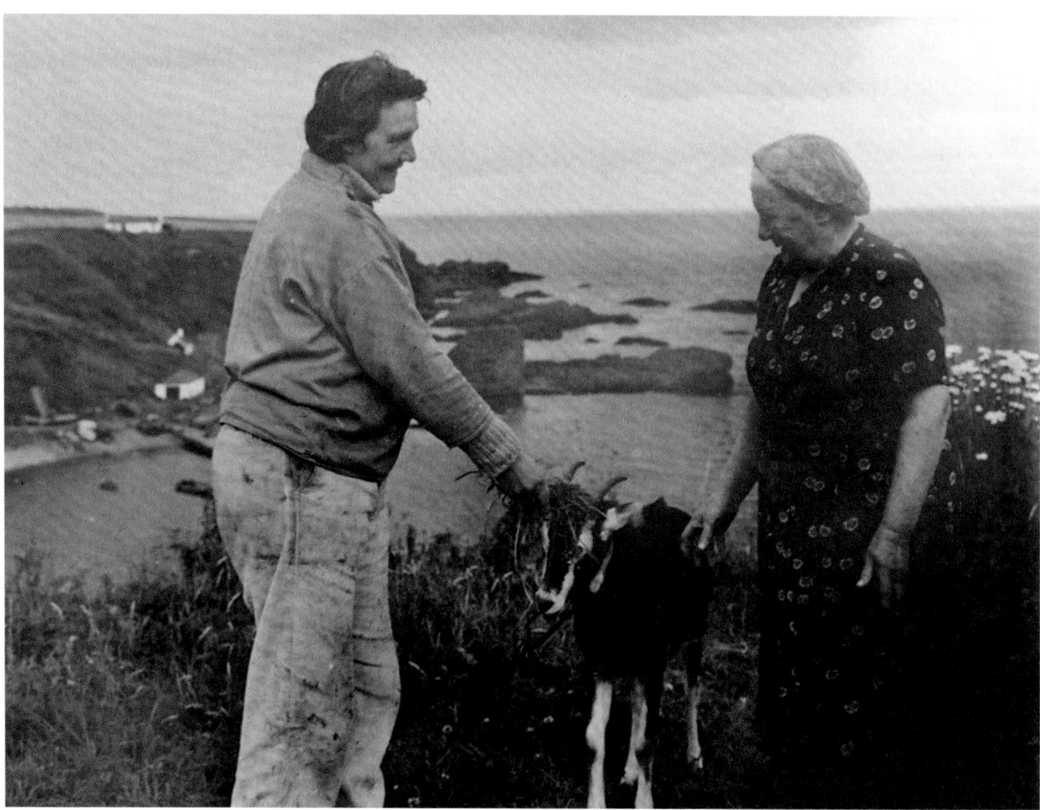

Fig.20 | Eardley with Mrs Taylor and her goat, called Sooty, *c.*1960
Private collection, courtesy of Ron Stephen
Photo by Audrey Walker

Initially called the Masson's Inn, it was run by Davina Masson. It was a porter house – a house with a licence to sell alcohol. There was a shed at the front that served as a shop: there she sold basic goods, cigarettes and sweets (for groceries and meat, the villagers went to Duncan's Shop). Eardley was one of her best customers: she always had a supply of mixed boiled sweets, pan drops or mints on her easel – never in a bag, but always in a rolled-up paper cone. Around 1953 the Inn was acquired by the Cormack family from Aberdeen, who remodelled it and built a bar at the back and renamed it the Creel Inn, the name it still carries.

In 1959 the chance to buy a property emerged. The house called Bridgend, but known to everyone as 'Sarah's Cottage' (after a previous owner, Sarah Smith), had been bought by Angus Neil in April 1958 for £30. It is likely that Eardley lent him the money since Neil never had any himself and he was always borrowing money from her. Then in May 1959 Neil sold Sarah's Cottage to Eardley, for the same price.[58] She can have lived there for only a few months, for in December 1959, Eardley bought No.18 for £250 from the Estate of Martha Beattie.[59] Then in January 1960, Eardley transferred part of Sarah's Cottage – the 'store' to the north-west of the house known as the Old Post Office – back to Neil, and sold the house itself to the artist James Morrison and his wife Dorothy.[60]

Why this flurry of activity, and why did she move out of No.1, the cottage she clearly loved above all others? It seems that she was obliged to, following a decision to condemn the South Row of cottages, which were declared unfit for habitation.[61] Sarah's Cottage seems to have been a stop-gap, and the fact that it lacked a sea view must have bothered her. Mrs Beattie's death in November meant there was a rare opportunity to buy one of the seafront cottages, and by 1959 Eardley's work was selling well and the price was not an issue. Eardley wrote to Walker:

> *Mrs Beattie has died. I'm wondering about the house. I'd sell Sarah's. I don't know. At least the windows look out on the sea. Maybe I'll write to Mrs Peacock first and see if she'll sell me No.1. Then I could floor it at least. And I really don't mind about water and lavy. In fact I like the primitiveness ...*[62]

No.18 was reasonably big, having a spare room, and mains water and electricity. In letters written to her mother soon after moving in, Eardley noted that she had bought a zinc bath and had four electric plug sockets fitted.[63] Now a property owner, the following year, for the first time, she gave her Catterline address, not her mother's Bearsden address, in particulars printed in the Royal Scottish Academy and Royal Glasgow Institute catalogues, where she exhibited most years.

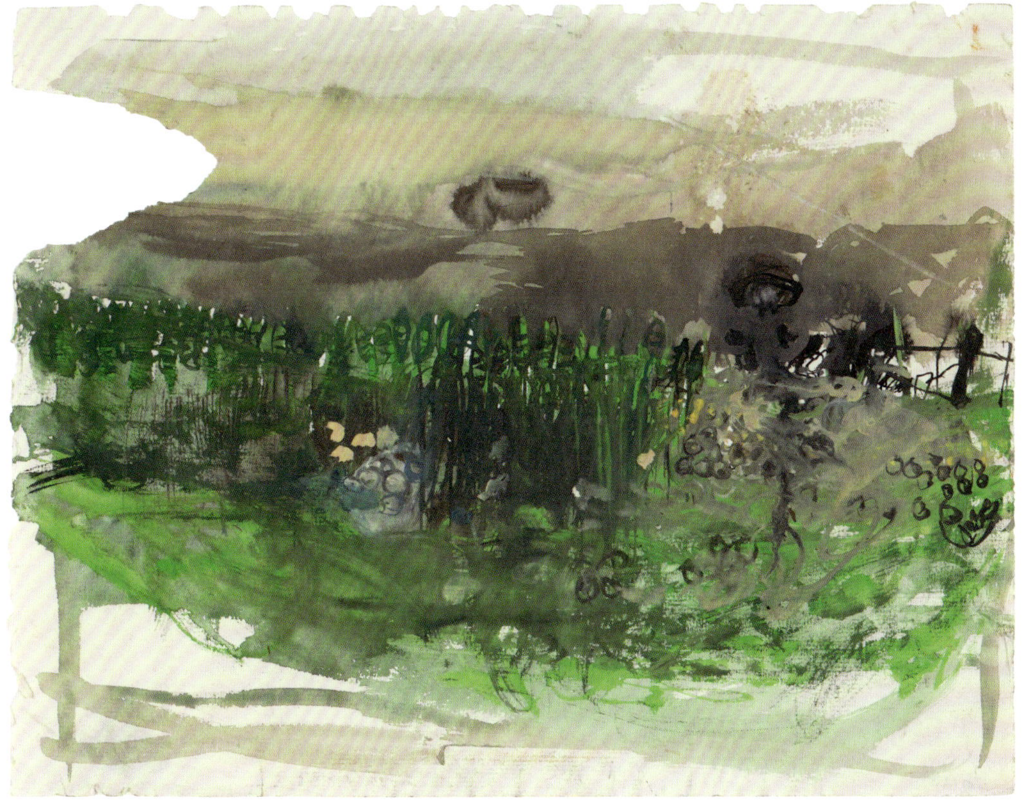

Fig.21 | Joan Eardley, *Green Corn and Flowers at a Field's Edge*, *c.*1960–62
Watercolour, gouache and ink on paper, 24.7 × 32.5 cm
Scottish National Gallery of Modern Art, Edinburgh

Eardley may have had more creature comforts at Sarah's Cottage and at No.18 than she had had at No.1, but this did not make her happier – quite the contrary. In letters to Walker she repeatedly stated that she missed living in No.1, which she described as 'the absolutest best and most beautiful spot in the whole village'.[64] One of the problems with No.18 was that, being in the centre of the village, she had to pass by other people's doors and would inevitably get drawn into idle chat. Eardley noted in a letter to her mother: 'Mrs [Gardener] nips out of hers every time I go past. And you know what Mrs Taylor is like! However it is nice that they are so friendly. Only when you're wanting to get on, it's a bit trying.'[65] The decision to condemn the South Row of cottages was reversed and Eardley continued to rent No.1 from Mrs Peacock, keeping it as a store for paintings. Most of the landscapes she painted in her last years were done in the fields beyond and behind the cottage [fig.16]. In August 1962 she wrote from No.18 to Margot Sandeman:

> *I've got a series of paintings going at the end of my old cottage – the one you stayed in – No.1 – almost the same spot as I painted last year. I never seem to find I want to move. It's a lovely spot as no one comes near and I can always work away undisturbed. I just go on from one painting to another. ... it's oats this year – barley it was last year – so it's a bit different and there's a wee wind-blown tree and that's all. But every day and every week it looks a bit different – flowers come and go and the colour grows – so it seems silly to shift about. I just leave my painting table out there, and my easel and palette. And I have another painting table down here and I paint my flowers in pots when I don't feel like being up there. Painting reduced to its minimum!!*[66]

The large seascapes also belong to these last years, from about 1960 [plates 90–93]. She painted these works right on the shore, usually near the pier or on the Makin Green, but occasionally further along, beyond the salmon bothy, often in appalling weather. In these works, the sea and sky occupy the whole picture surface, to produce something akin to American Abstract Expressionism. Eardley was no ingénue and kept abreast of contemporary trends in art. When asked, in 1961, to name the artists who interested her, she thought first of Jackson Pollock and the Tachistes.[67] But asked about Joseph Mallord William Turner and William MacTaggart, she said that she did not much like Turner's art and knew little about MacTaggart.

In January 1963, the opportunity to buy No.1 from Mrs Peacock came. The price was £35. *Catterline in Winter* [plate 59], one of Eardley's greatest paintings, was created that month, during an exceptionally

Fig.22 | Catterline, from the Makin Green, *c.*1960
Photo by Audrey Walker, courtesy of The Scottish Gallery, Edinburgh

hard winter. It was painted from the footpath in front of the Coastguard Buildings, just beside No.18, but looks out at the South Row, with No.1 at the extreme left. By this time, Eardley's reputation was well established. That year she was made an Academician at the Royal Scottish Academy. A film on her was produced by the Scottish Arts Council. Her work sold well too: her solo exhibition at the Roland, Browse and Delbanco gallery in London in May 1963 was a great success. Aberdeen Art Gallery and Glasgow Art Gallery had bought her work some years earlier, and the recently opened Scottish National Gallery of Modern Art bought *The Wave*, 1961 [plate 90] in January 1962 for £120 and *Children and Chalked Wall 3*, 1962–63 [plate 47] in June 1963 for £165. She was in fact well off; but it was also clear that she was not well.[68] She had suffered headaches for some time, and brushed them off in conversations with neighbours. In May 1963 she was in London, preparing for her show at Roland, Browse and Delbanco, and began to feel seriously ill. She saw a doctor and relayed the prognosis in a letter to Lil Neilson, a young artist she had met at Hospitalfield College of Art and who had become a close friend:

> *The doctor said my bosom had gone into a multiple cist, so I guess I'd better see my own doctor when I get back. She gave me more little white pills, and seems hopefull* [sic] *enough. So I'm not bothering too much, but it would be interesting apart from anything else to see what the other side of the medical profession has to say.*[69]

A few days later she was feeling worse, writing again to Neilson:

> *I intend to go the rounds of the galleries. Though my bosom has been playing up quite a bit and making me feel a bit below par. I'll have to get something done I'm afraid, for it is definitely worse. God what a life. I hate it when bodies go wrong like this. I'm really quite frightened about this bosom. Though I suppose there's perhaps no need to be. But I'll need to see another doctor I think.*[70]

In June she was admitted to Aberdeen Royal Infirmary. She had breast cancer, and it was spreading and badly affecting her sight. She wrote to Walker: 'My headache and lack of sight continues so I'm pretty well confined. But as you know I'm in good hands. Though I must say I'm nearly crackers with the not seeing. For me this is the end!'[71] She was transferred to Killearn Hospital, north of Glasgow, and died there on 16 August 1963, aged forty-two. Her ashes were scattered on the shore at Catterline by the Makin Green [fig.22].

After Eardley's death, Ruby Coull, who lived in one of the Coastguard Buildings, wrote to Walker, expressing her sympathies:

> *We all miss Joan so much, you see in a small village like this we are like one big family and we can't spare one, the place is so empty and quiet when one of us goes, and is never quite the same again. We just cannot believe we won't see Joan standing down at the harbour with her easel in all kinds of weather. Just now she would have been in the harvest field. She lived so quietly among us and was accepted as one of us. We knew she wasn't keeping well and going in to hospital for treatment but never realised how ill, and when we asked her how she was she just passed it off with a smile and said she wasn't feeling too bad. But it is better that she didn't have to suffer too long and her eyesight gone altogether. I pass her wee house a few times every day and it's awful to see the closed door.*[72]

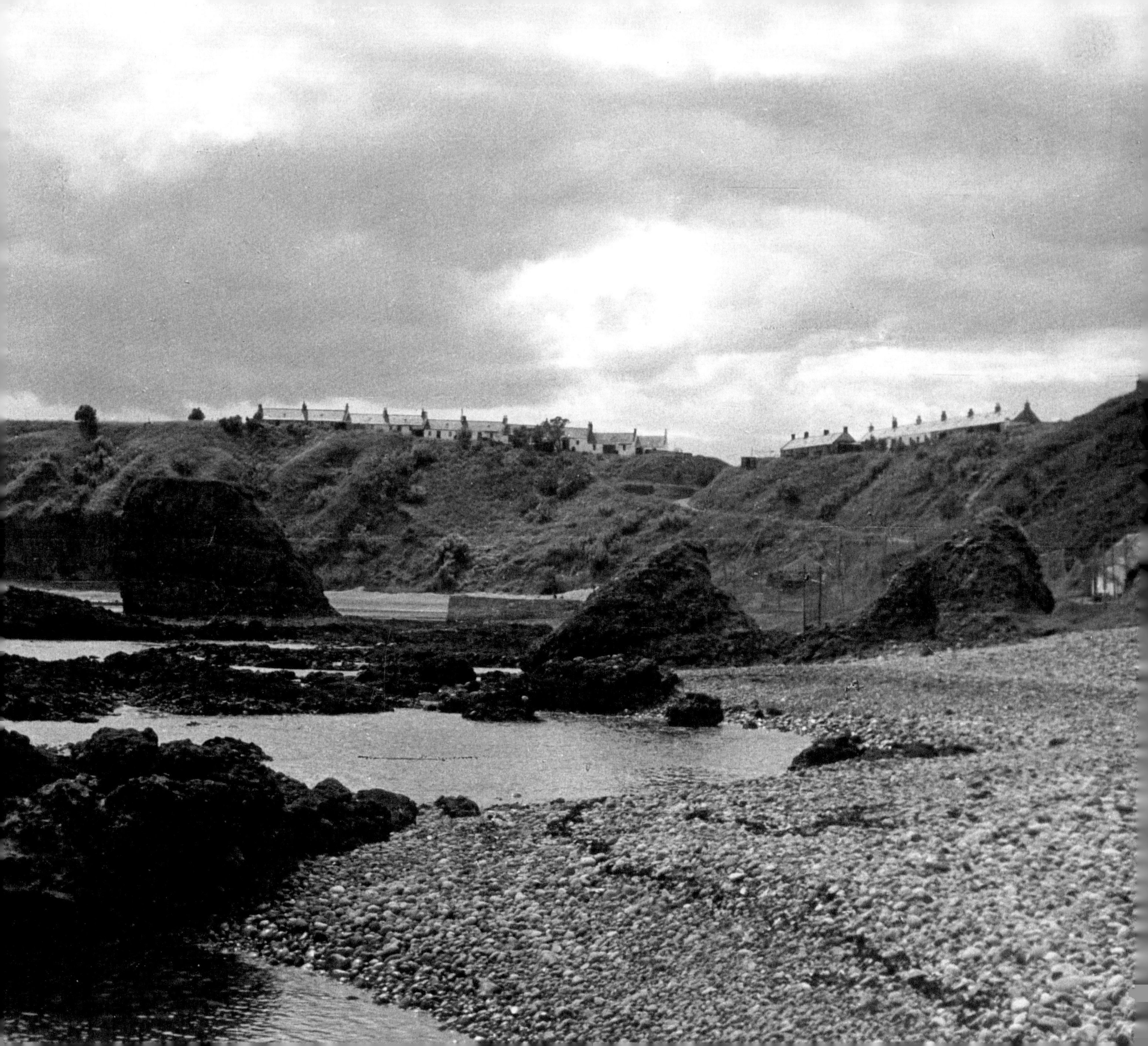

Early Paintings of Catterline

Eardley's earliest paintings of Catterline, done between 1951 and 1954, were painted in the northern part of the village (see map p.125). *Catterline Coastguard Cottages*, 1951 [plate 49] was painted before she settled in the village, probably when she was staying in the local inn; the others were painted between 1952 and 1954, when she was staying at the Watchie.

Cornfield at Nightfall, 1952 [plate 50] shows the backs of houses Nos 19–22, Eardley's nearest neighbours when she was based at the Watchie. The corn stooks are drying, so this is evidently late summer (the view no longer exists: a school and playing field were built on the site in about 1955). *Winter Landscape*, 1954 [plate 51] shows the same strip of cottages from behind, but from slightly further back, allowing the cottage known as Sarah's Cottage to come into view on the right, beyond which is the garage of 'J. & A. Stephen, Carriers and Motor Hirers'. No.1a Coastguard Buildings is glimpsed just behind that.

Sarah's Cottage, *c.*1954 [plate 52] was painted from the field depicted in *Cornfield at Nightfall* and *Winter Landscape* but instead of looking south, Eardley is looking west. It shows Sarah's Cottage on the right, and on the left the home belonging to William Masson, whose sister-in-law Davina Masson owned the Masson's Inn. The middle section was his workshop – and on the other side he had a small shed that served as the village Post Office, where you could buy stamps and make telephone calls. Sarah's Cottage is the white building on the left of the earlier *Catterline Coastguard Cottages*, 1951 [plate 49]. The land in the centre, the 'Tumley', belonged to William Masson, who used it for market gardening. In the distance are the Coastguard Buildings, seen from behind; the communal wash-house is in the centre, behind No.3. The Masson's Inn (which became the Creel Inn in about 1953) can be seen to the far right. This view no longer exists either: the council built the three Burnside Cottages on the Tumley in about 1954.

Catterline Cottages with Figure on Path, *c.*1953–54 [plate 53] depicts the same strip of Coastguard Buildings, but this time from the front, as well as Nos 19–22 to the right. The large house on the extreme left is the Station Officer's House. The path leads, in the opposite direction, back to the Watchie. Had Eardley shifted her position slightly to the left, she would have shown us the harbour and sea below, but these were subjects that held little interest for her at the time.

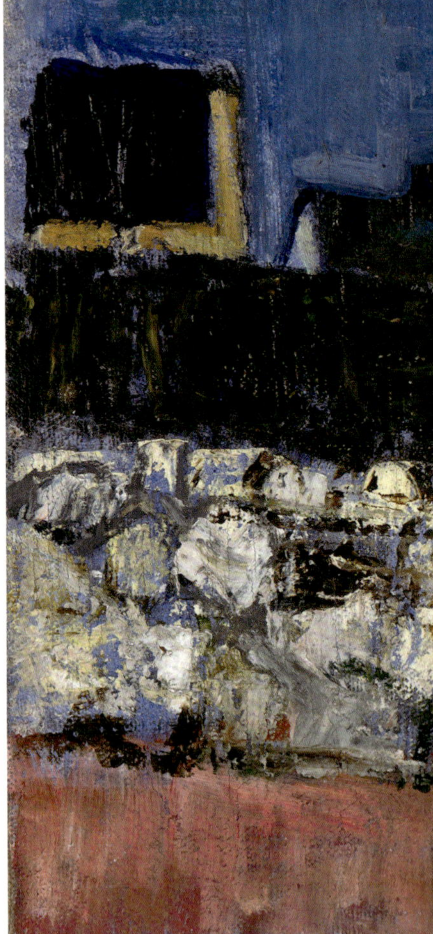

49 *Catterline Coastguard Cottages*, 1951

Oil on canvas, 35.6 × 83.8 cm

Glasgow Life (Glasgow Museums) on behalf of Glasgow City Council

Purchased 1952

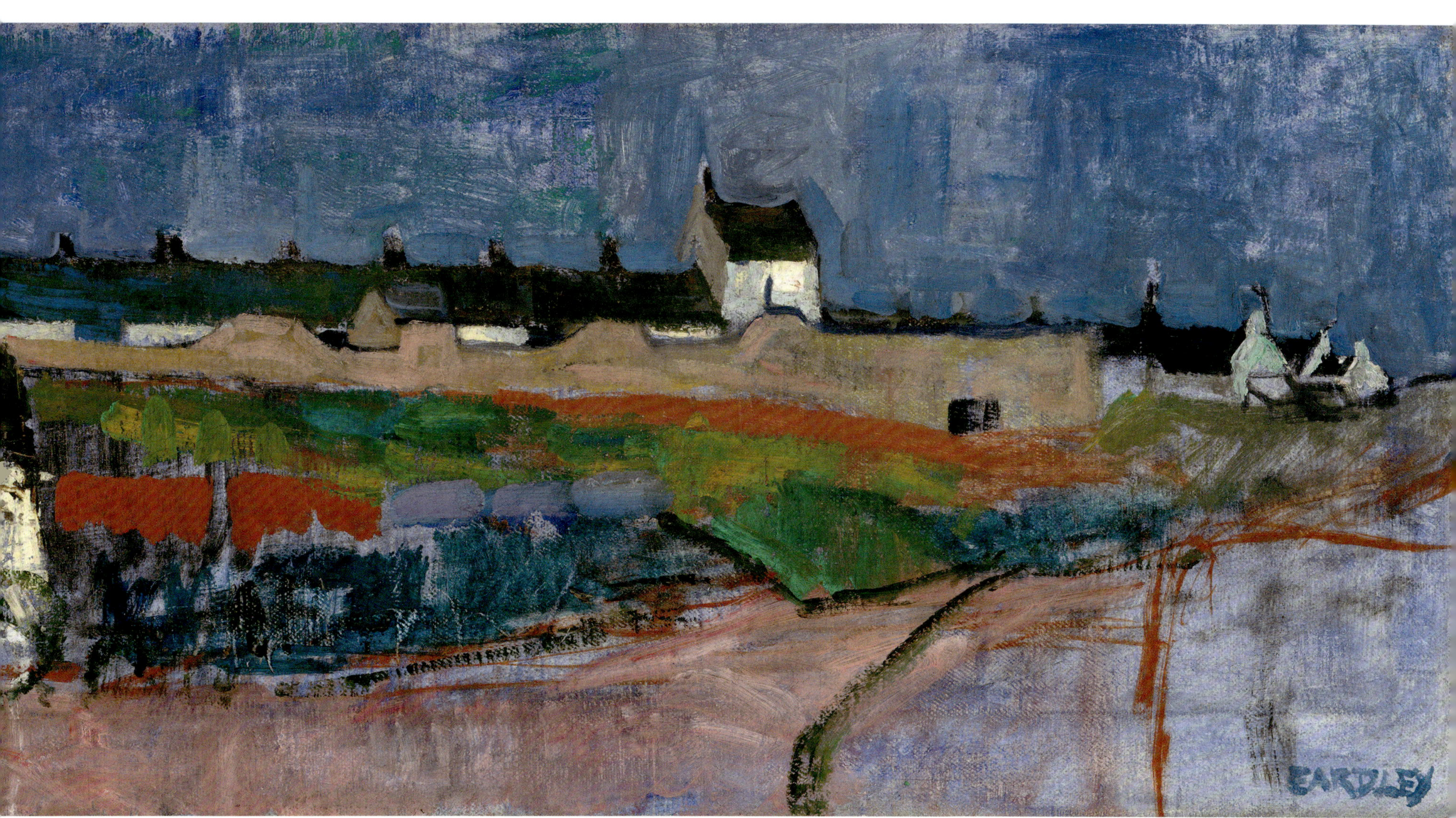
EARDLEY

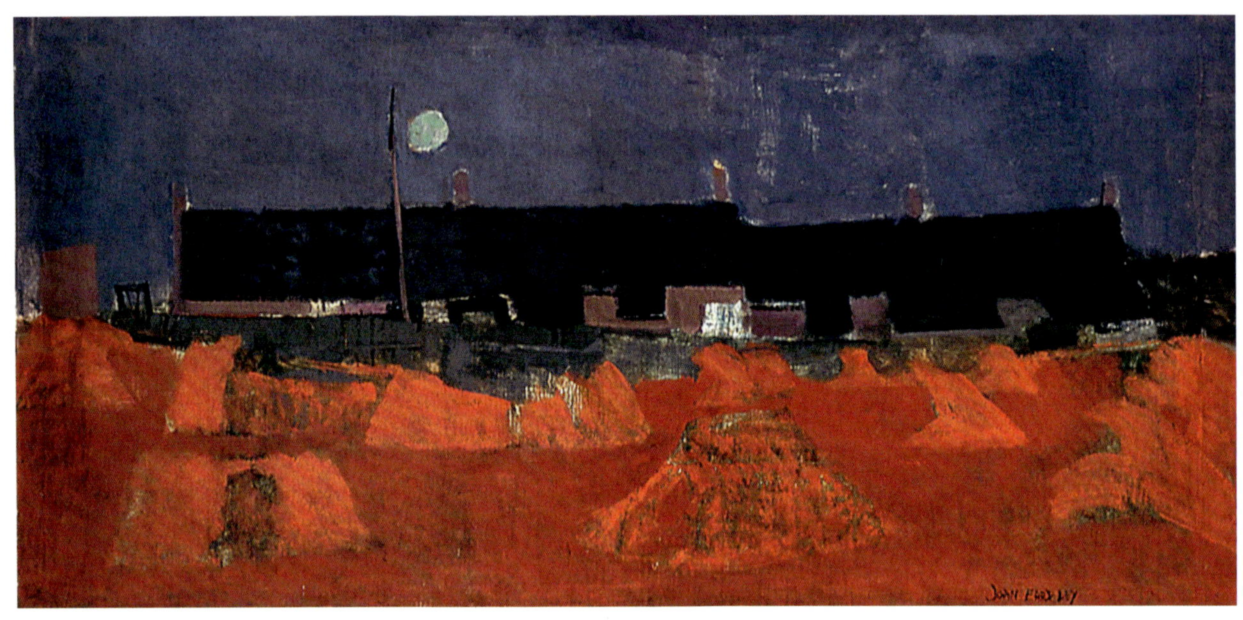

50 *Cornfield at Nightfall*, 1952

Oil on canvas, 66 × 136 cm
Aberdeen Archives, Gallery and Museums
Purchased with the aid of grants from the National Fund for Acquisitions and the Pilgrim Trust and with the assistance of the Friends of Aberdeen Archives, Gallery and Museums, 1990

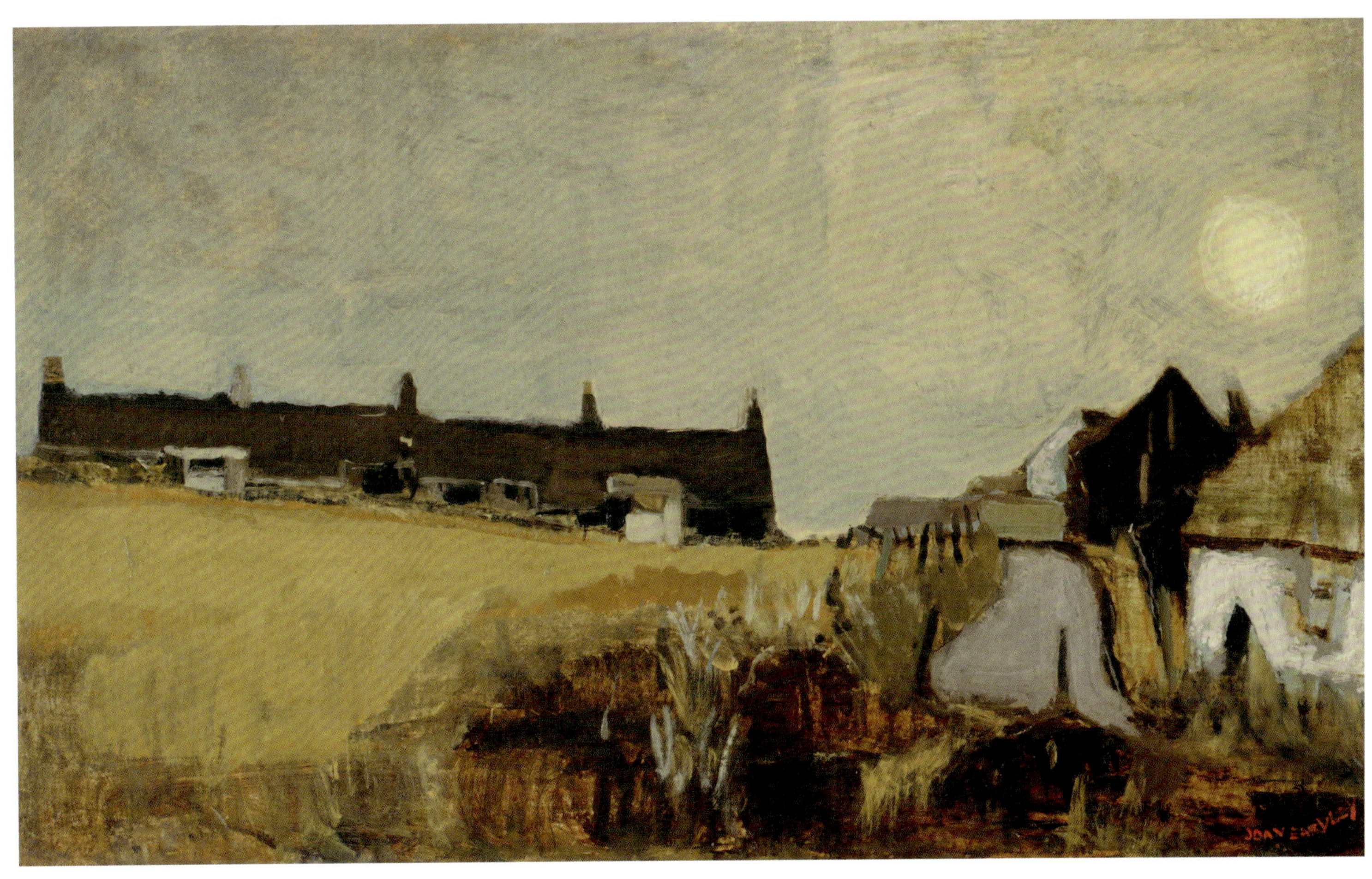

51 *Winter Landscape*, 1954

Oil on canvas, 66 × 96.5 cm
Southwark Art Collection, Southwark Council, London
(Not shown in exhibition)

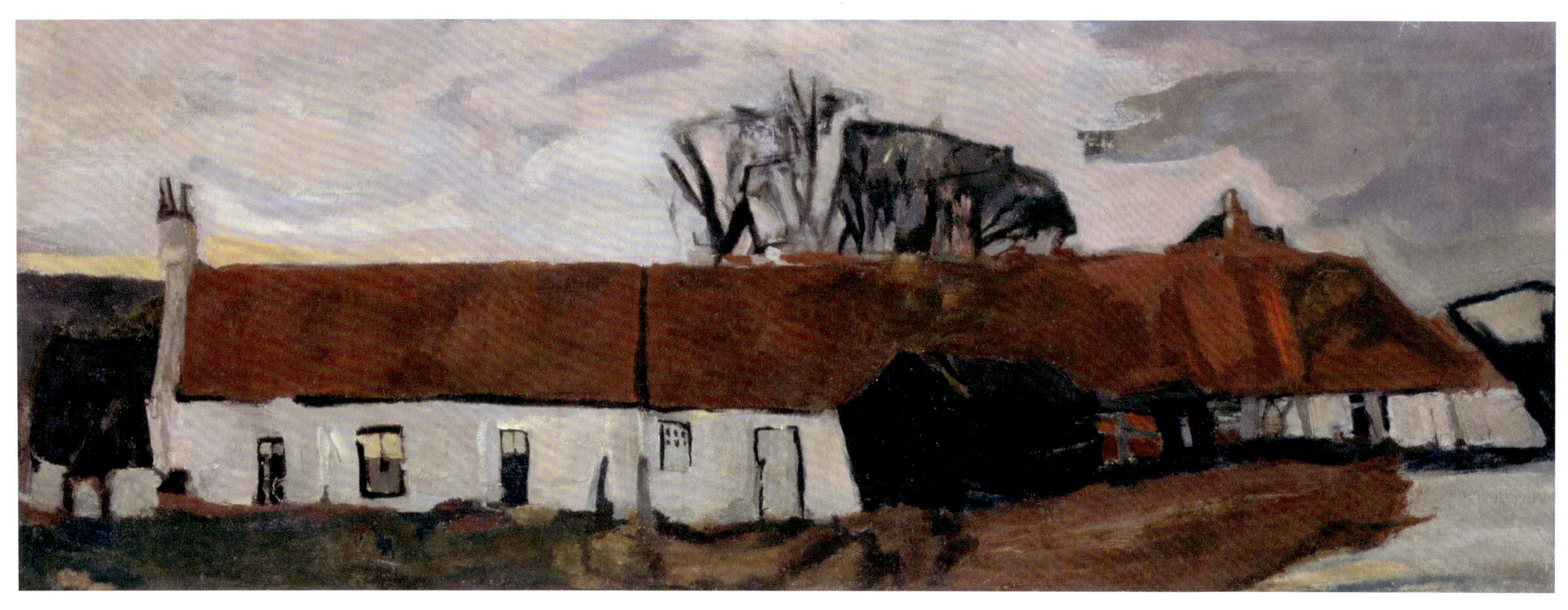

52 *Sarah's Cottage*, *c.*1954

Oil on canvas, 48.3 × 132.2 cm

Aberdeen Archives, Gallery and Museums

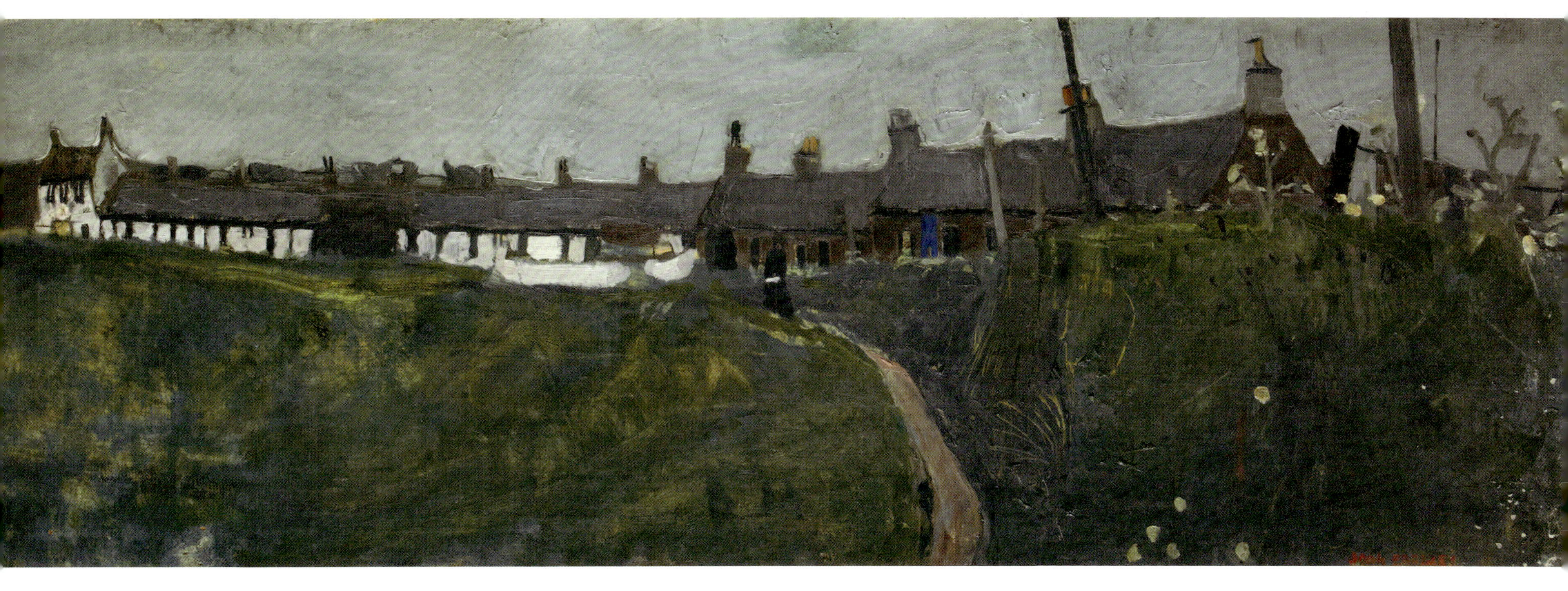

53 *Catterline Cottages with Figure on Path*, c.1953–54

Oil on canvas, laid on board, 40.5 × 150 cm

Private collection

The South Row of Cottages

In 1954 Eardley rented No.1 Catterline, the little cottage on the southern end of a strip of ten cottages known as the South Row. The cottage appears in many of Eardley's drawings and paintings from this time. It is sometimes depicted from a viewpoint roughly outside the Coastguard Buildings, looking south, featuring at the left end of the row, with a windswept tree showing up a little further along to the left [plates 54–59]. To the right in many of these views, we see the gable end of No.12, owned by Mr Watt, with the lean-to shed that was used for storing nets [plates 54, 58 & 59]. In several of these views, the sun is shown roughly above No.12, indicating that it is afternoon.

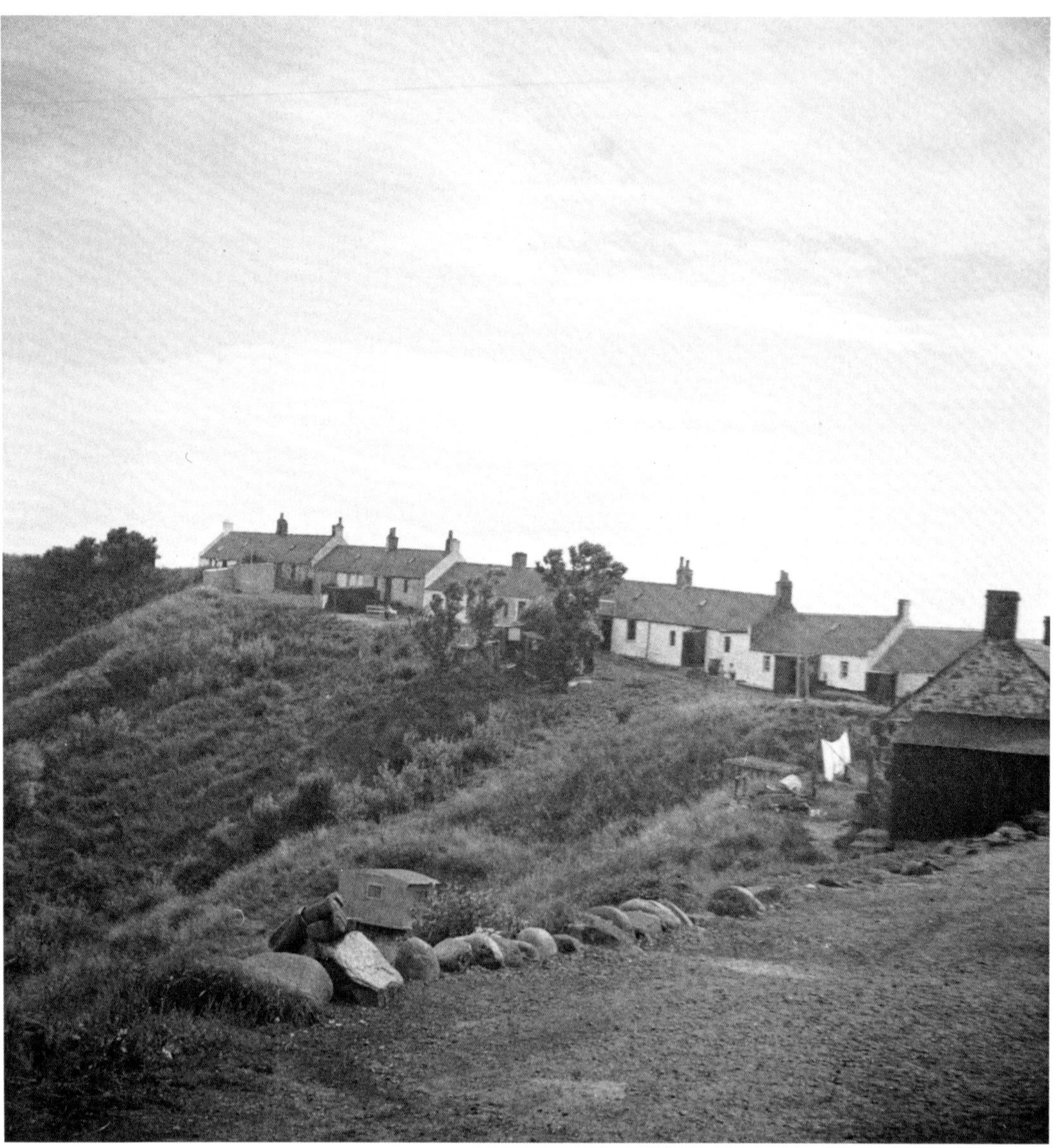

54 *Row of Cottages, Catterline*, *c.*1960–63
Silver gelatine print, 10.5 × 9.5 cm
Joan Eardley Archive, Scottish National Gallery of Modern Art, Edinburgh
Presented by the artist's sister, Mrs P.M. Black, 1987

55 *Row of Cottages, Catterline*, *c.*1960–63
Black ink and watercolour on paper, 20.2 × 25.1 cm
Scottish National Gallery of Modern Art, Edinburgh
Presented by the artist's sister, Mrs P.M. Black, 1987

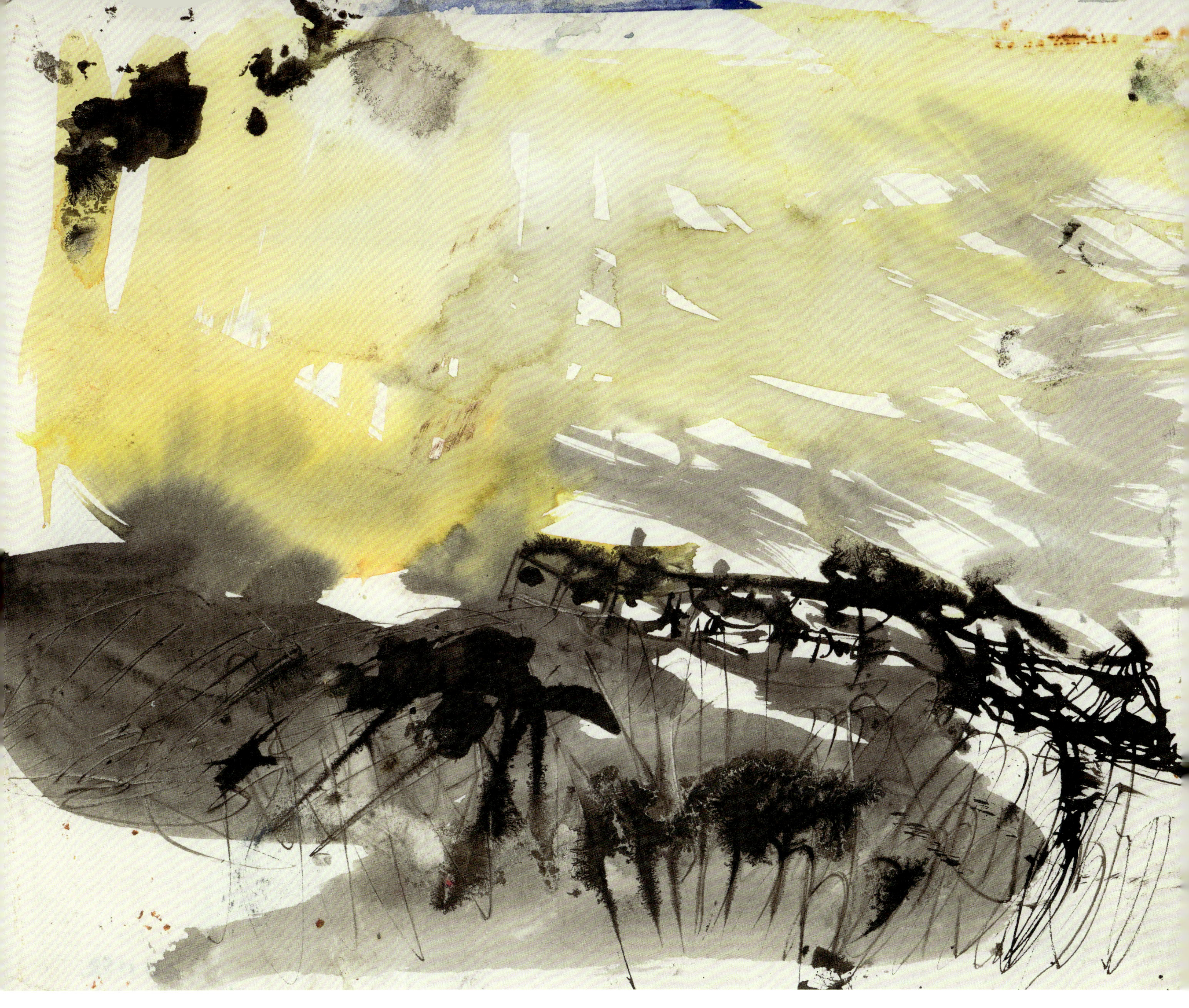

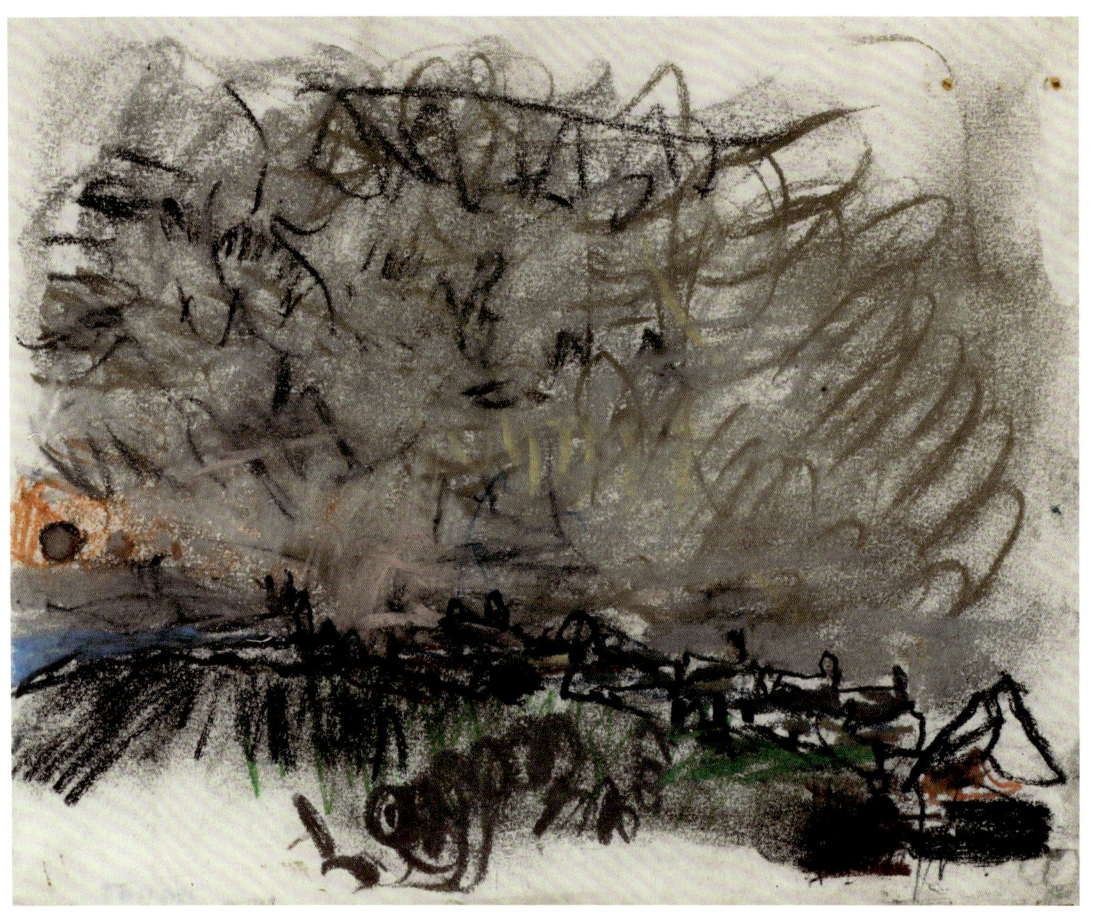

56 *Stormy Sky over Catterline, c.*1960–63

Pastel on paper, 20.2 × 25.2 cm
Scottish National Gallery of Modern Art, Edinburgh
Presented by the artist's sister, Mrs P.M. Black, 1987

57 *Cottages on a Grey Stormy Day, c.*1963

Oil on canvas, laid on board, 10.5 × 36.5 cm
Private collection

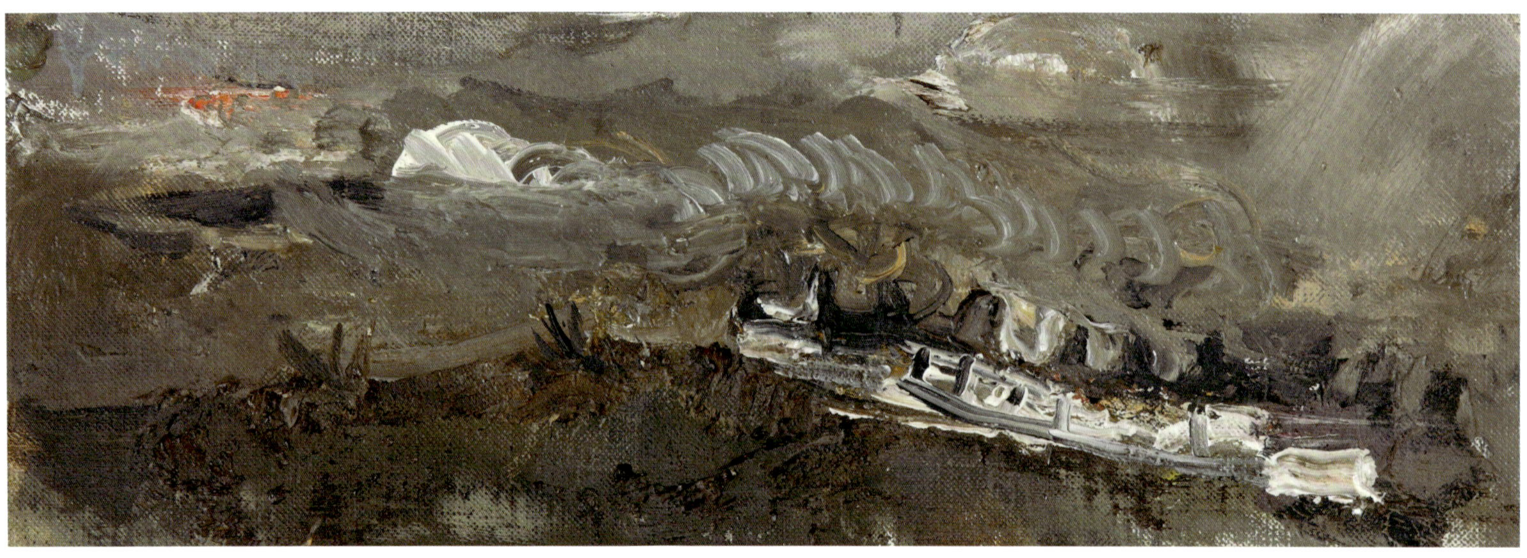

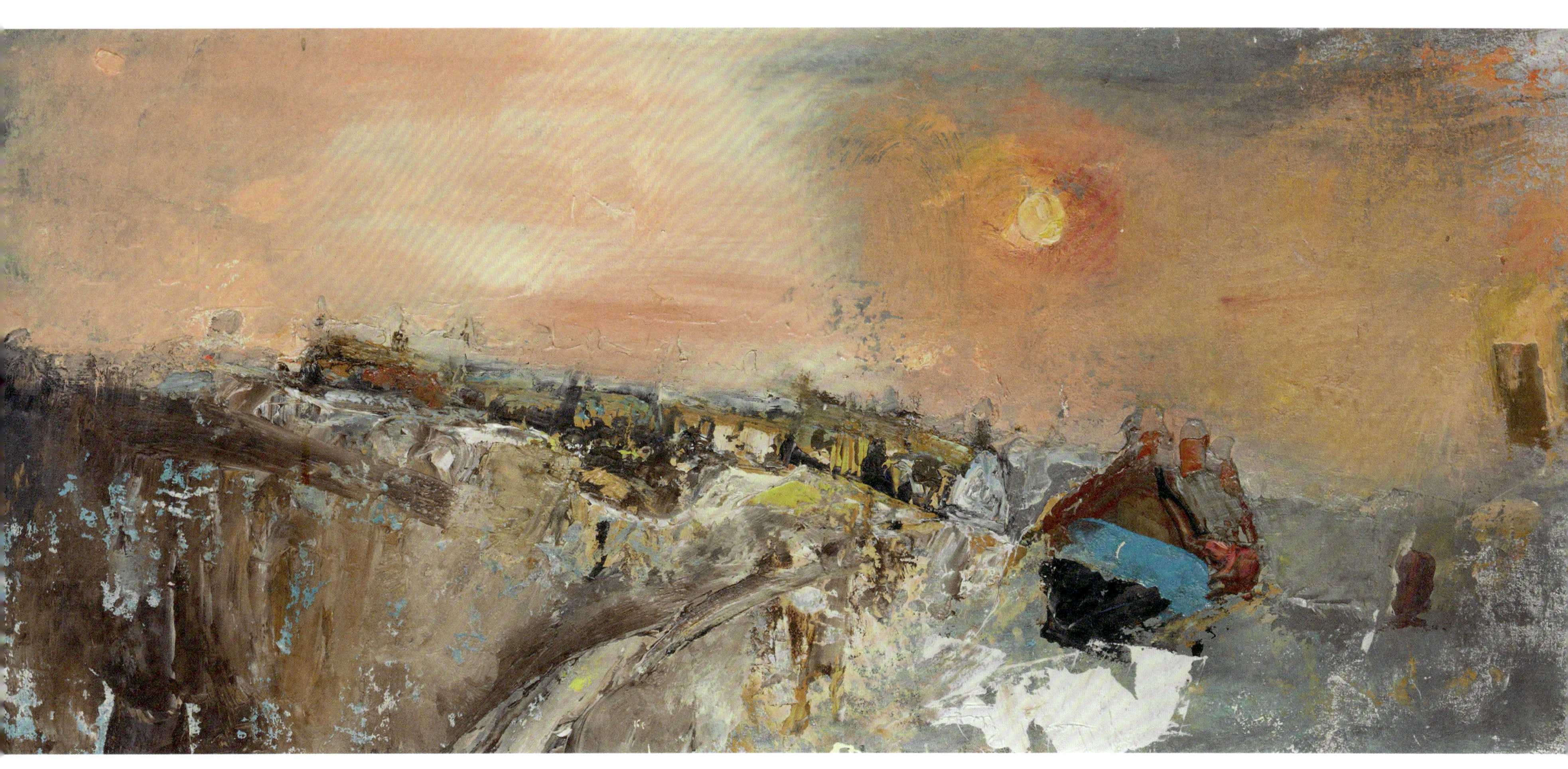

58 *Winter Day, Catterline*, *c.*1957–60

Oil on calico, laid on board, 30 × 69 cm

Private collection

59 *Catterline in Winter*, 1963

Oil on board, 120.7 × 130.8 cm
Scottish National Gallery of Modern Art, Edinburgh
Purchased 1964

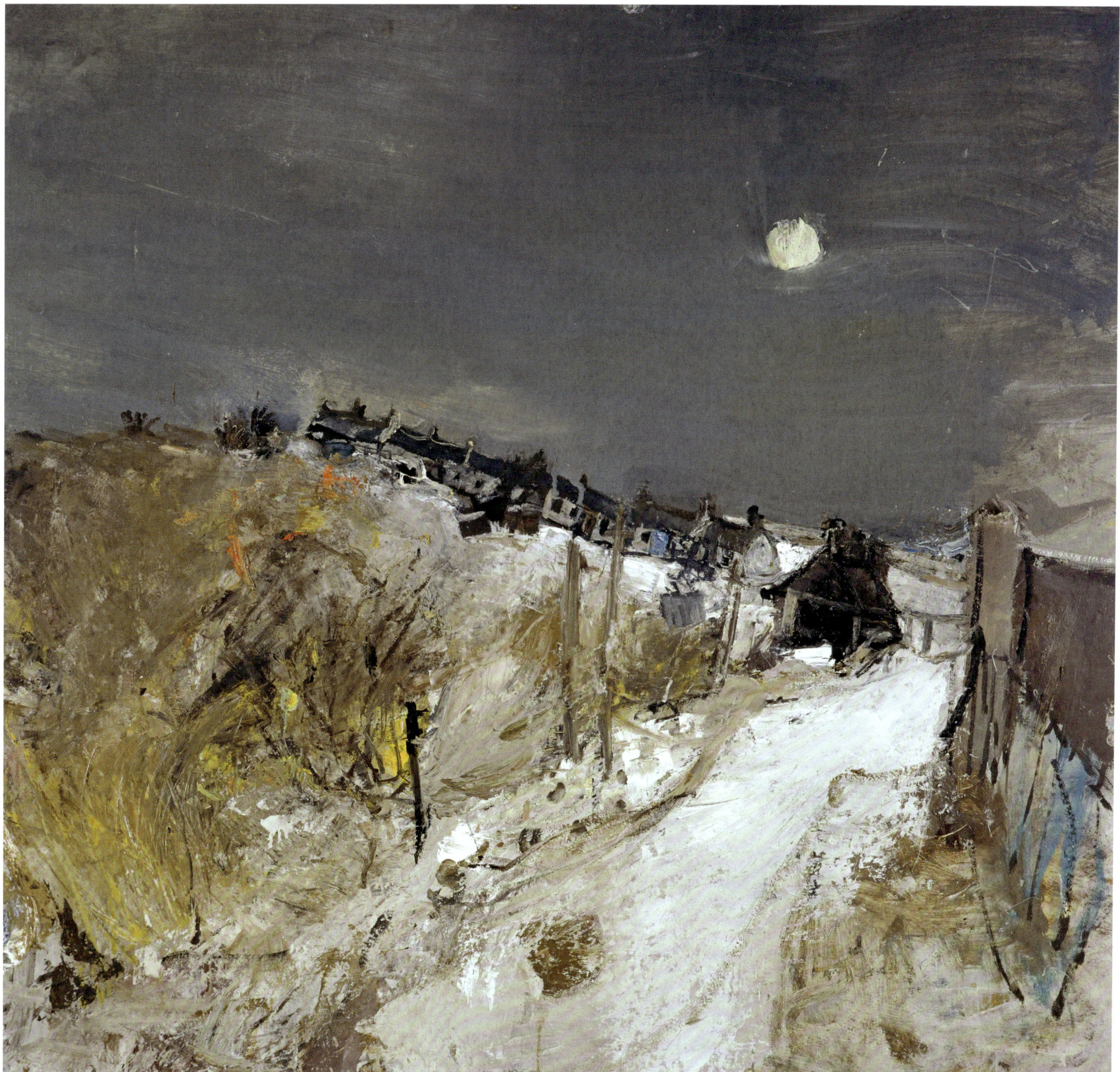

Around No.1 Catterline

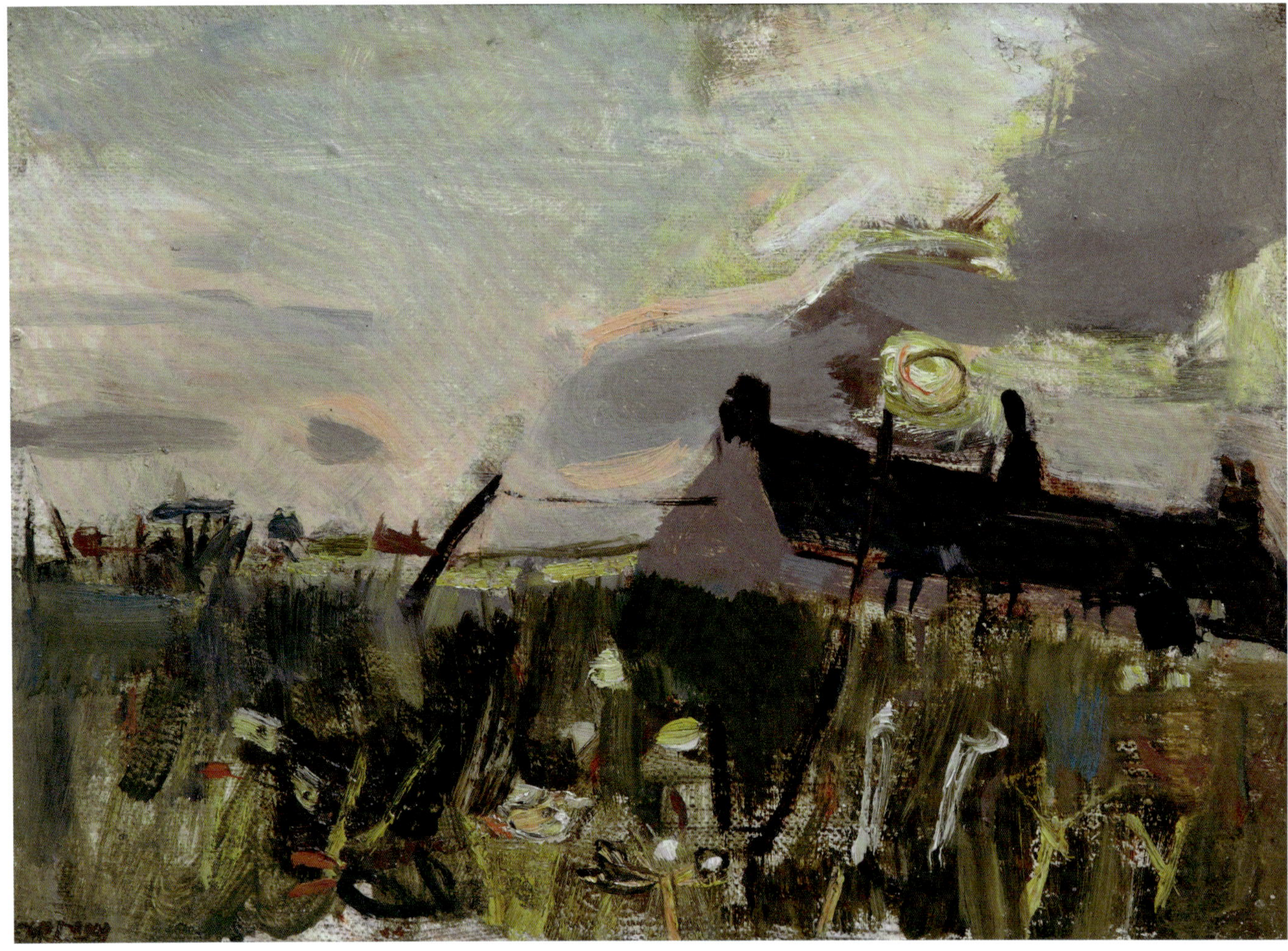

60 *Cottages, Catterline*, *c.*1954–56
Oil on canvas, 25 × 35 cm
Private collection

Sometimes Eardley painted her cottage at No.1 South Row from the back gardens that were used for growing vegetables. Occasionally she shows the beehives [plates 61–63], which were kept there by Bill Coull, who lived in one of the Coastguard Buildings. At other times she painted her cottage from the south side [plates 60 & 67].

She painted the fields behind on many occasions, and especially the edge of the field, to the south of the house, where the hedgerow flowers grew [plates 69–76]; or the vista beyond, looking north-west over the fields called The Reath, which were part of the nearest farm, the Mains of Catterline [plates 64 & 65].

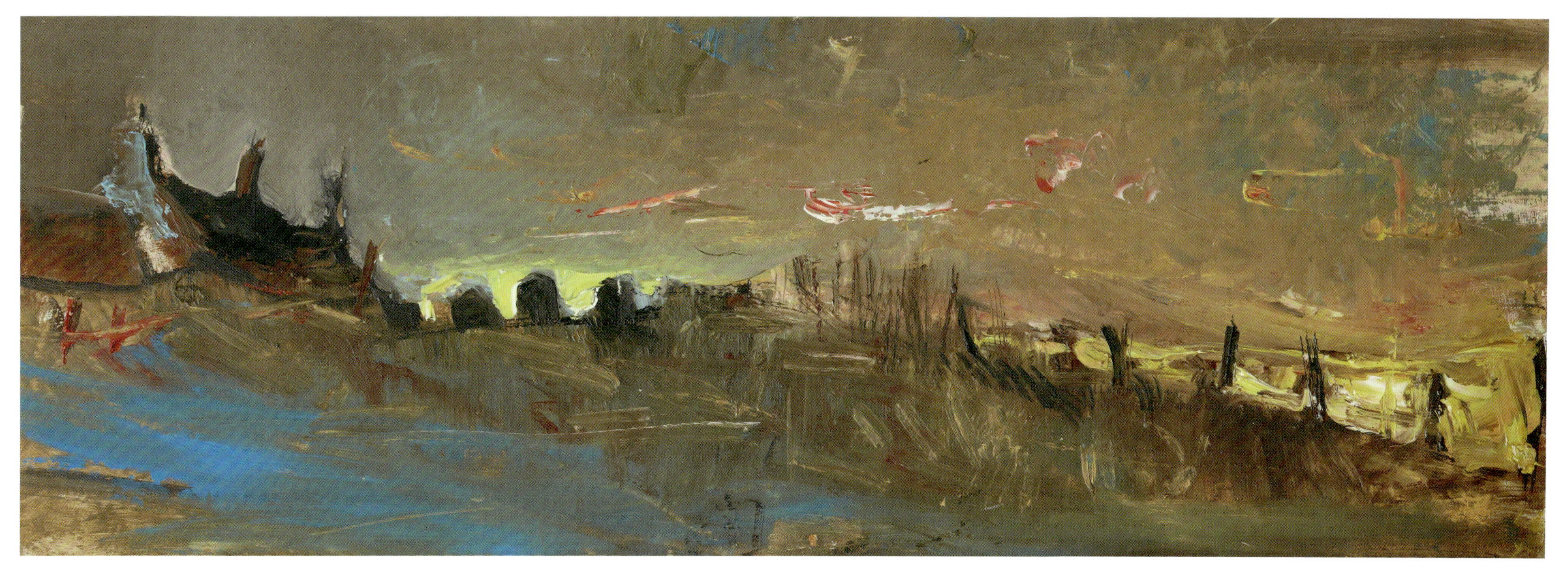

61 *Cottages, Beehives and Winter Sunset*, *c*.1961–62
Oil on board, 26 × 71 cm
Private collection

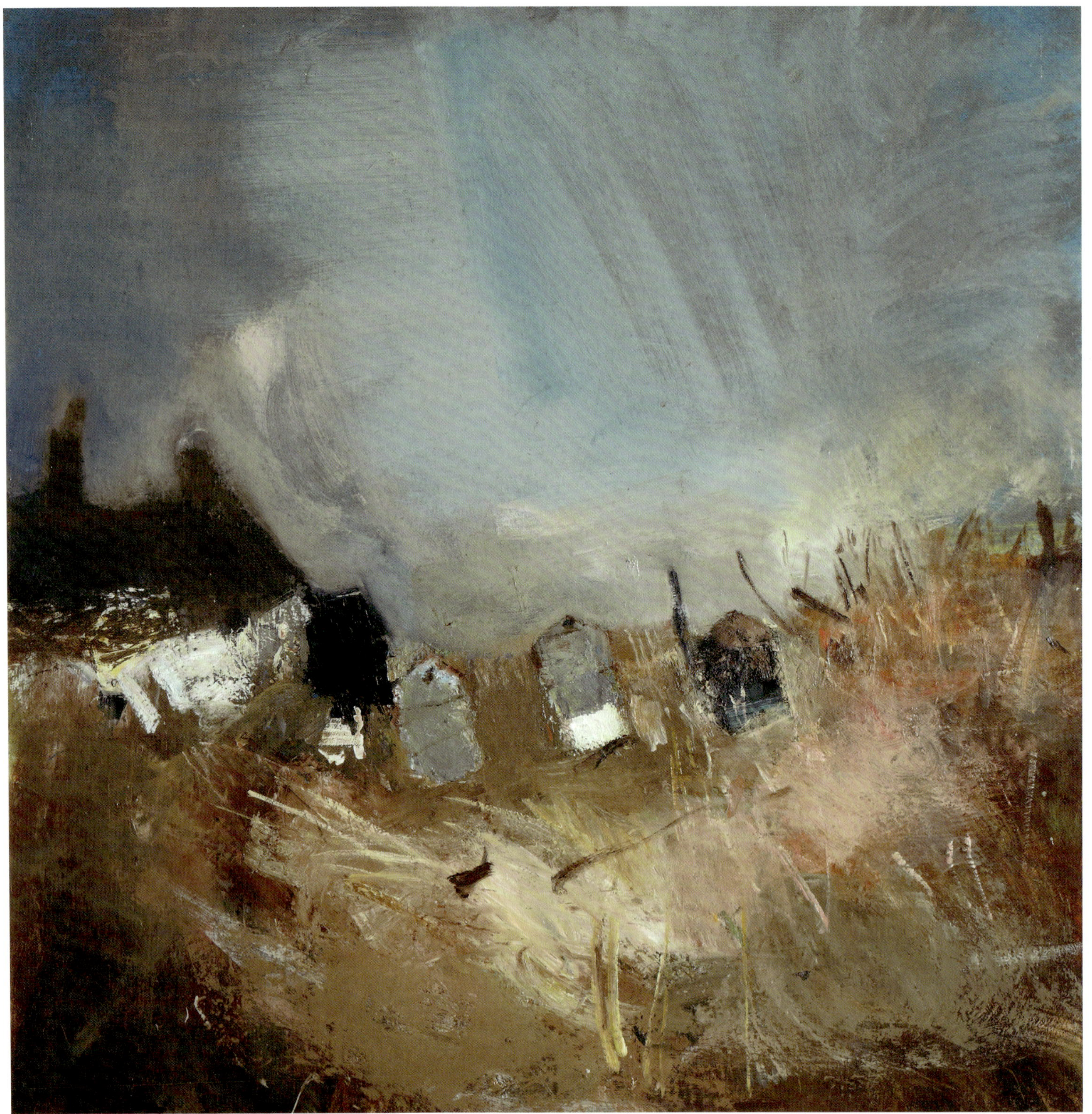

62 *Beehives*, *c.*1961
Oil on board, 100 × 100 cm
Private collection

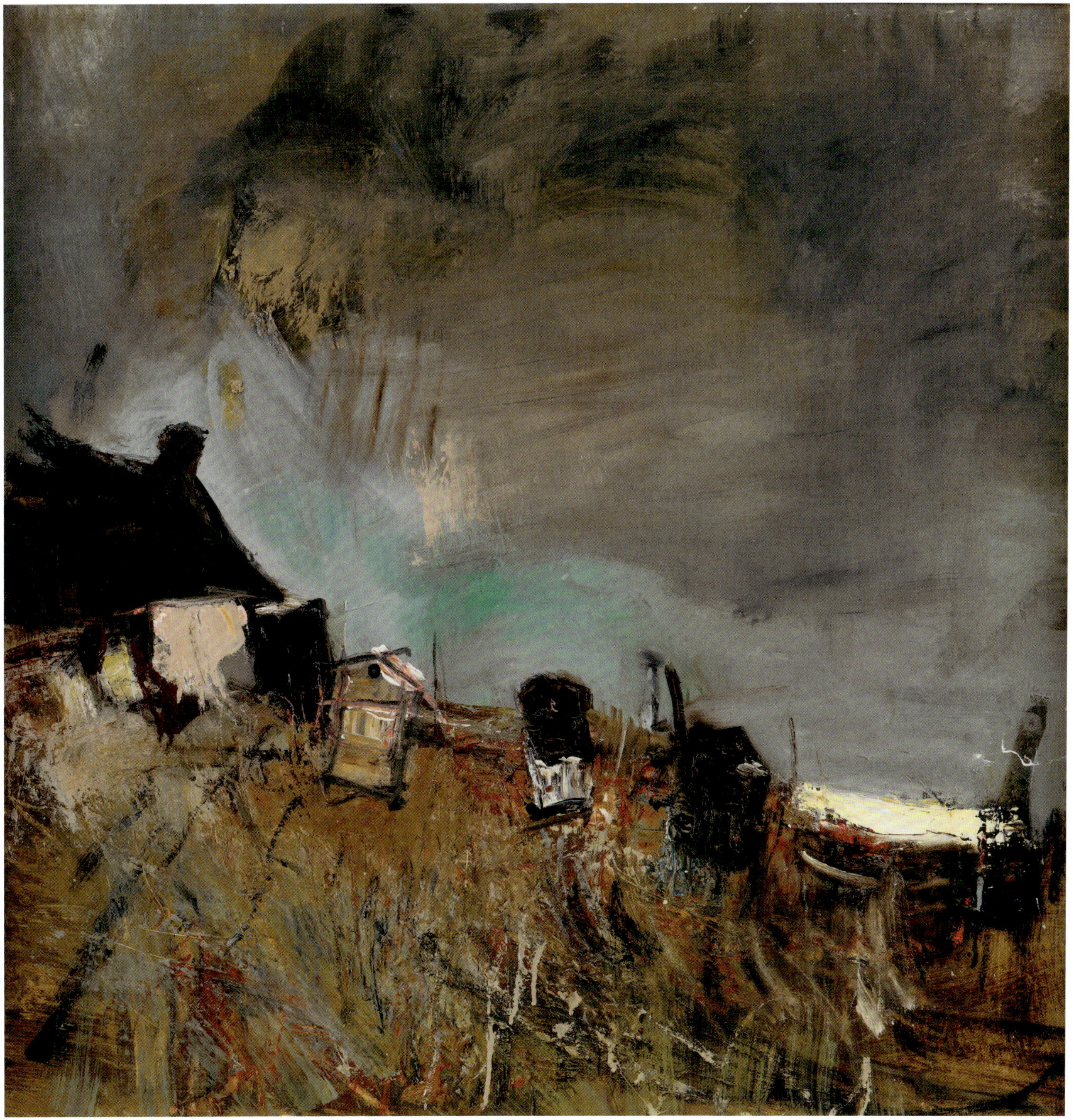

63 *Beehives, Storm Approaching*, 1961
Oil on board, 98.5 × 97.8 cm
NatWest Group

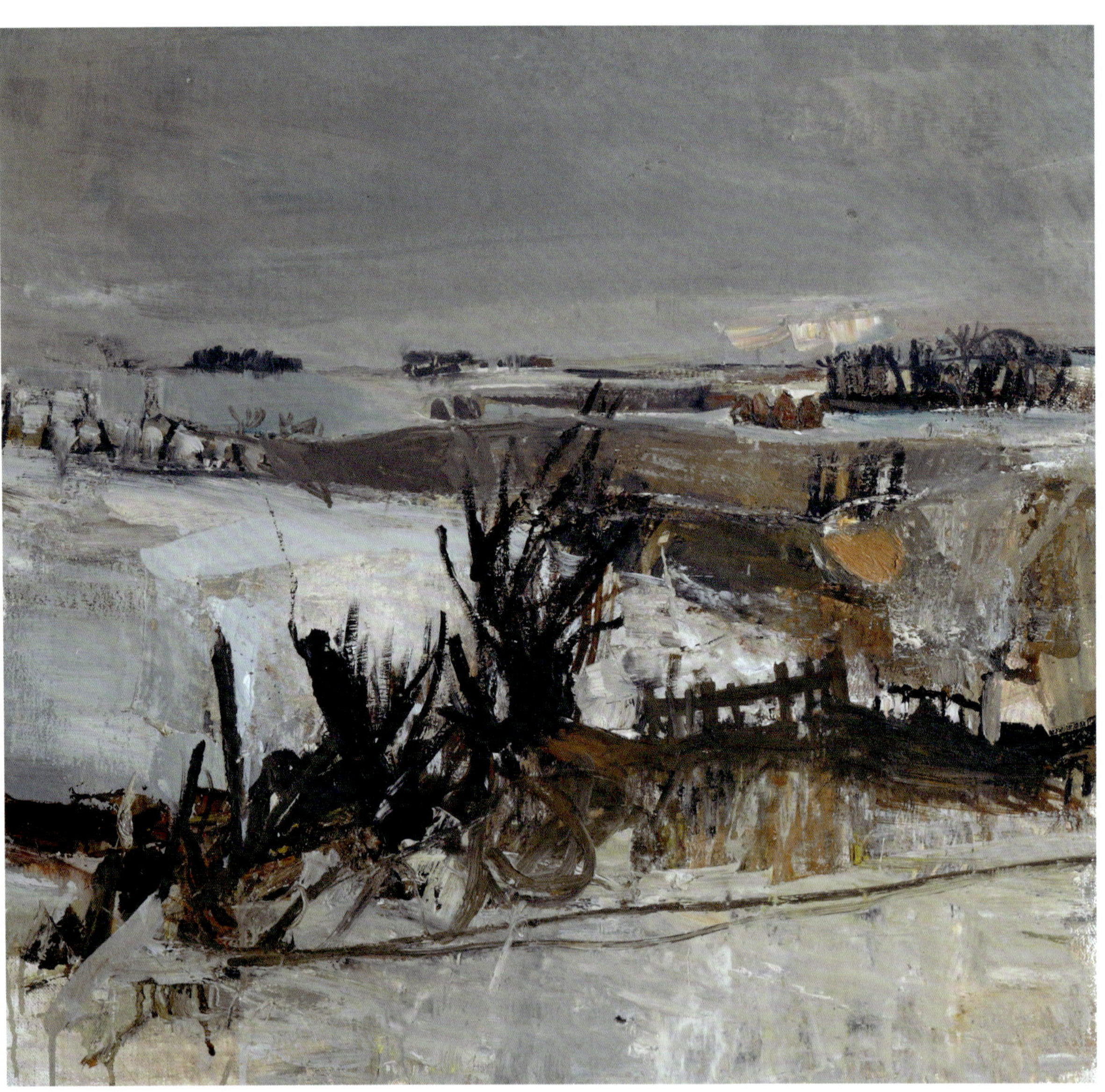

64 *Fields under Snow*, 1958
Oil on canvas, 68 × 73 cm
Private collection

65 *Snow*, 1958
Oil on board, 101.5 × 113.5 cm
Scottish National Gallery of Modern Art, Edinburgh
Bequeathed by David Murray Burns, 2003

Fields under Snow and *Snow*, both 1958, show the same vista, seen from behind the South Row of cottages, looking north towards the Mains of Catterline farmstead. Eardley must have painted *Snow* from within or near her back garden, and we see her neighbouring cottages; to paint *Fields under Snow* she had moved further north, closer to the fence.

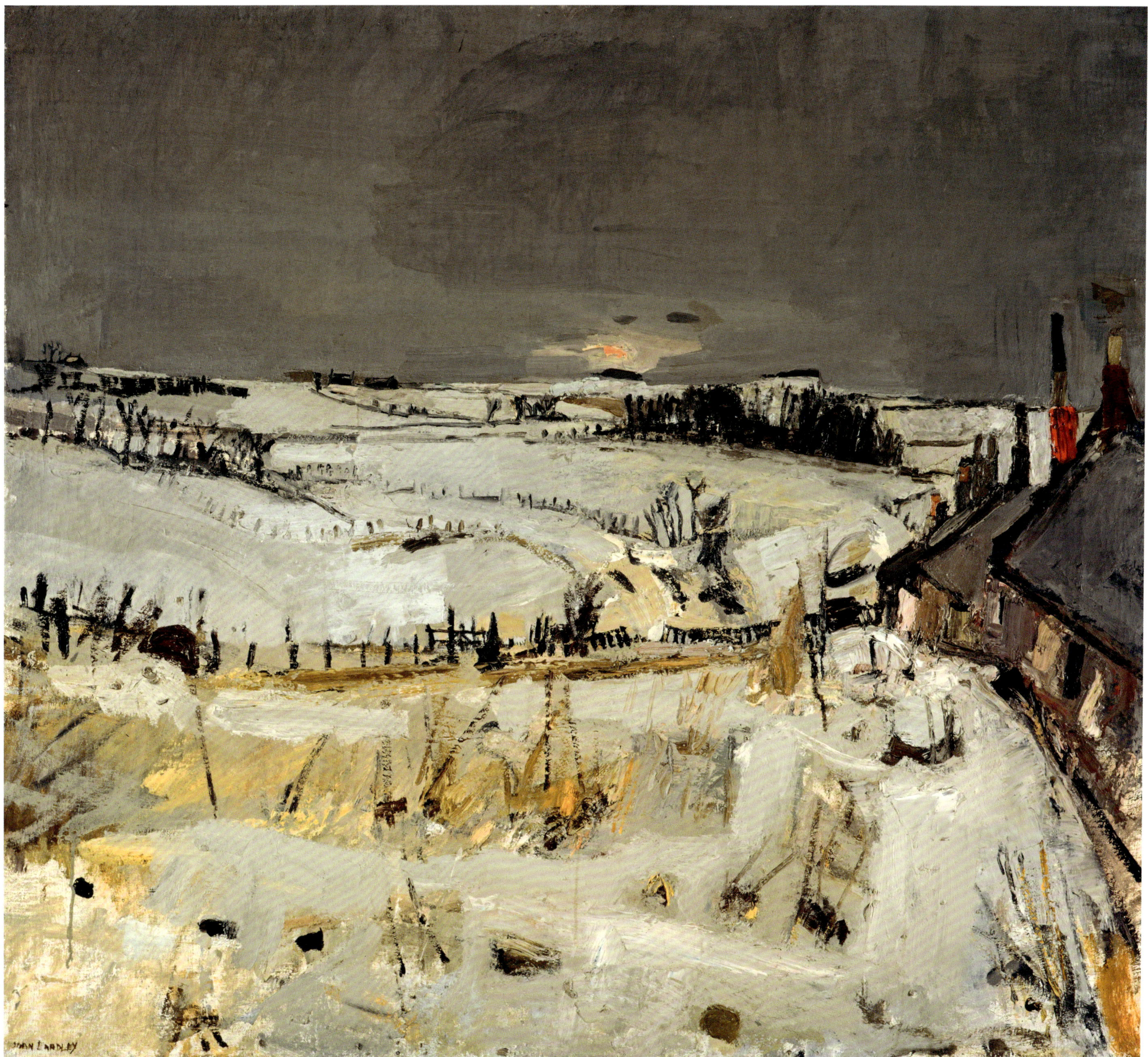
JOAN EARDLEY

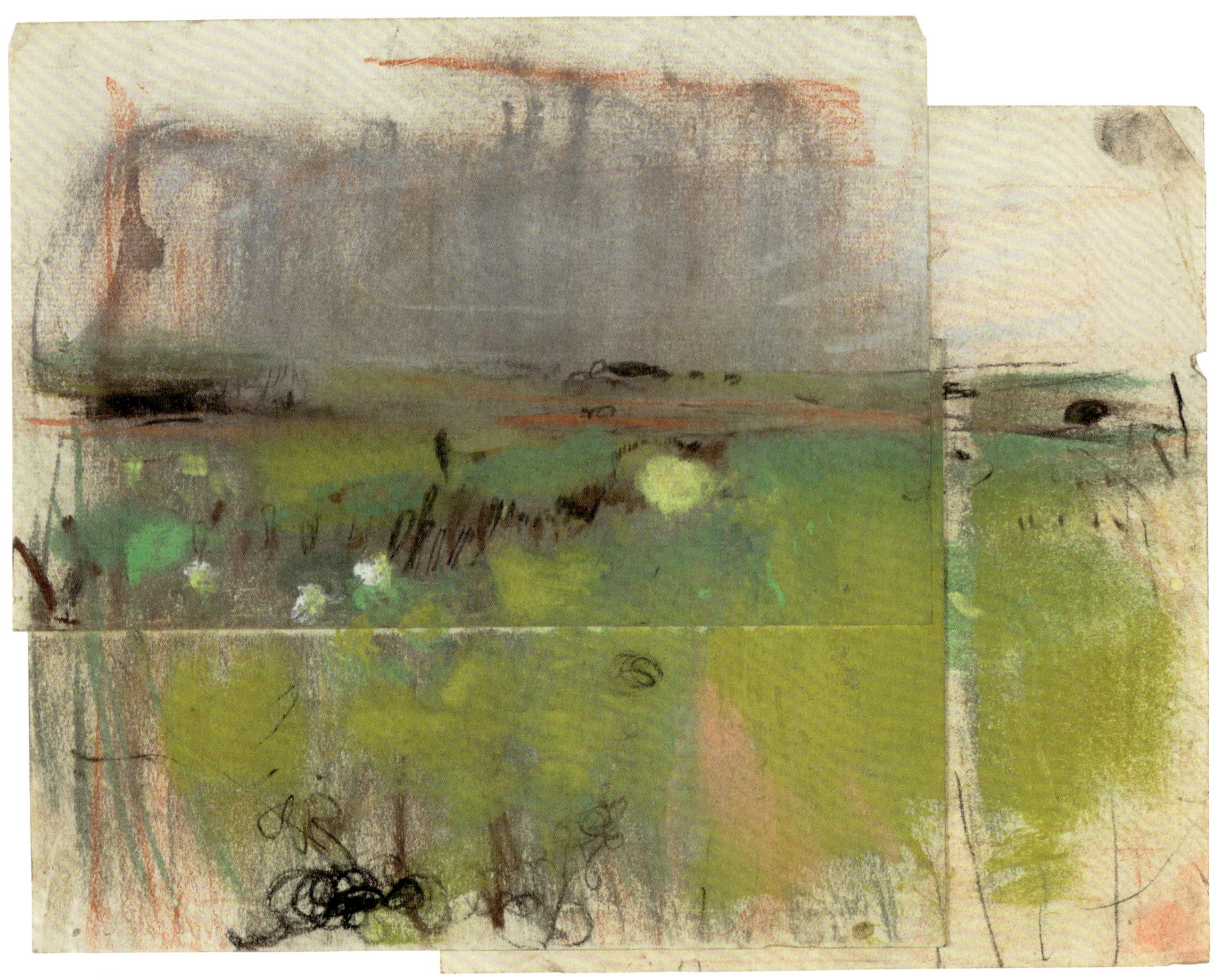

66 *Landscape of Flat Fields*, c.1960

Pastel on three sheets of paper, 23.5 × 30.5 cm
Scottish National Gallery of Modern Art, Edinburgh
Presented by the artist's sister, Mrs P.M. Black, 1987

67 *The Cornfield*, 1962

Oil on board, 88.9 × 101.6 cm
Abbot Hall Art Gallery, Kendal
Bequeathed by Guy Howard, 1992

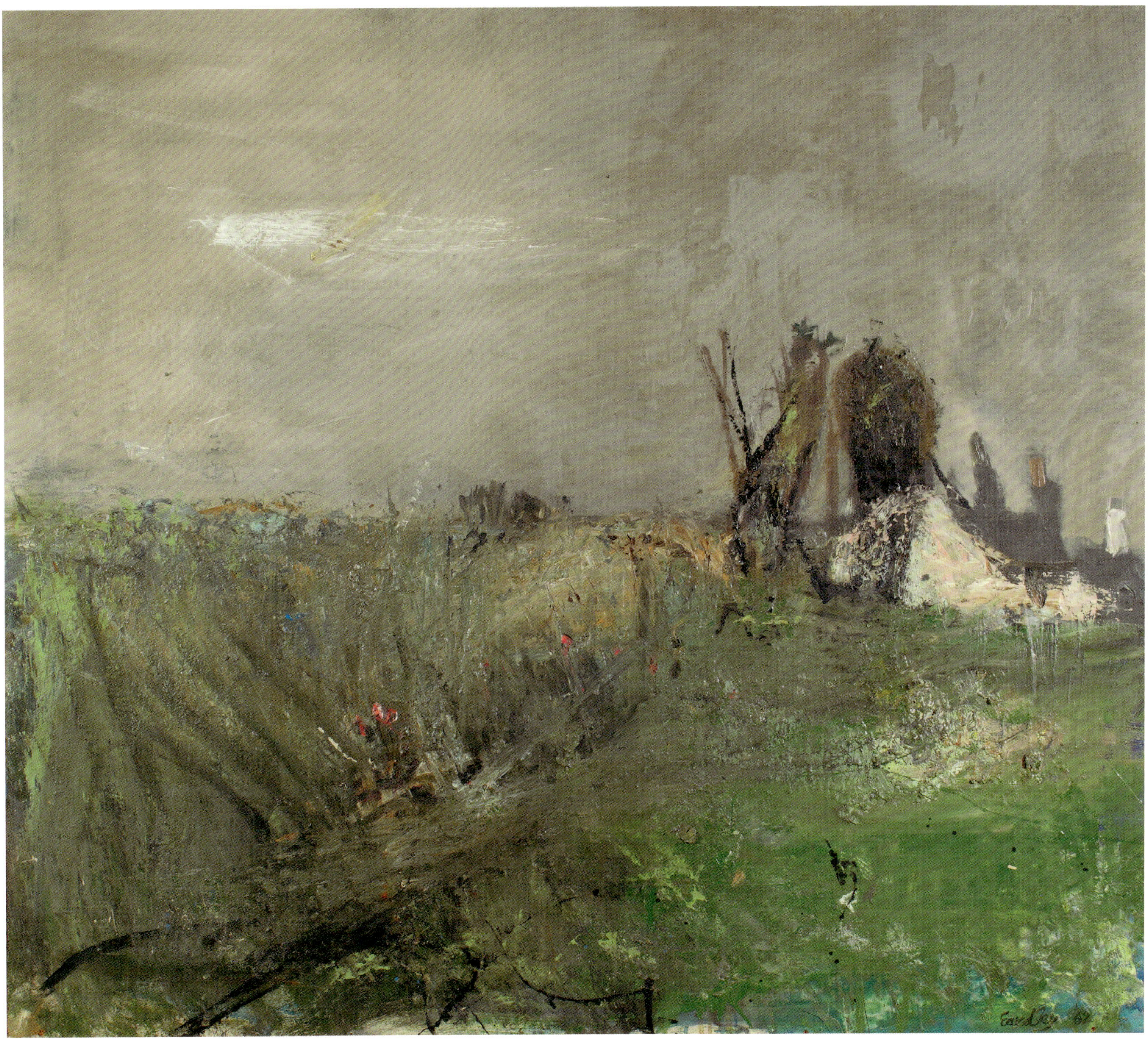
Eardley

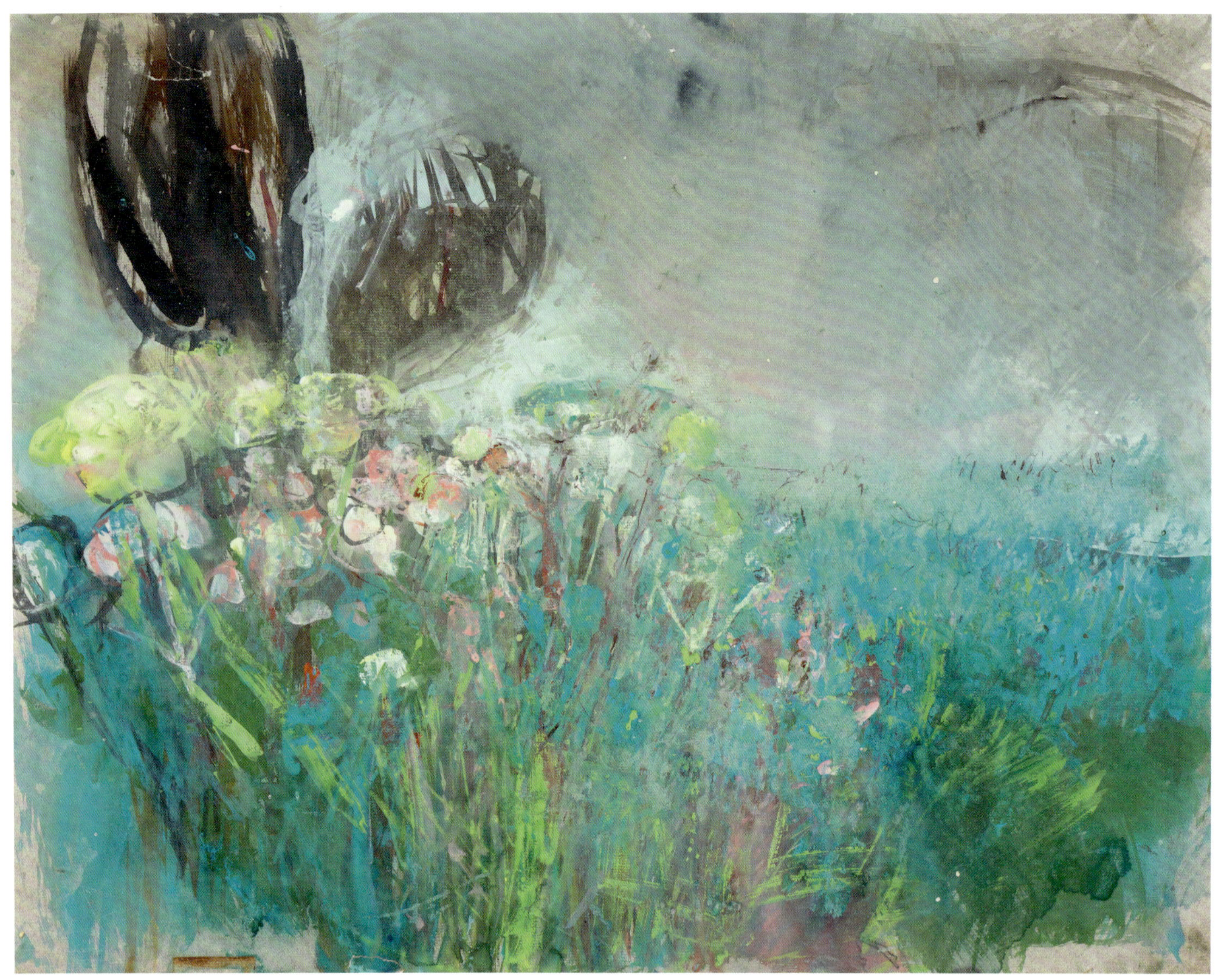

68 *Field with Wild Flowers*, *c*.1960–62

Gouache on grey paper, 49.7 × 64.5 cm
Scottish National Gallery of Modern Art, Edinburgh
Presented by the artist's sister, Mrs P.M. Black, 1987

69 *Summer Fields*, *c*.1961

Oil and grasses on board, 106 × 105 cm
Scottish National Gallery of Modern Art, Edinburgh
Bequeathed by Mr R.R. Scott Hay and presented by
Mrs M.E.B. Scott Hay, 1984

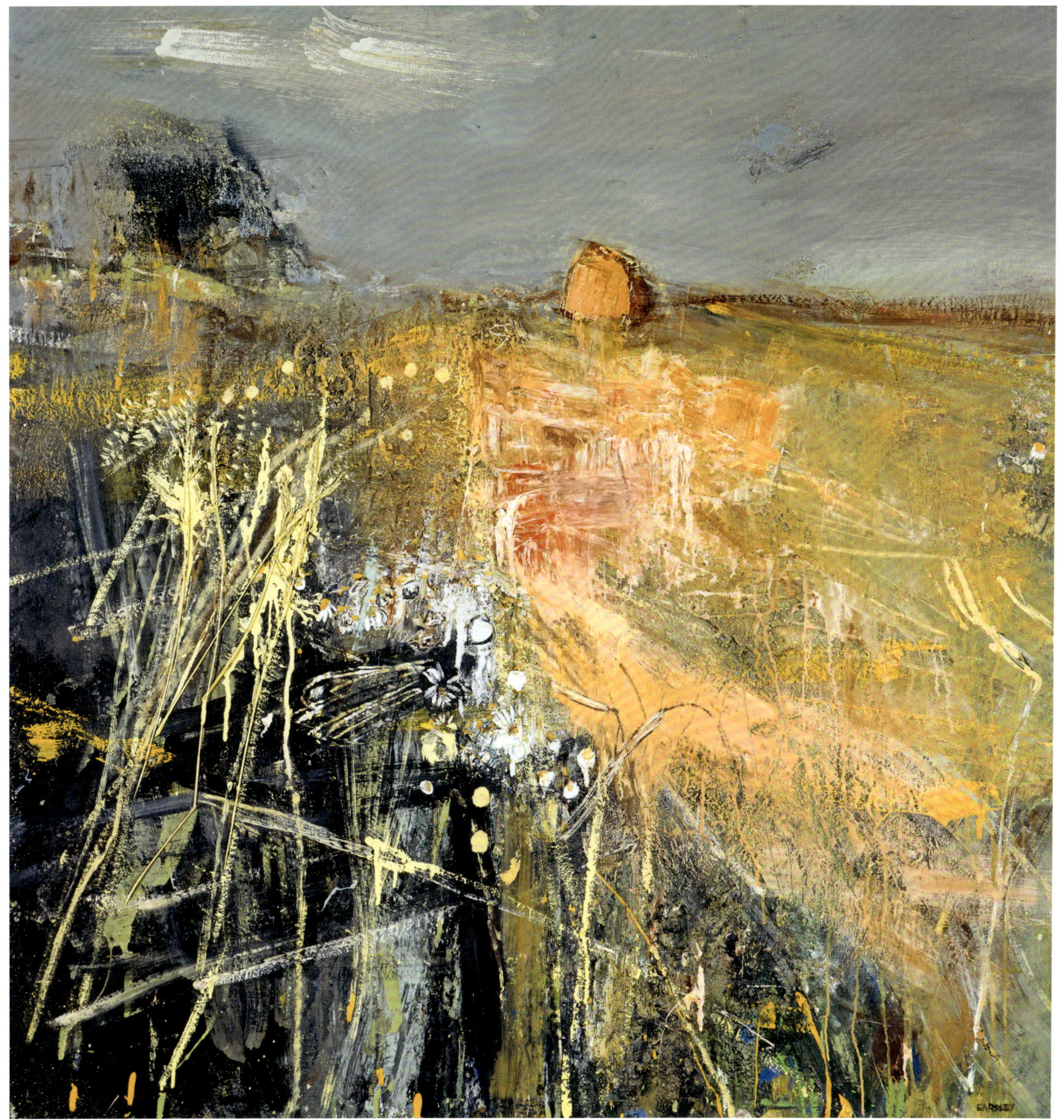

70 *July Fields*, *c.*1959

Oil on canvas, 52.7 × 61 cm
City Art Centre, Edinburgh Museums and Galleries

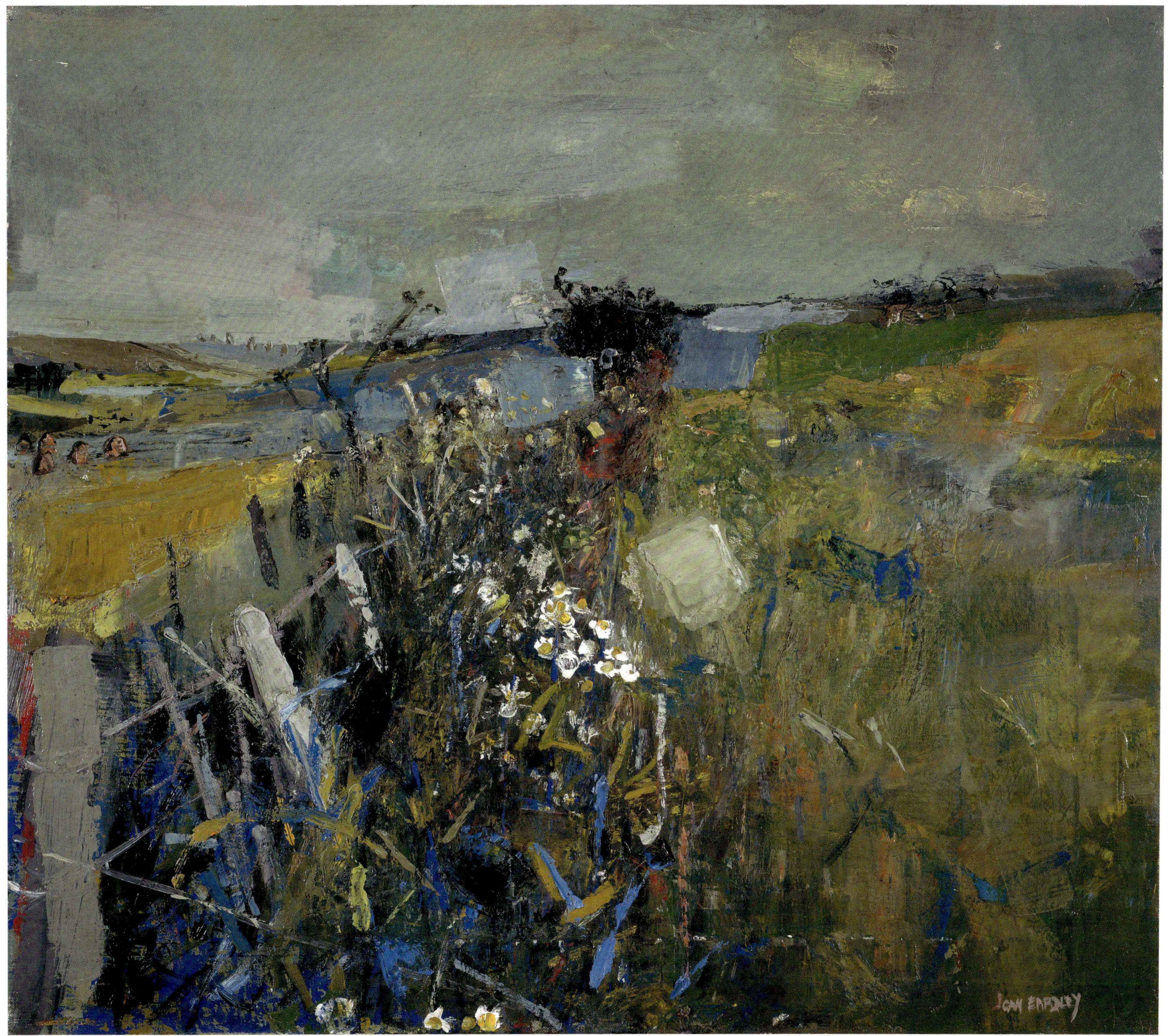
JOAN EARDLEY

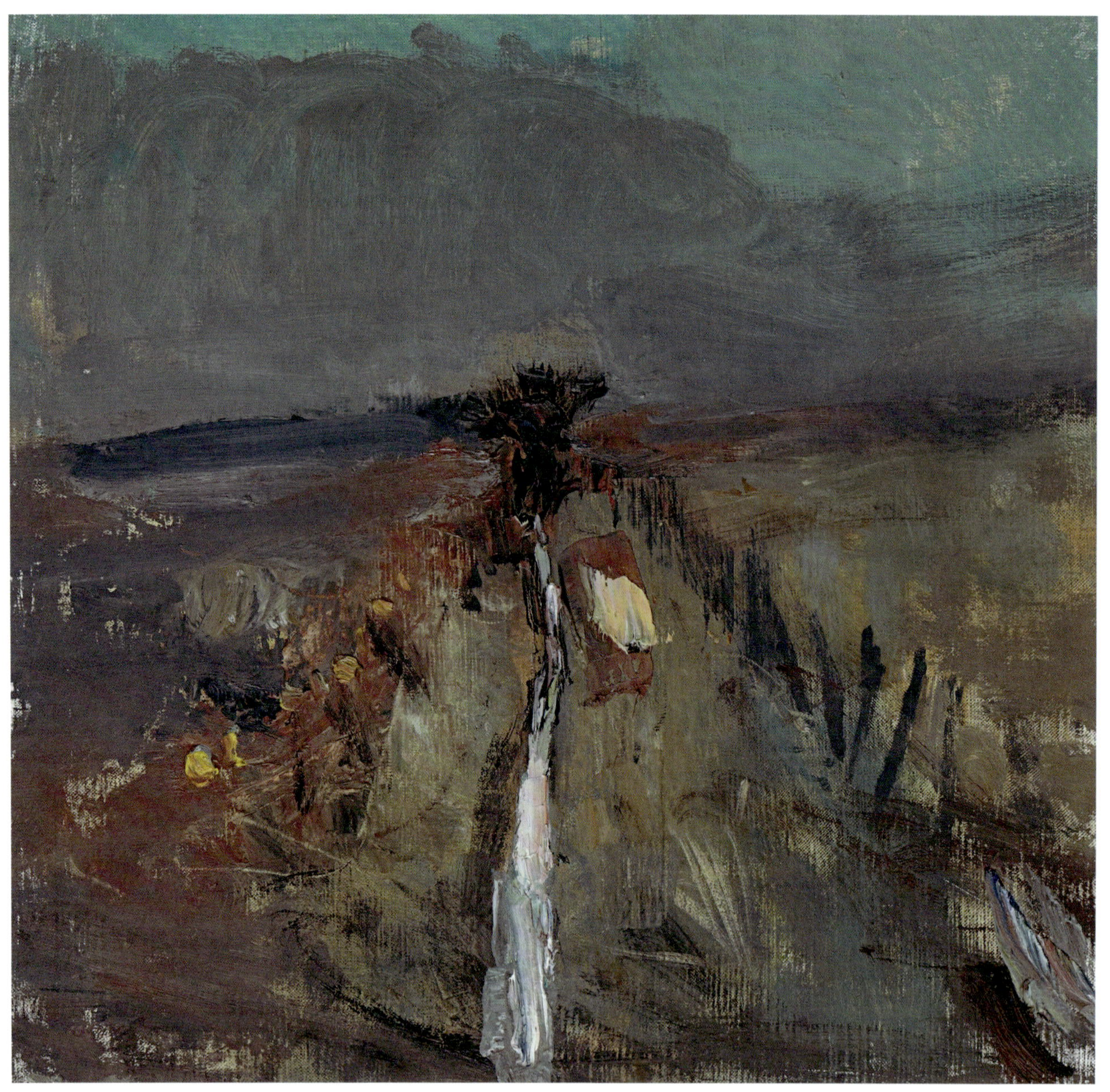

71 *Catterline Landscape*, *c.*1960–63

Oil on board, 47 × 49.5 cm

Cyril Gerber Fine Art, Glasgow

72 *Fields, Catterline*, *c.*1960–63

Oil on board, 104.5 × 121 cm

Cyril Gerber Fine Art, Glasgow

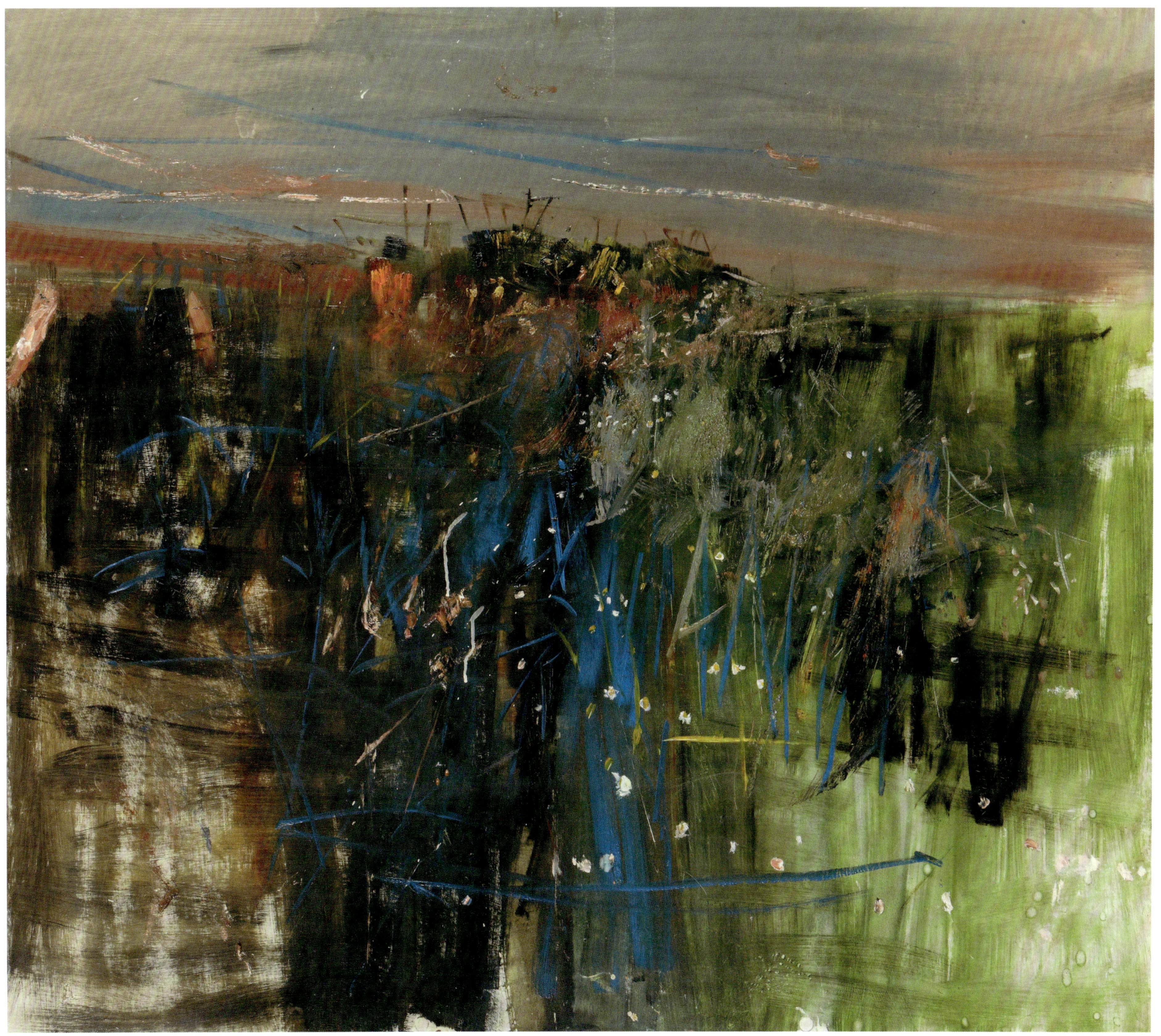

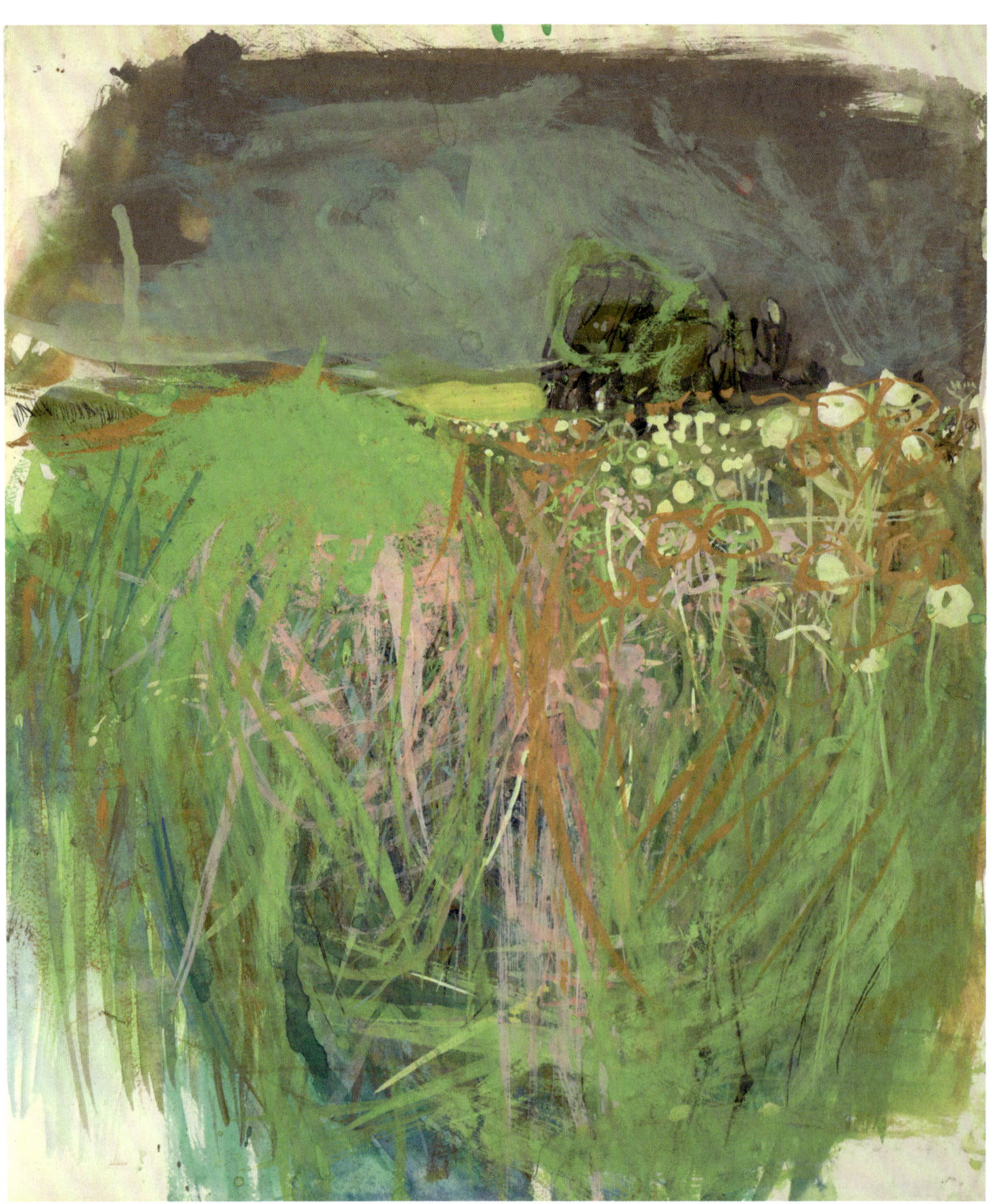

73 *Hedgerow with Grasses and Flowers*, c.1962–63

Gouache and oil on paper, 37.5 × 33 cm
Scottish National Gallery of Modern Art, Edinburgh
The Henry and Sula Walton Collection: bequeathed 2012

74 *Harvest*, 1960–61

Oil and grit on board, 118.1 × 118.1 cm
Scottish National Gallery of Modern Art, Edinburgh
Scott Hay Collection: presented 1967

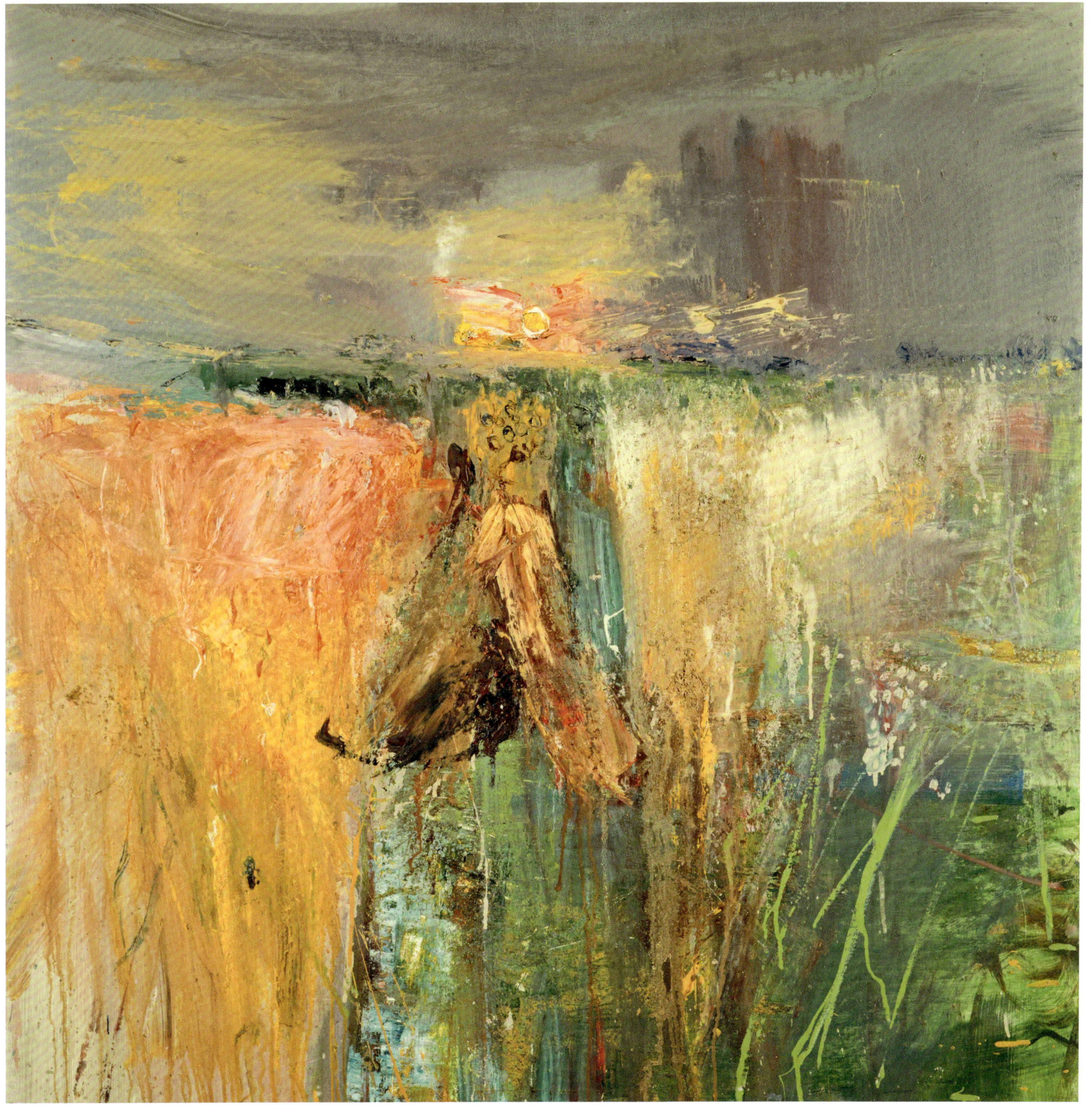

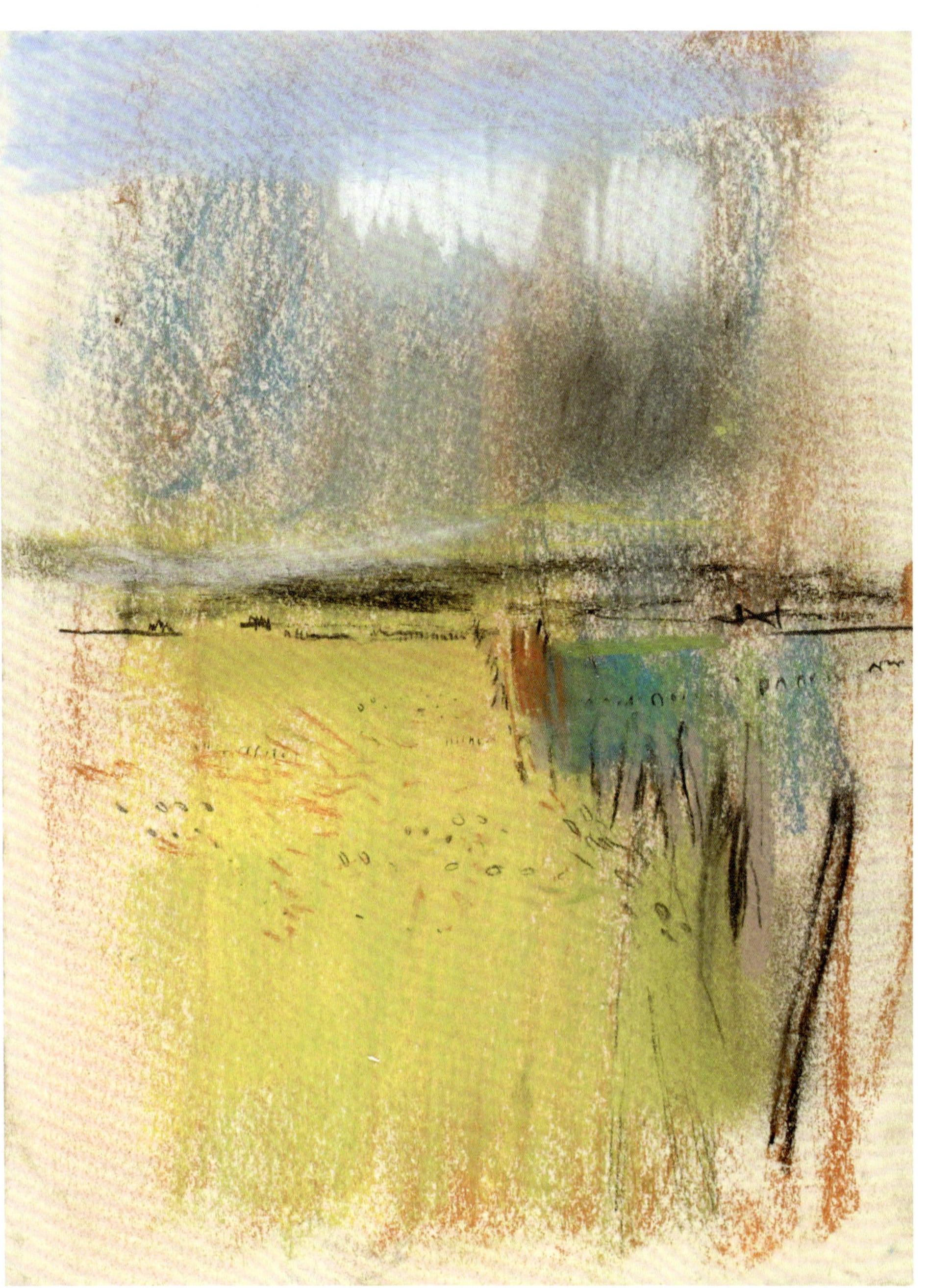

75 *Cornfield and Wide Horizon*, *c*.1960–62

Pastel on paper, 18.1 × 13.5 cm
Scottish National Gallery of Modern Art, Edinburgh
Presented by the artist's sister, Mrs P.M. Black, 1987

76 *Seeded Grasses and Daisies*, 1960

Oil, grass stalks and seedheads on board, 121.9 × 133.3 cm
Scottish National Gallery of Modern Art, Edinburgh
Purchased with funds given by an anonymous donor, 1964

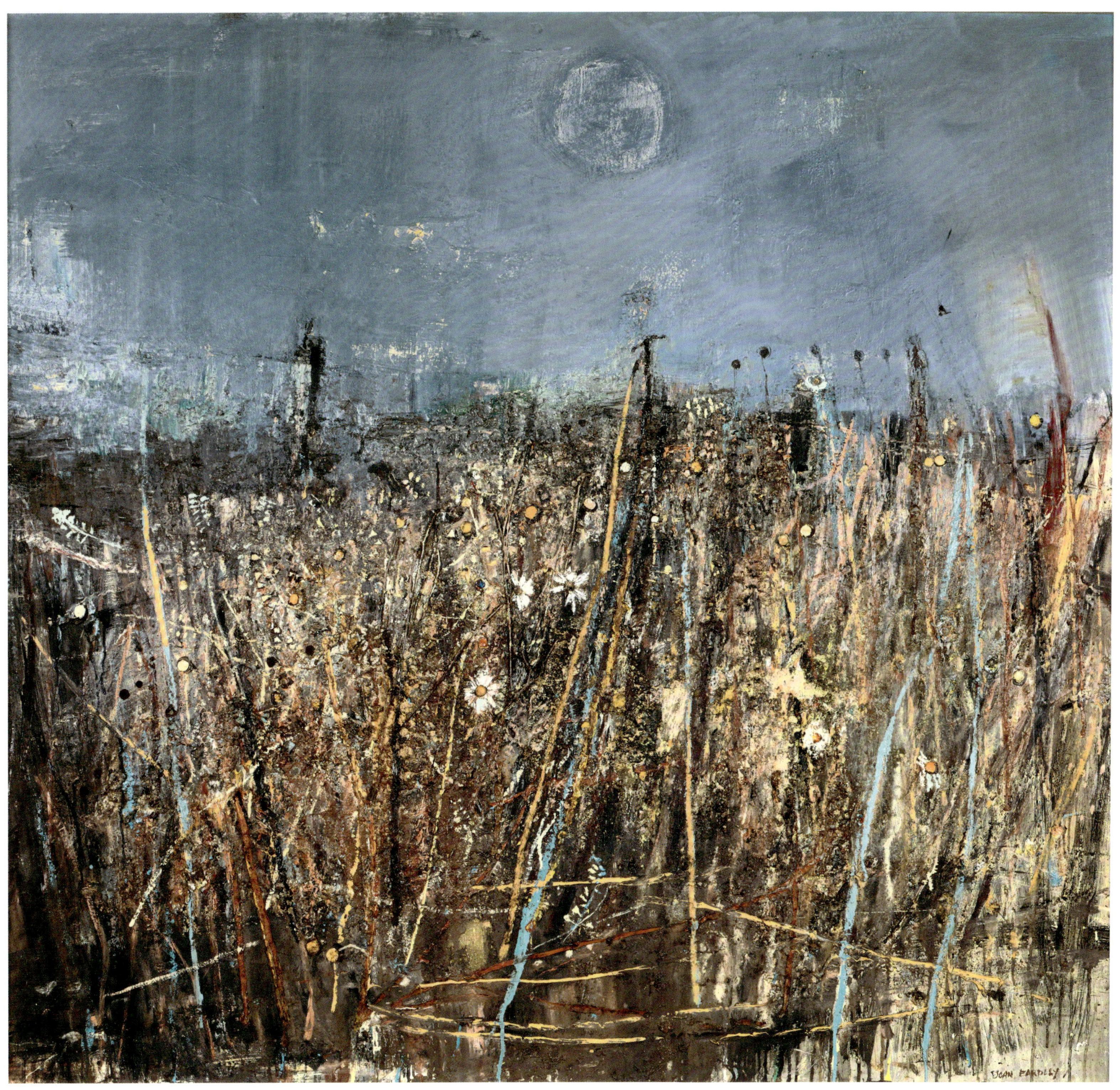
JOAN EARDLEY

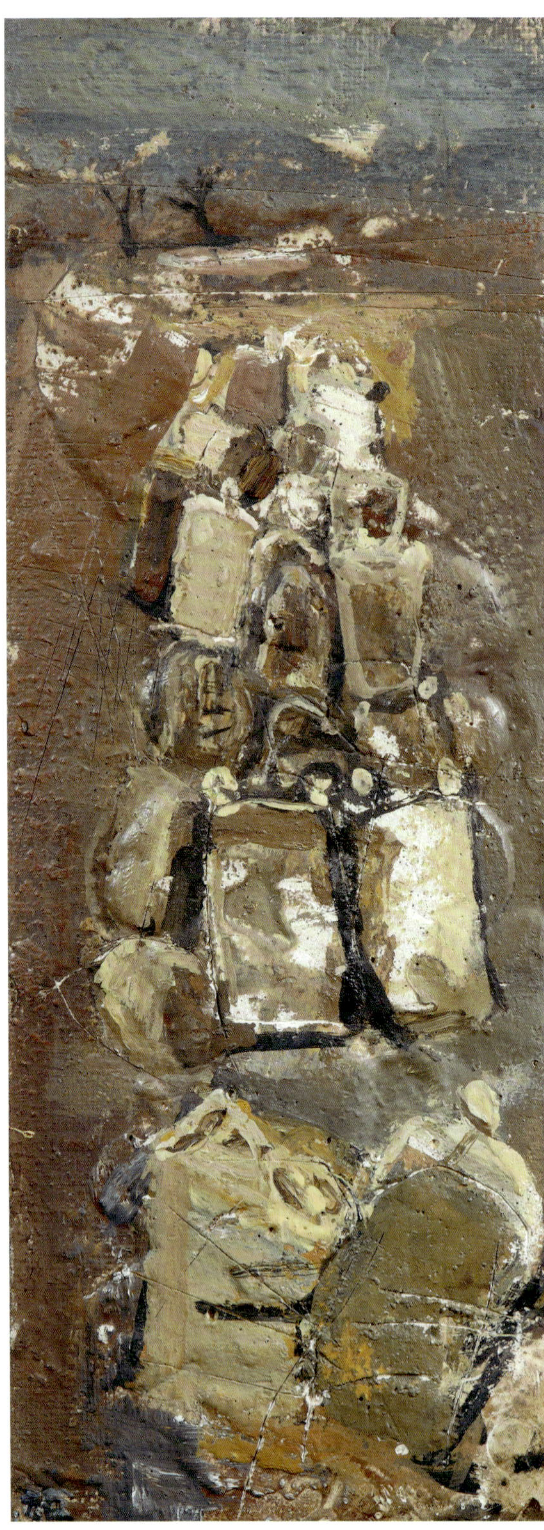

77 *Bagged Potatoes 1*, *c.*1960

Oil on board, 42 × 16 cm
The University of Edinburgh Art Collection
Bequeathed by Hope Scott, 1989

78 *Sheep Feeding in a Field of Turnips*, *c.*1960

Black ink and watercolour on grey paper, 49.6 × 64.6 cm
Scottish National Gallery of Modern Art, Edinburgh
Presented by the artist's sister, Mrs P.M. Black, 1987

79 *Sheep and Neeps*, *c.*1960

Oil on board, 20.5 × 50 cm
Private collection

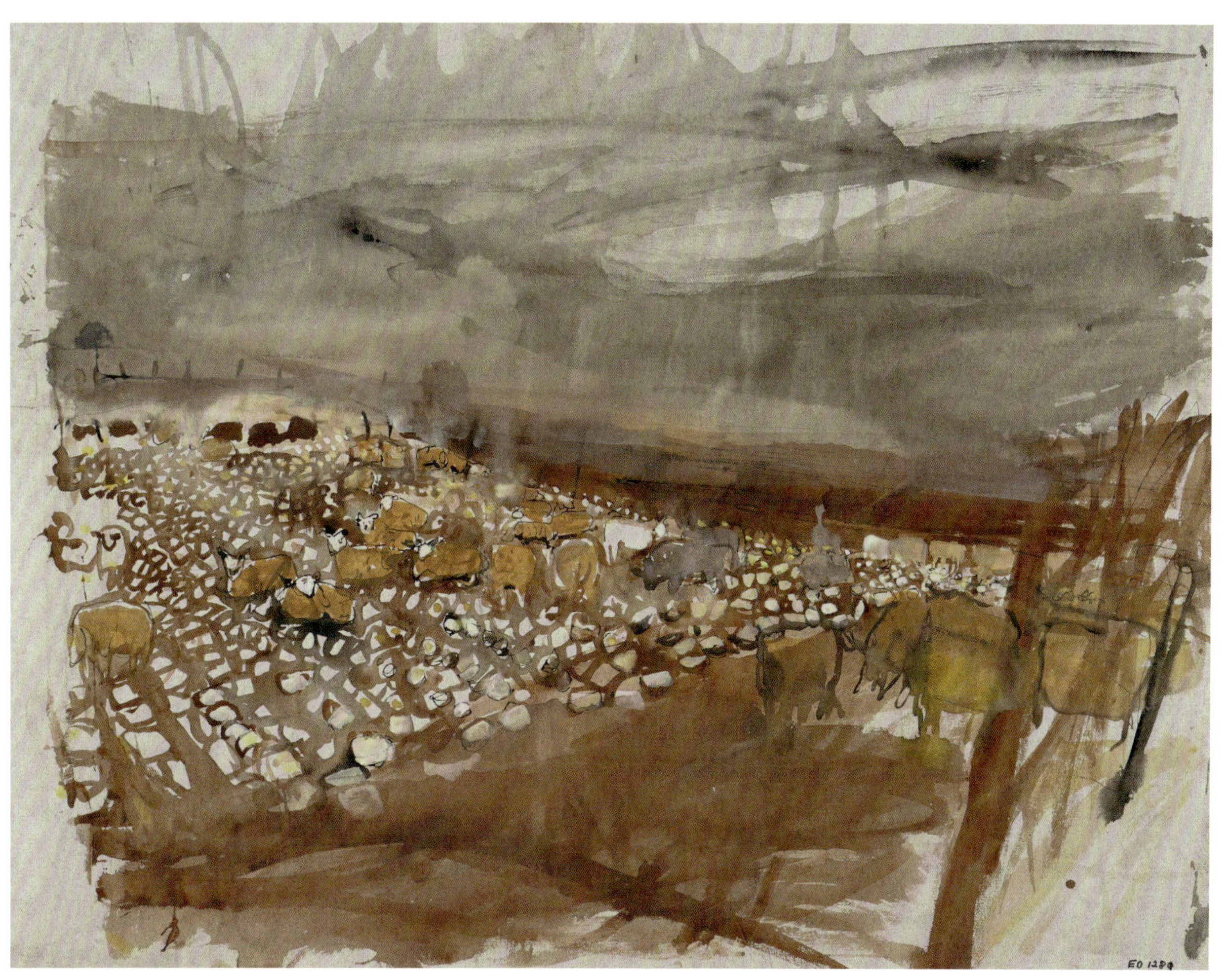

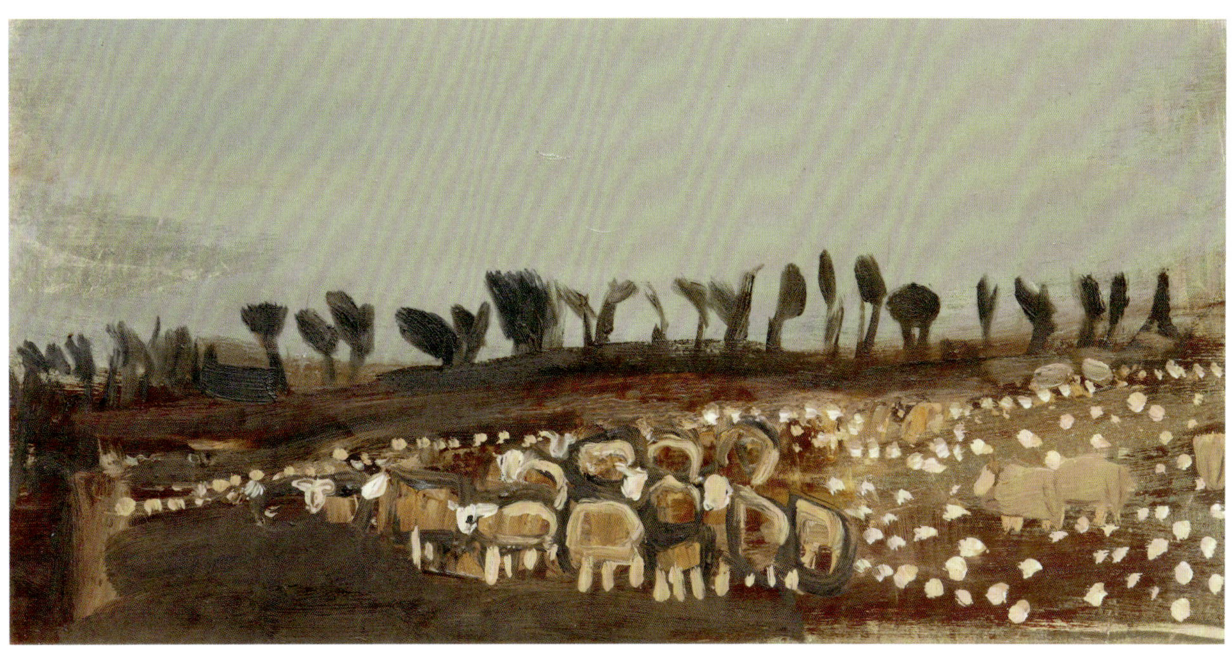

Beach and Sea

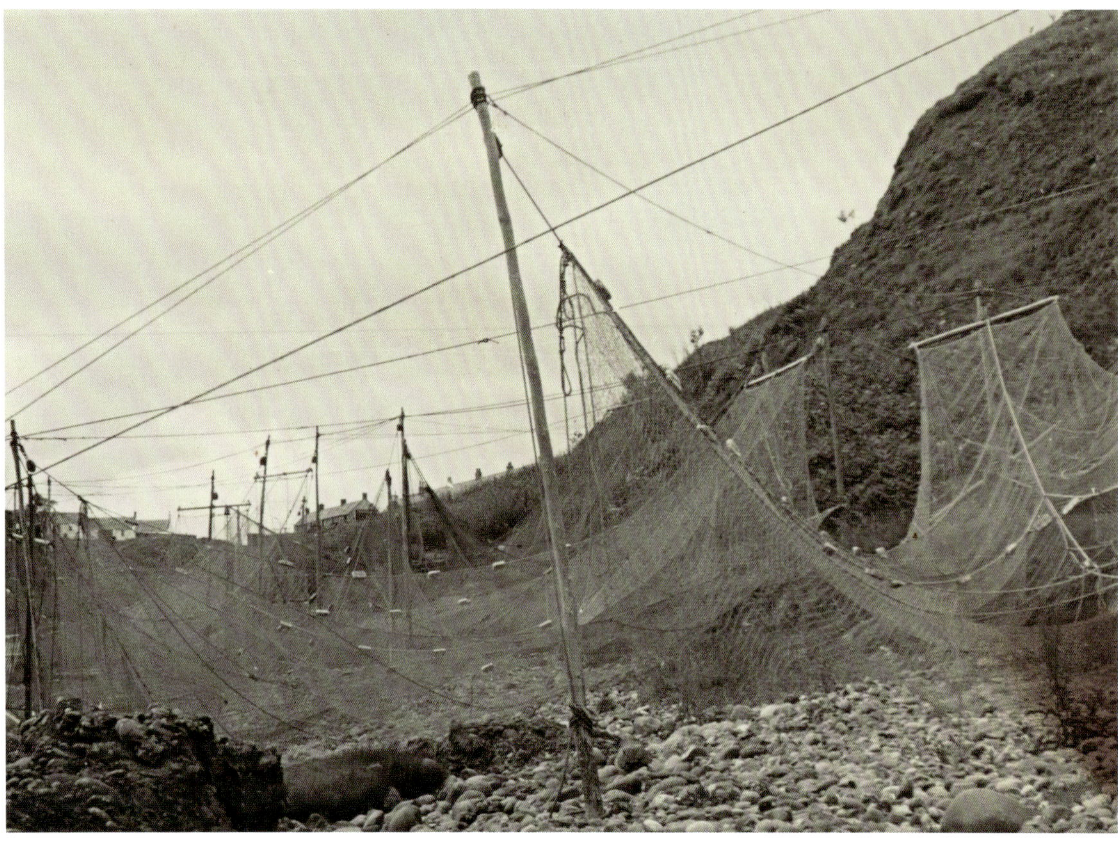

80 *Beach at Catterline with Nets*, c.1956
Silver gelatine print, 15.9 × 21.4 cm
Joan Eardley Archive, Scottish National Gallery of Modern Art, Edinburgh
Presented by the artist's sister, Mrs P.M. Black, 1987

Eardley took a particular interest in fishing nets before living in Catterline: she drew them in Arbroath, where she had a postgraduate year in 1947, and two years later in Italy, when on her student scholarship travels. In 1951 she exhibited a painting, *Drying Salmon Nets*, at the Society of Scottish Artists' annual exhibition in Edinburgh. This could have been painted at Catterline, but it is not certain. Regardless, the subject of the fishing nets seems not to have attracted Eardley much in her early years in the village.

Around 1956, however, Eardley began seriously and consistently to draw, paint and photograph the salmon nets at Catterline. They were hung up to dry on the shore beyond the salmon bothy, in an area known as the Makin Green. In a letter to Walker, written in 1956, Eardley states:

> *A perfect day so far ... I mustn't sit here and write to you, much as I want to. There's these old nets to be tackled! Awful thought because I'm frightened of them a bit – but I find on sunny days such as this that it is only possible to see them in the morning. So I must go.*[73]

Salmon were attracted to the freshwater burn that flowed into the sea at Catterline, although by the time Eardley lived there in the 1950s salmon fishing was in steep decline. The fish were caught in bag nets (a type of net unique to the Scottish coastline), which were anchored about fifty metres out from the shore.[74] Up to ten of these bag nets would be set. The rights for salmon fishing were held by Joseph Johnston and Sons of Montrose, who owned all the nets used by the Catterline fishermen, as well as the one salmon fishing boat, called a coble. Because the salmon swam close to the shore, the cobles had no keel and were flat bottomed. In Eardley's day, the coble was skippered by Harry Wylie who had a crew of five. The salmon bothy, just beyond the pier on the shore, can be seen in many of Eardley's paintings: a place to shelter in bad weather, it had bunk beds and a fire. On a good day as many as fifty salmon would be netted; on a bad day, as few as two. Salmon fishing in Catterline ceased altogether in 1975 when the last salmon fisherman retired.

On the beach, the nets were supported on larch poles over five metres tall, which remained in place on the Makin Green throughout the salmon fishing season.[75] They became a favourite motif for Eardley. Often, behind, and even through the nets, we glimpse the salmon bothy and, up above, the Watchie. After her death in August 1963 Eardley's ashes were scattered on the beach at the Makin Green. In 1964 Eardley's mother gave a painting of the nets drying on the Green (a smaller variant of plate 83) to the people of the village; it has remained there, hanging in the Creel Inn, ever since.

81 Study for *Drying Salmon Nets*, *c.*1956

Pastel on two sheets of yellow paper, 21.5 × 38.5 cm
Scottish National Gallery of Modern Art, Edinburgh
Presented by the artist's sister, Mrs P.M. Black, 1987

82 Study for *Drying Salmon Nets*, *c.*1956

Pastel on yellow paper, 20 × 25.5 cm
Private collection

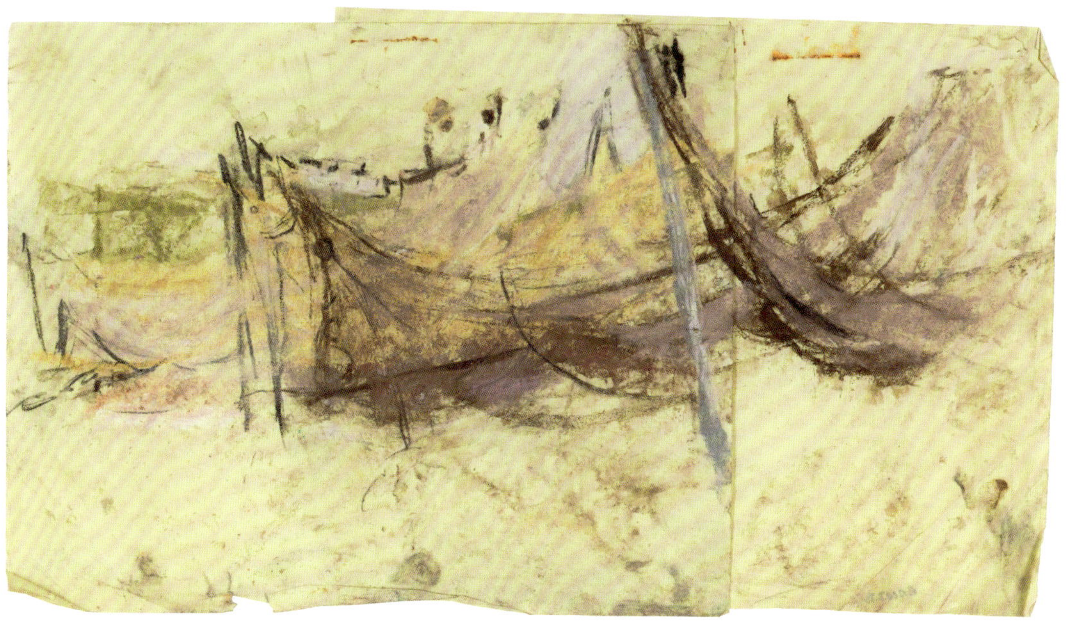

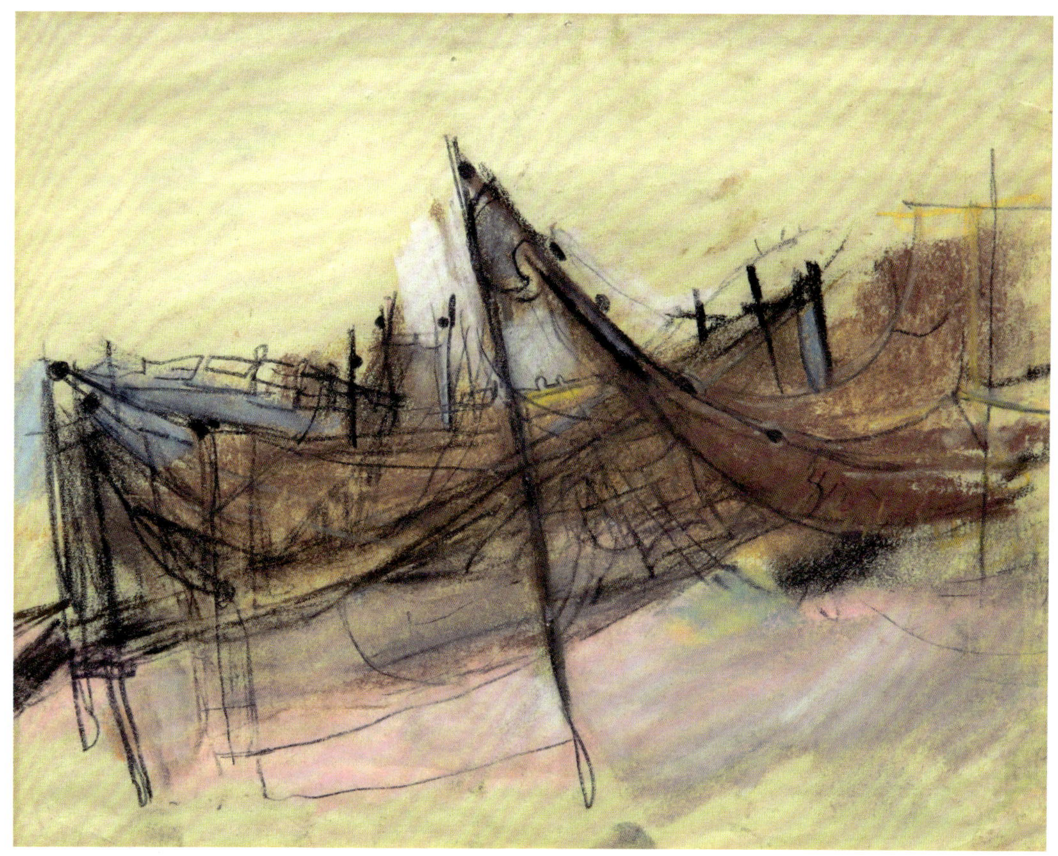

83 *Drying Salmon Nets*, 1956

Oil on canvas, 68.7 × 153.8 cm

Private collection

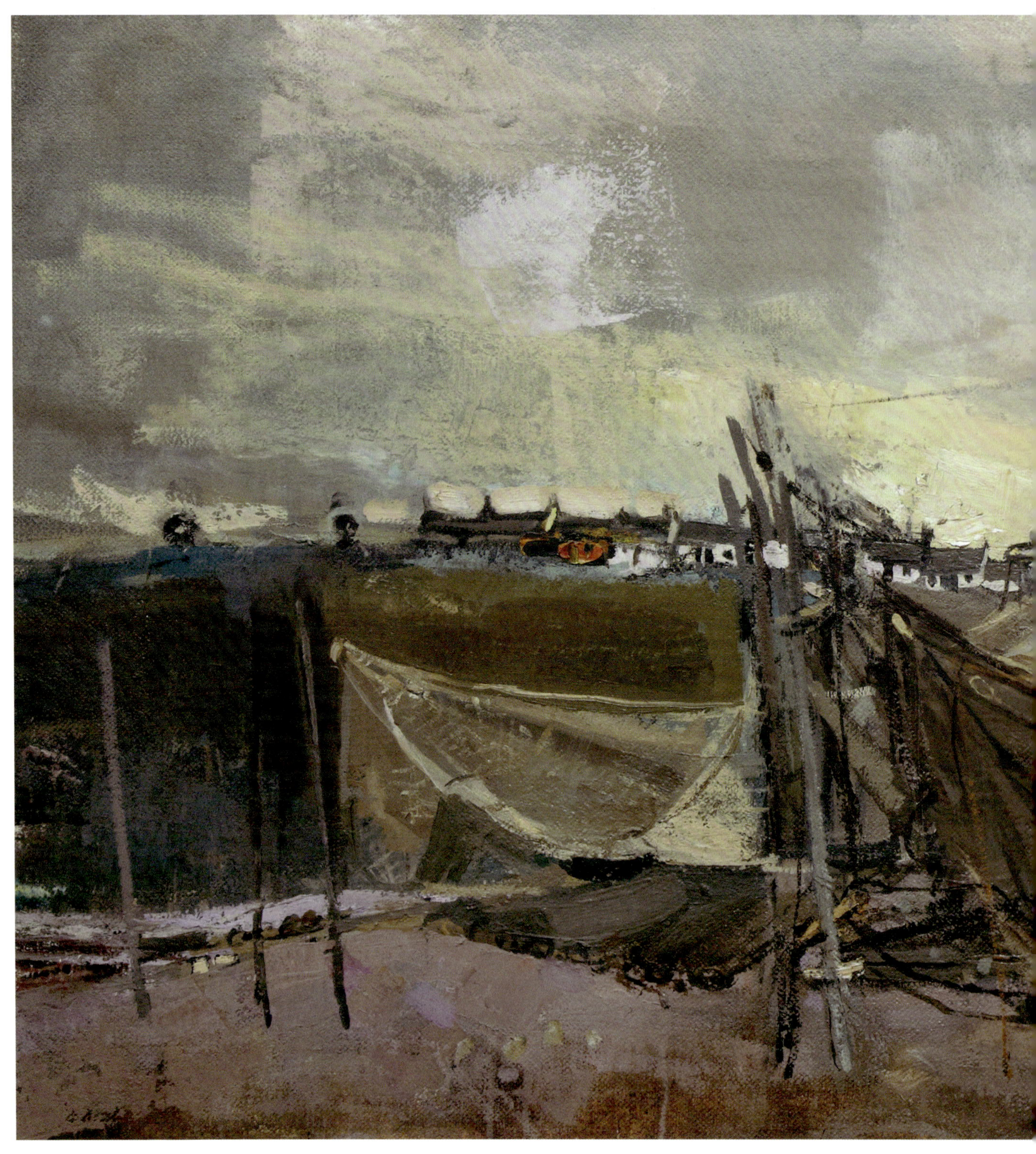

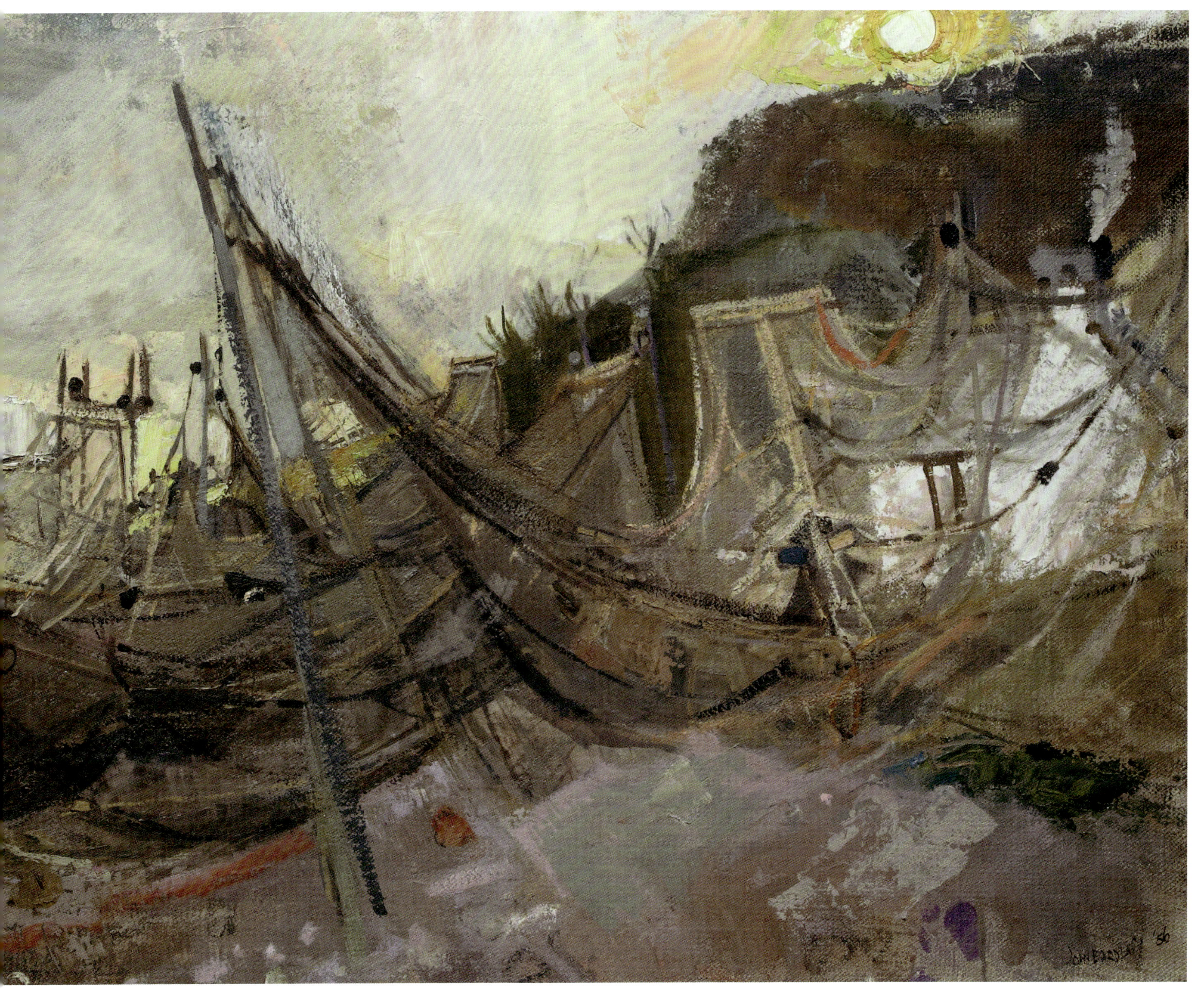

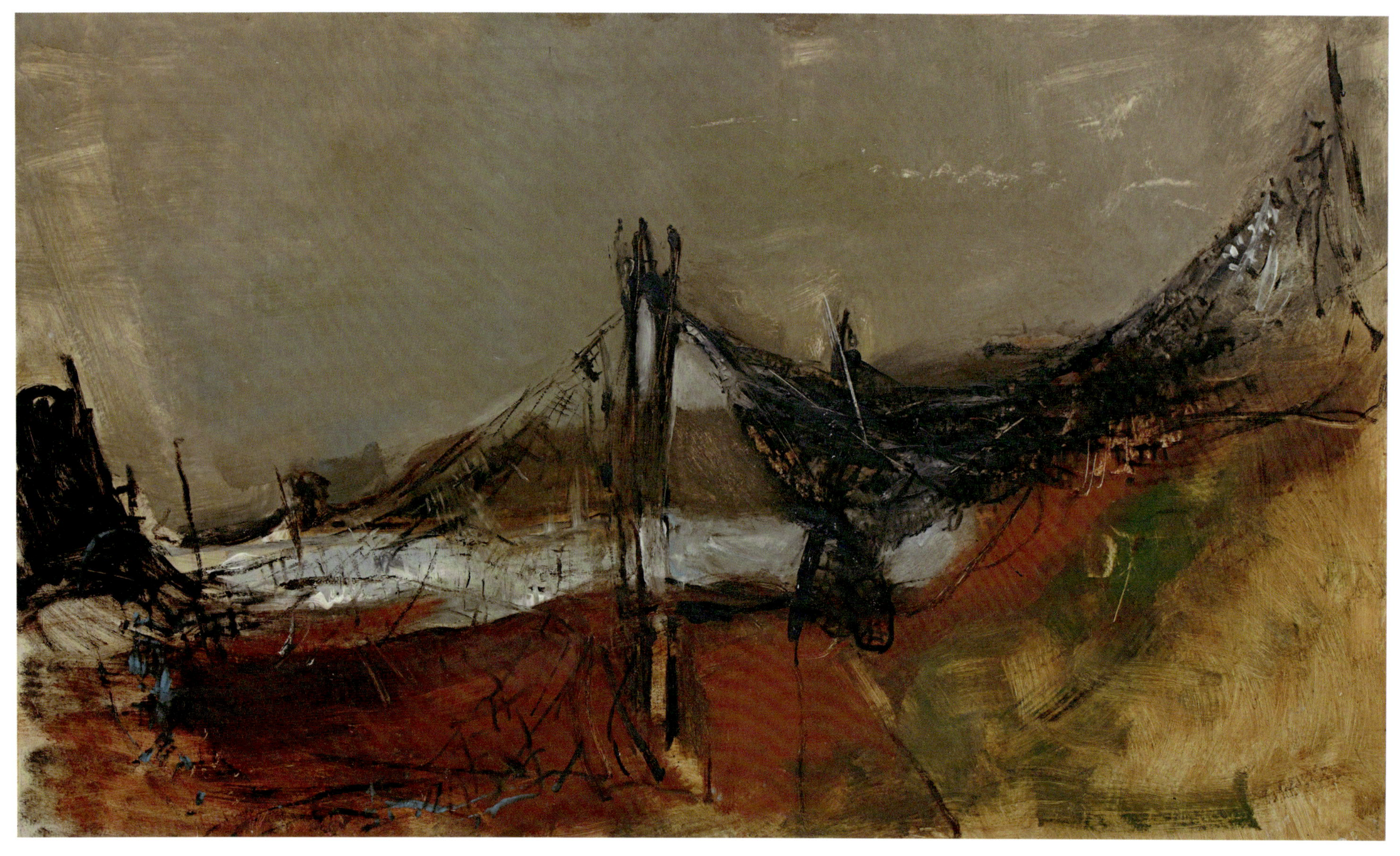

84 *Fishing Nets, Catterline*, *c.*1962
Oil on board, 97.8 × 167.6 cm
Cyril Gerber Fine Art, Glasgow

85 *Salmon Nets 1*, *c.*1961–63
Oil on board, 111 × 122 cm
Abbot Hall Art Gallery, Kendal
Gift from P.F. Scott, 1986

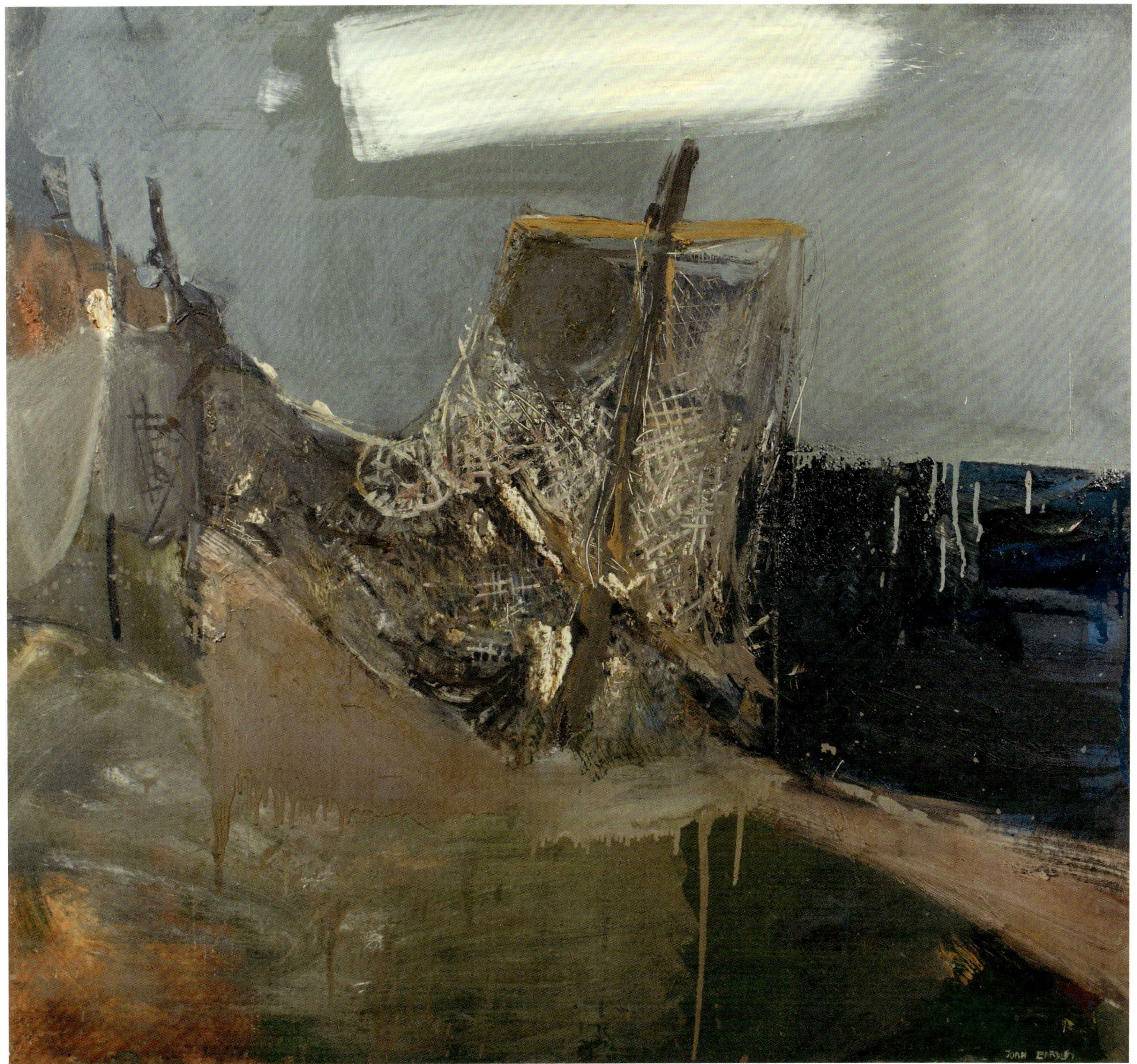
JOAN EARDLEY

Boats on the Shore and the Sea

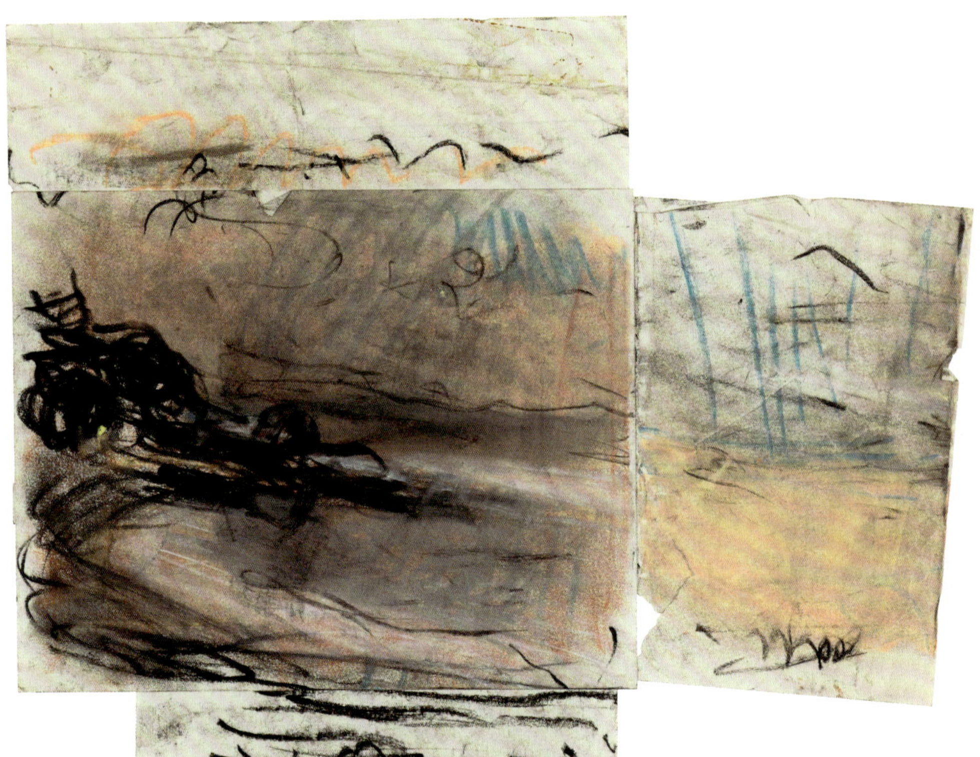

There were six fishing boats operating from Catterline in the 1950s. *The Meanwell* (A271) belonged to Andrew Stephen and his brother Jim; *The Hopeful* (A267, painted black) was an identical type of boat (both were built in 1907) that belonged to another family called Stephen (another Jim Stephen, whom Annette Soper married); *The Rose* and *The Mascot* (A440, painted dark green) both belonged to the Watt family; and *The Barbara* belonged to Bill Coull and Jim Moir.[76] *The Linfall* (A471), owned by Harry Wylie, is the blue boat most often seen in Eardley's pictures. *The Mascot* was the only boat to have a light; it was attached to a tall pole with a bent end. The boats were used for in-shore fishing – crabs and lobsters in creels, and haddock and cod on lines.

88 *Boats on the Shore*, *c.*1963
Oil on board, 101.6 × 115.6 cm
Scottish National Gallery of Modern Art, Edinburgh
Scott Hay Collection: presented 1967

86 *The Sea at Catterline*, *c.*1960–63
Pastel on four sheets of paper, 29.5 × 35.3 cm
Scottish National Gallery of Modern Art, Edinburgh
Presented by the artist's sister, Mrs P.M. Black, 1987

87 *Stormy Sky over Catterline Sea Shore*, *c.*1960–63
Pastel on two sheets of paper, 12.5 × 29.7 cm
Scottish National Gallery of Modern Art, Edinburgh
Presented by the artist's sister, Mrs P.M. Black, 1987

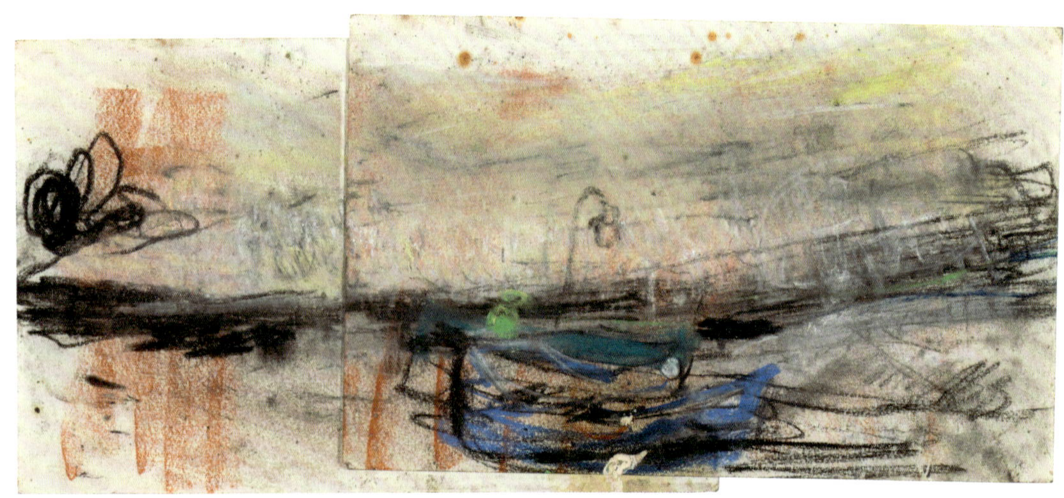

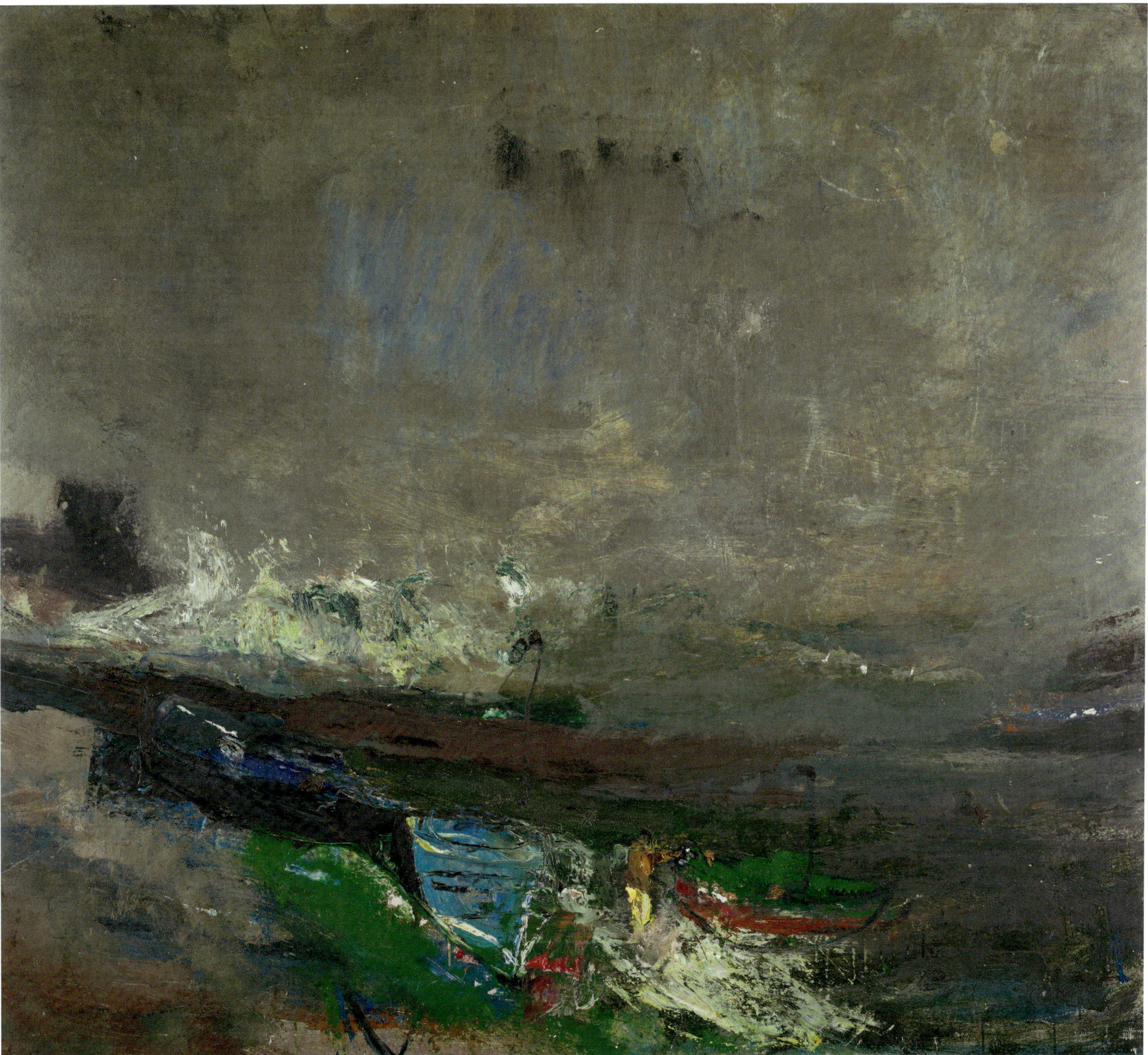

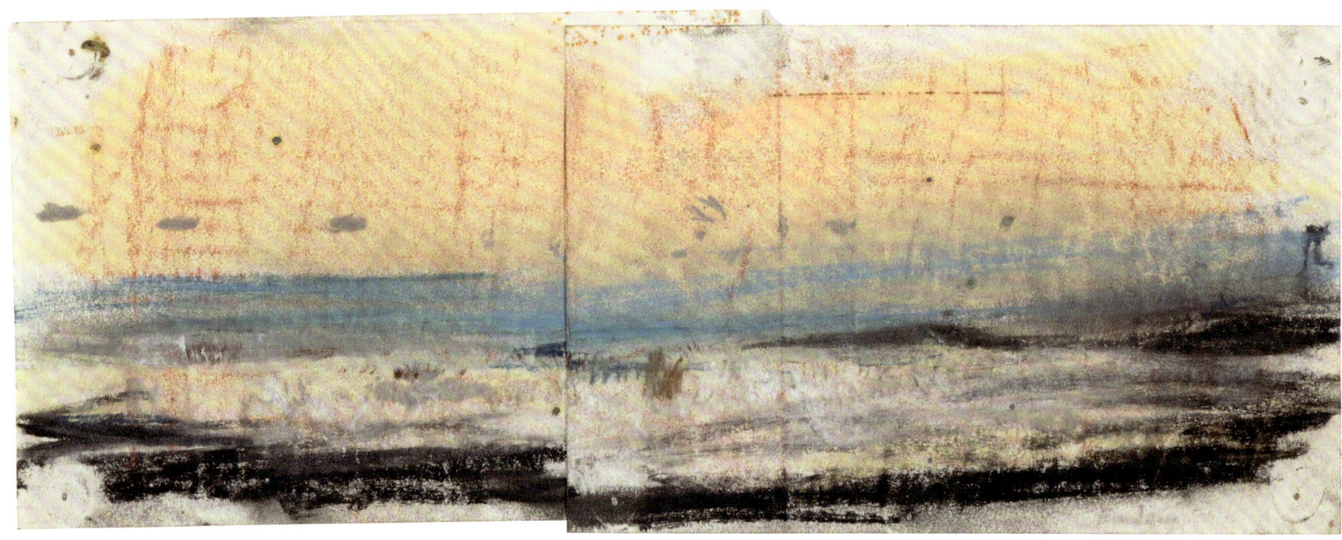

89 *The Sea at Catterline*, *c.*1960–63

Pastel on two sheets of paper, 13.2 × 34.2 cm
Scottish National Gallery of Modern Art, Edinburgh
Presented by the artist's sister, Mrs P.M. Black, 1987

90 *The Wave*, 1961

Oil and grit on board, 121.9 × 188 cm
Scottish National Gallery of Modern Art, Edinburgh
Purchased (Gulbenkian UK Trust Fund) 1962

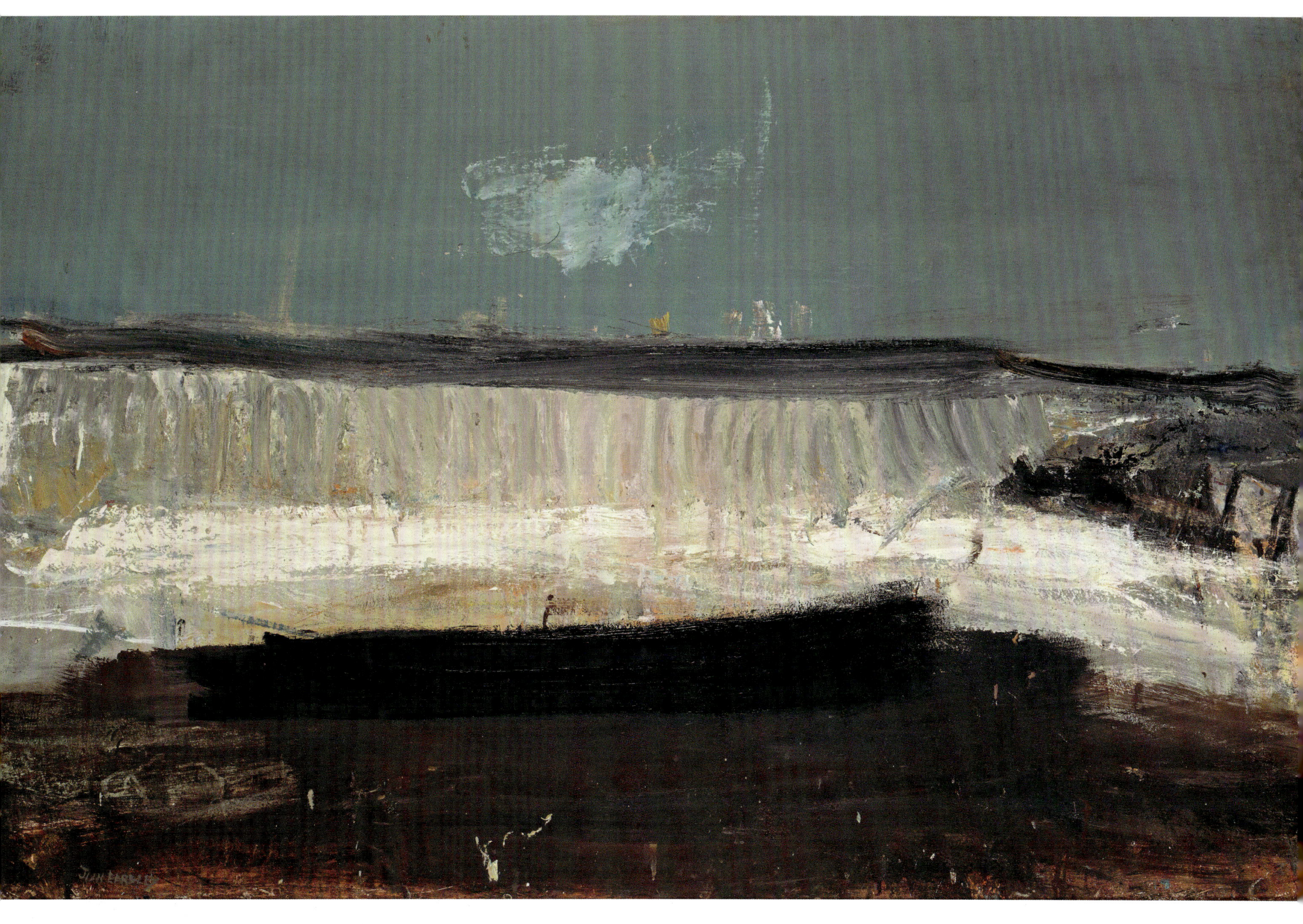

91 *January Flow Tide*, by 1960

Oil and collage on board, 88 × 156 cm

The University of Edinburgh Art Collection

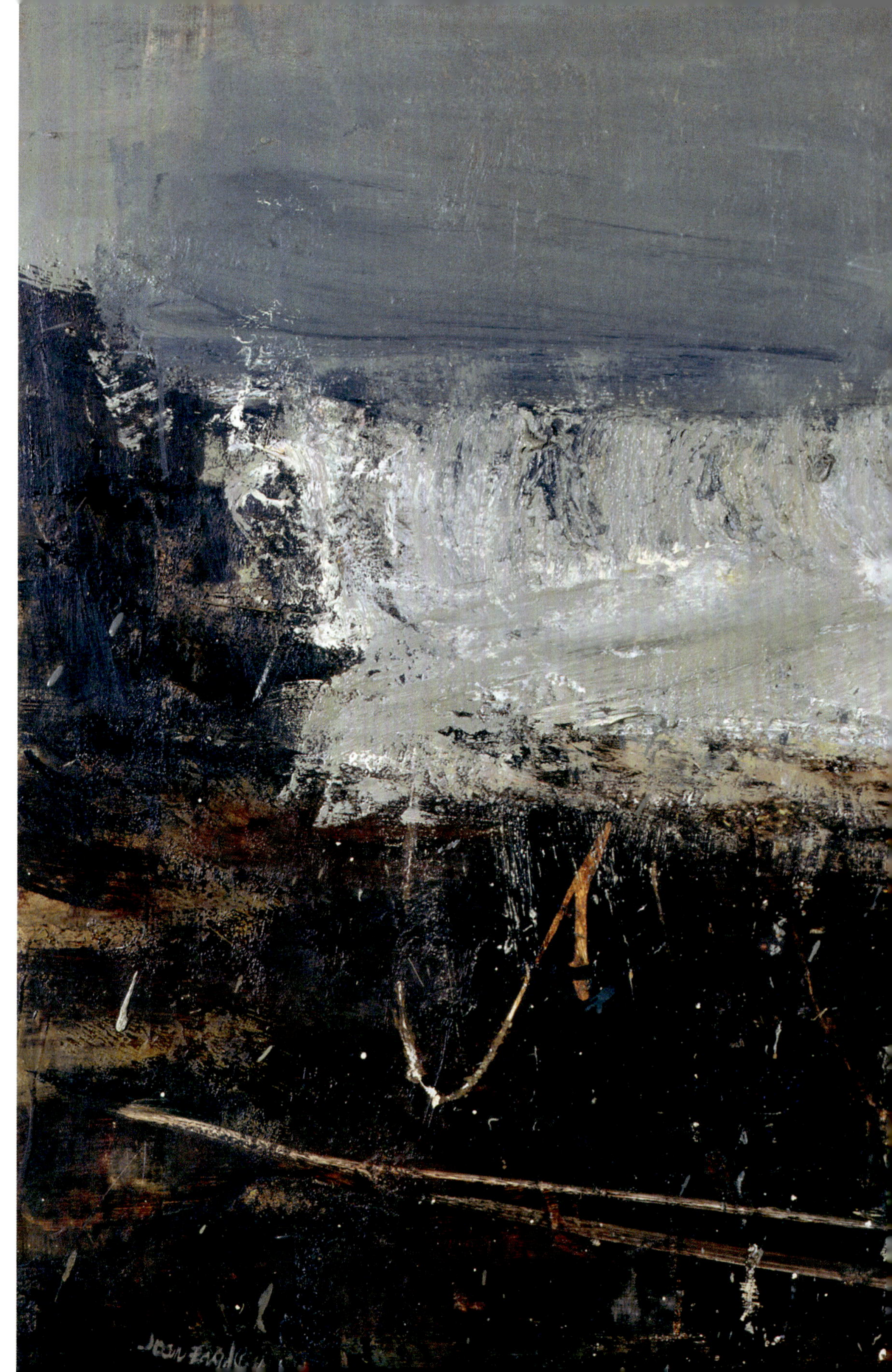

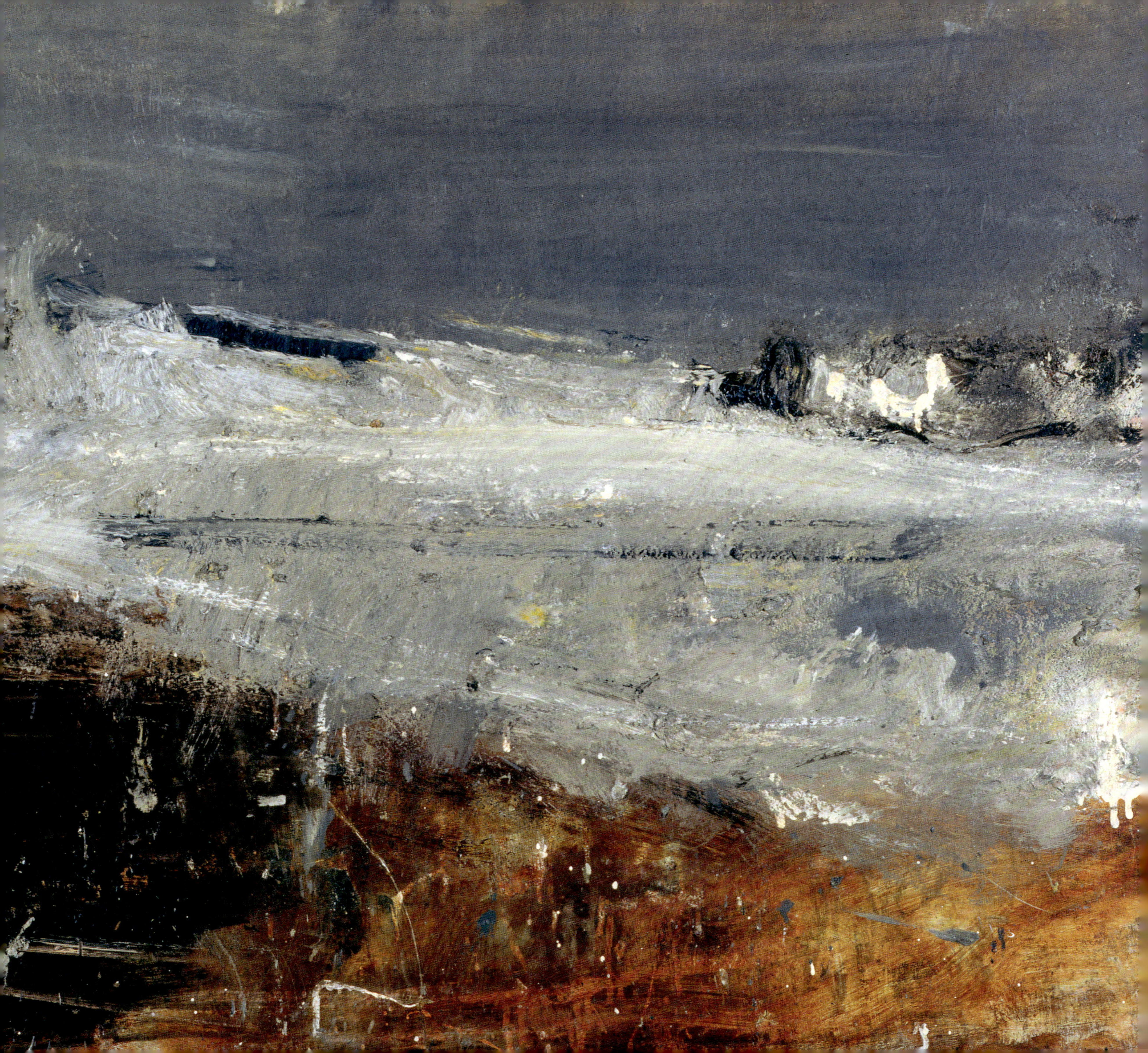

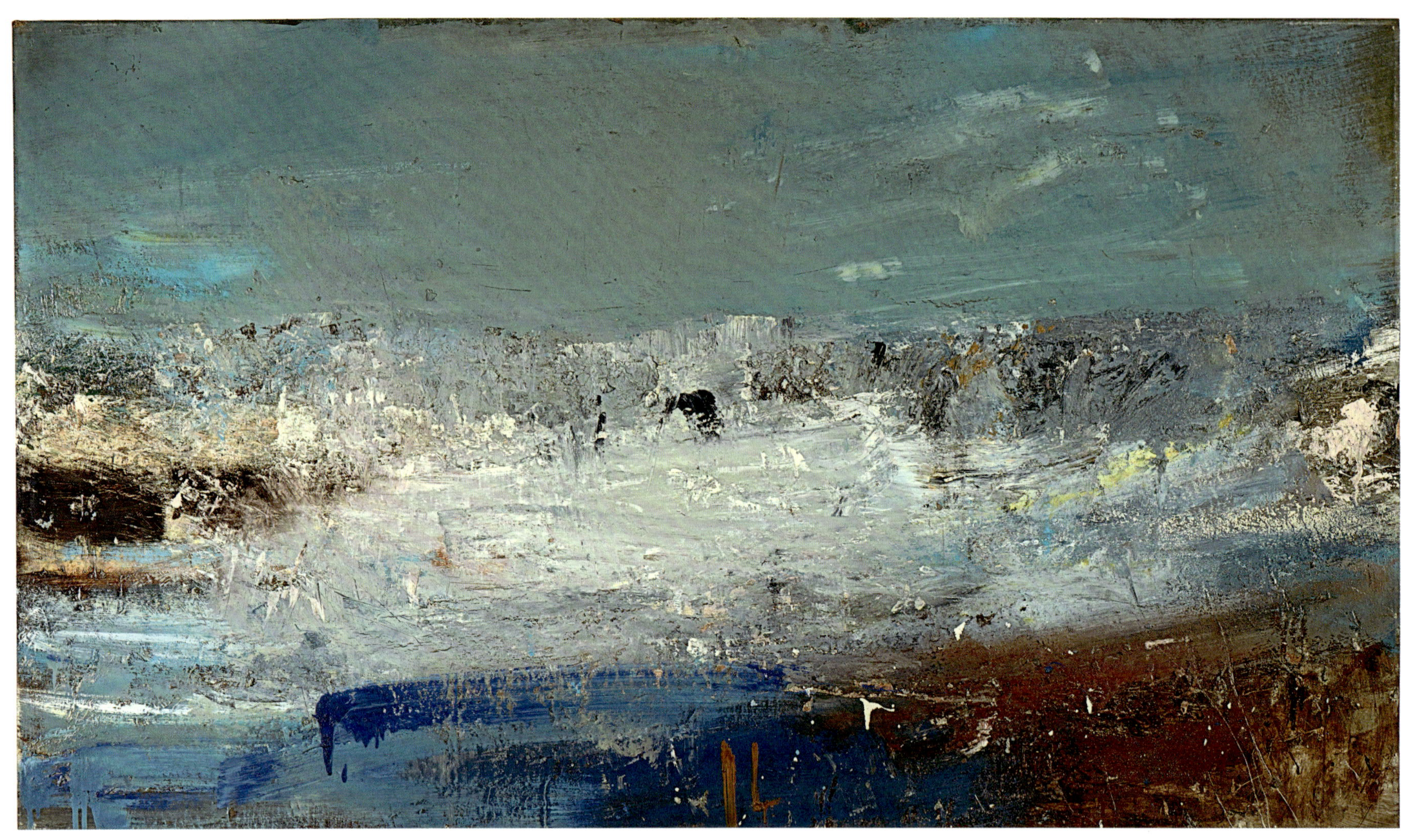

92 *Seascape (Foam and Blue Sky)*, 1962
Oil on board, 94 × 167 cm
Scottish National Gallery of Modern Art, Edinburgh
The Henry and Sula Walton Collection: bequeathed 2012

93 *Summer Sea*, 1962
Oil and collage on board, 122.2 × 183 cm
Royal Scottish Academy of Art & Architecture
(Diploma Collection)

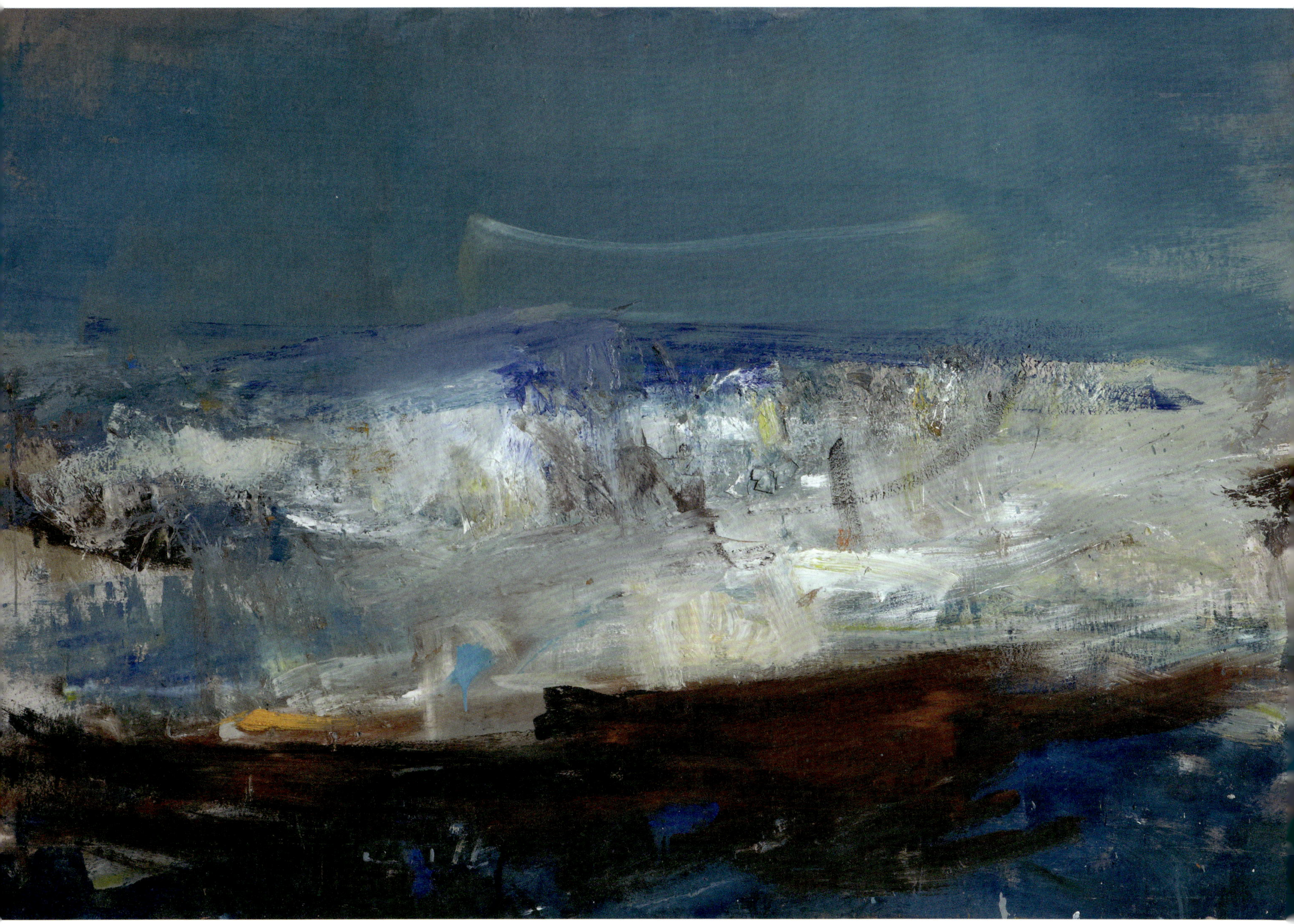

View of the Bay

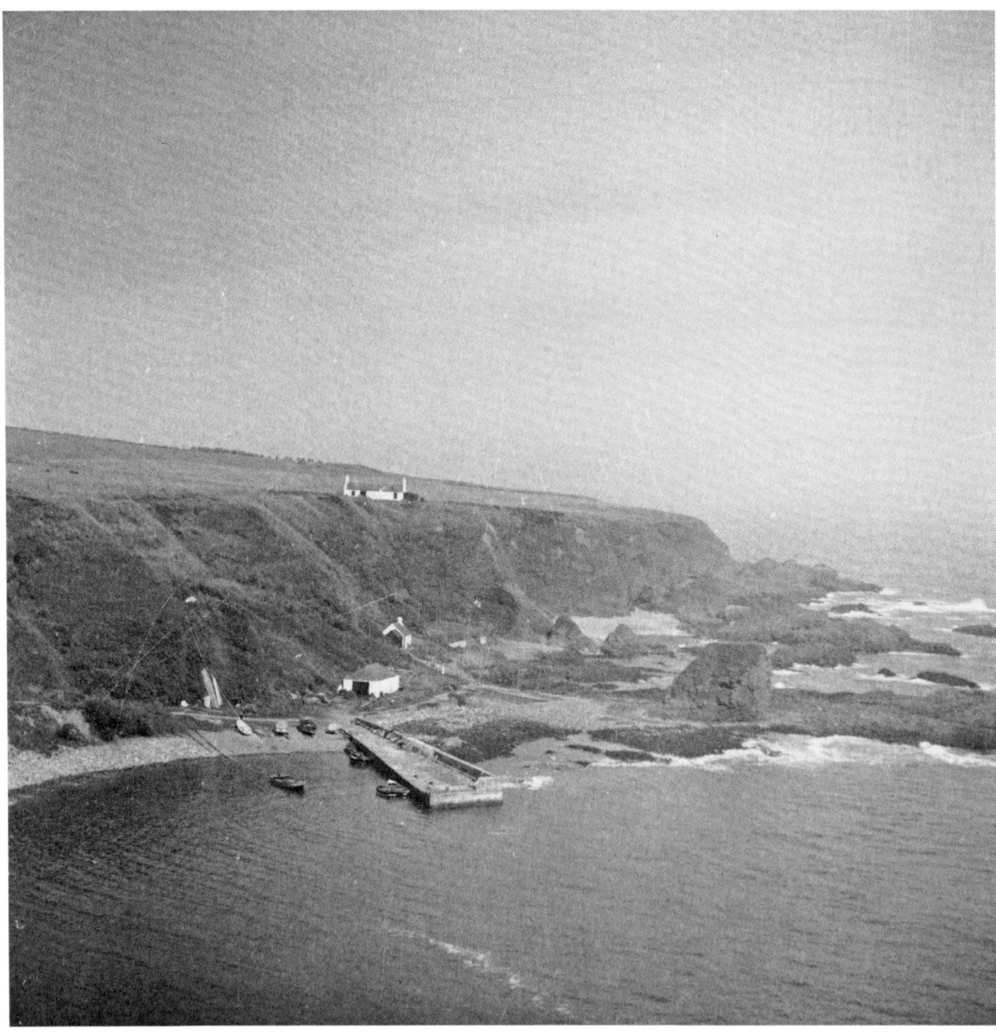

94 *Catterline Harbour*, *c.*1955–60
Silver gelatine print, 10.5 × 10.5 cm
Joan Eardley Archive, Scottish National Gallery of Modern Art, Edinburgh
Presented by the artist's sister, Mrs P.M. Black, 1987

This photograph shows the harbour and pier, viewed from the top of the steep cliff, outside Eardley's house at No.1 South Row. The boat shed is directly beyond the pier, and to the right of that is the salmon bothy. Above that, on the cliff, is the Watchie, where Eardley lived when she first stayed in Catterline. The Makin Green, where the salmon nets were hung up to dry and repair, is just beside the salmon bothy. The rocky mound to the right of the pier is the Kale Tap (on top of which the villagers once grew kale), a prominent feature in many of Eardley's paintings of the beach area.

95 *Winter Sea III*, *c.*1958

Oil on board, 55 × 82 cm
The Hunterian, University of Glasgow

96 *Winter Sea V*, 1958

Oil on canvas, 43.5 × 51 cm
Private collection

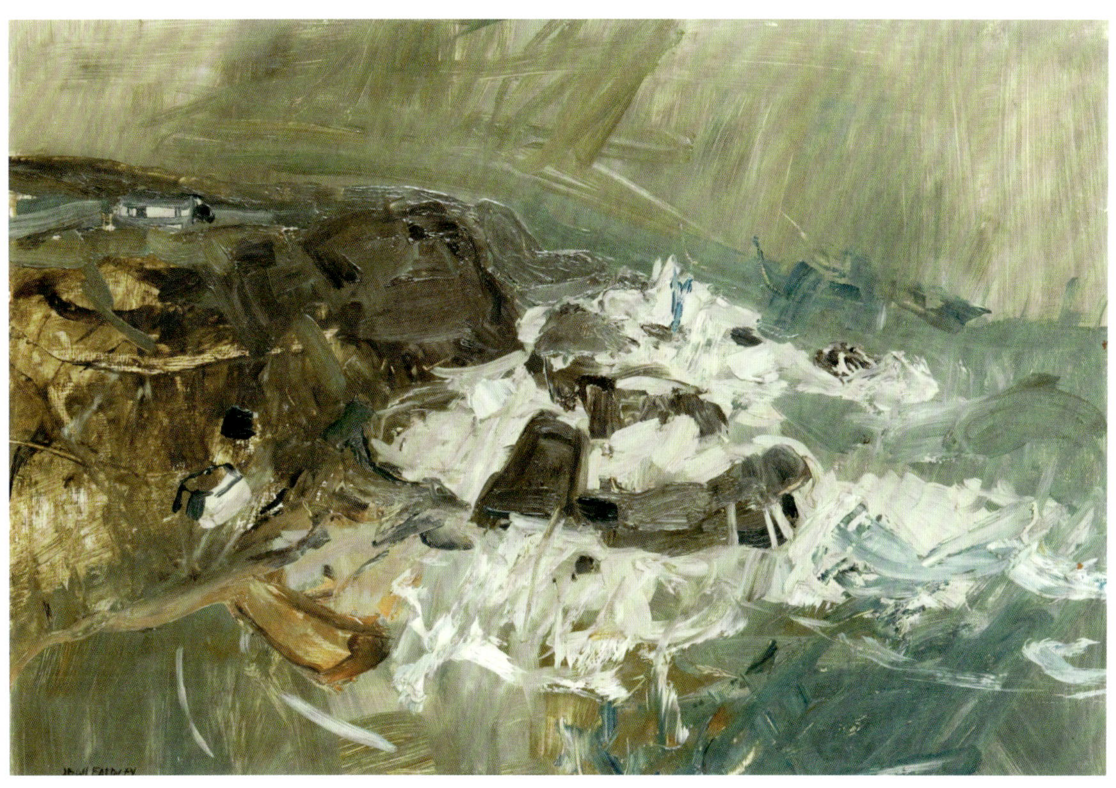

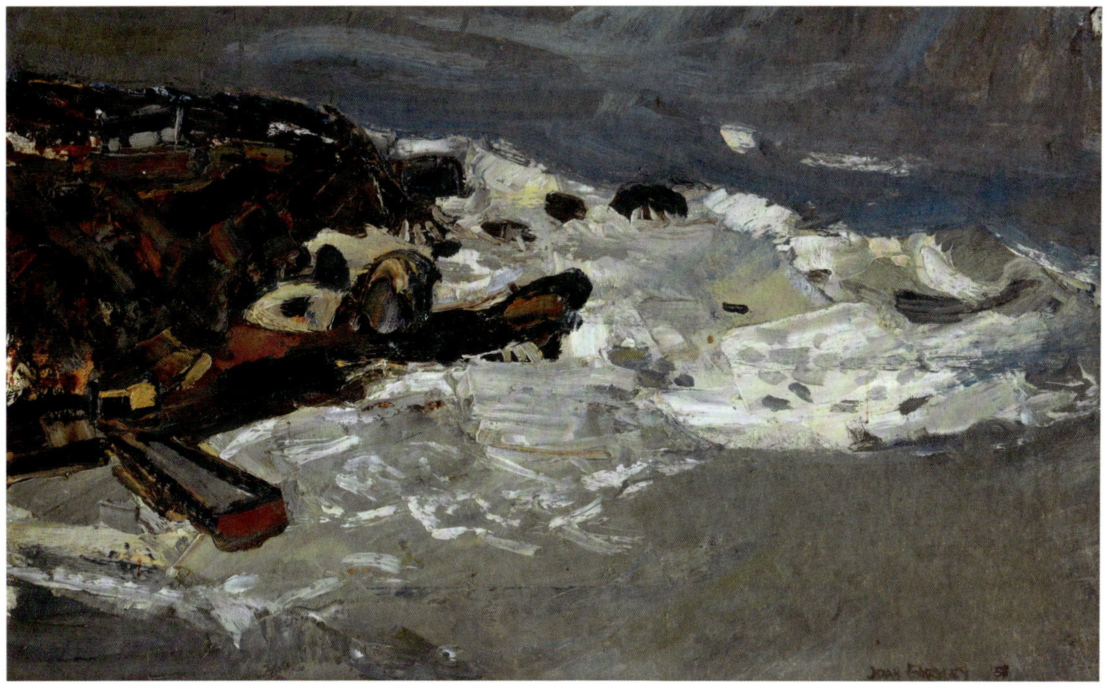

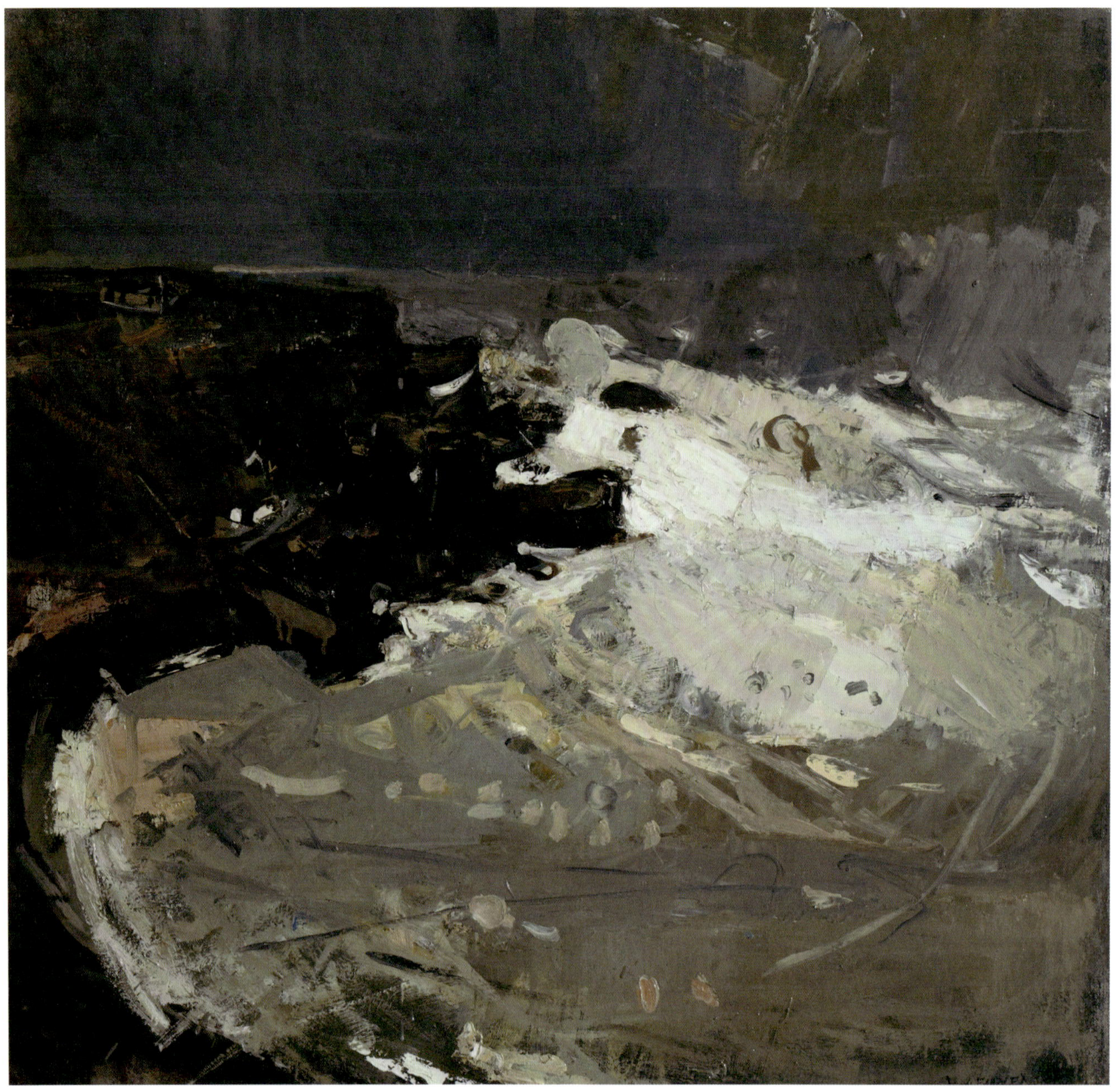

97 *Winter Sea*, 1958
Oil on canvas, 88.5 × 90 cm
Windyhill Collection, Kilmacolm

98 *Seascape*, 1956–58
Oil on board, 88.2 × 118.1 cm
City Art Centre, Edinburgh Museums and Galleries
Purchased with the assistance of the Jean F. Watson Bequest Fund and the National Fund for Acquisitions

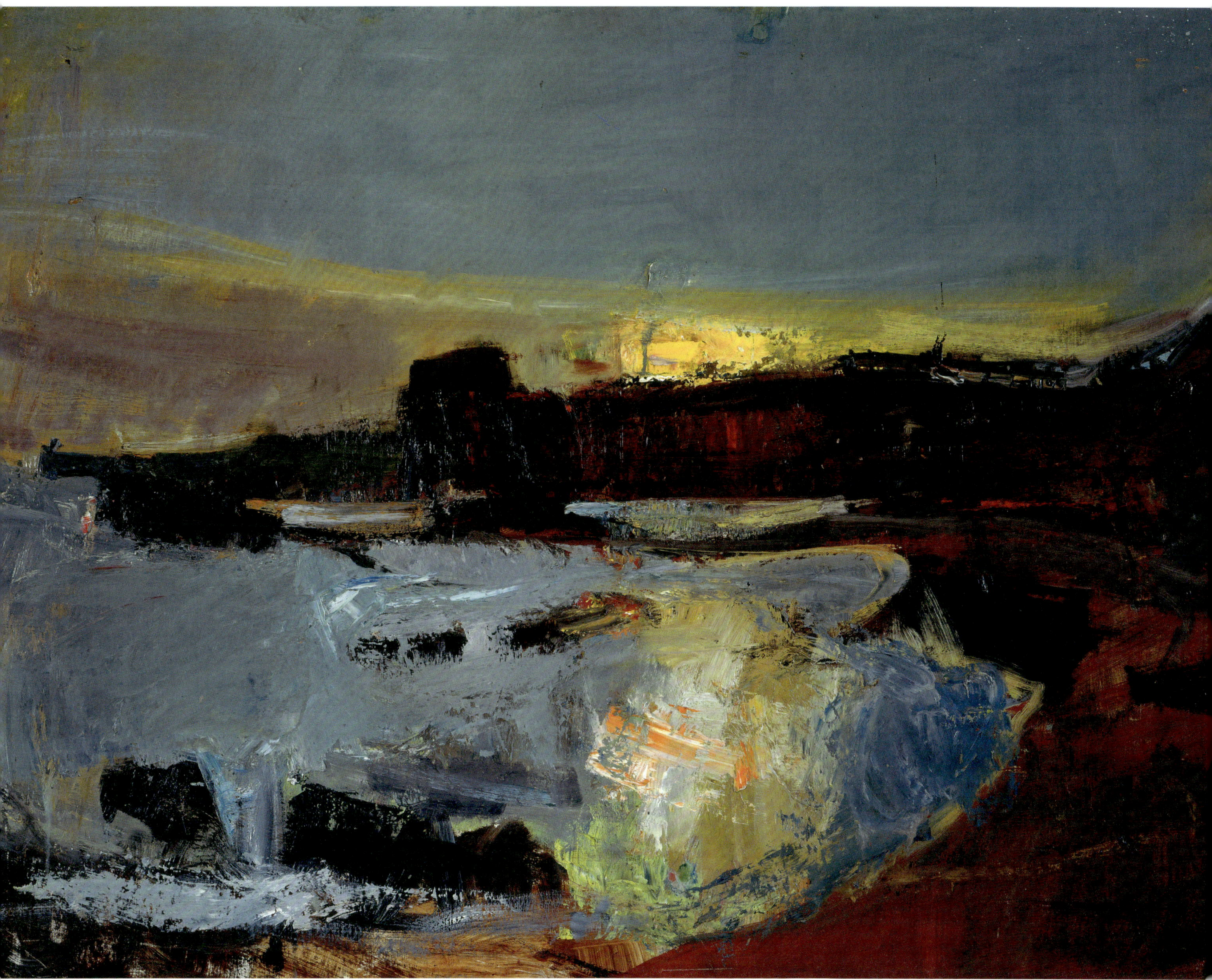

99 *Approaching Storm*, *c.*1963

Pastel on paper, 20.1 × 25.3 cm
Scottish National Gallery of Modern Art, Edinburgh
Presented by the artist's sister, Mrs P.M. Black, 1987

opposite, clockwise from top left

100 *Approaching Storm no.3*, *c.*1963

Pastel on paper, 20.1 × 25.3 cm
Private collection

101 *Approaching Storm no.5*, *c.*1963

Pastel on paper, 20.1 × 25.3 cm
Private collection

102 *Approaching Storm no.6*, *c.*1963

Pastel on paper, 20.1 × 25.3 cm
Private collection

103 *Approaching Storm no.8*, *c.*1963

Pastel on paper, 20.1 × 25.3 cm
Private collection

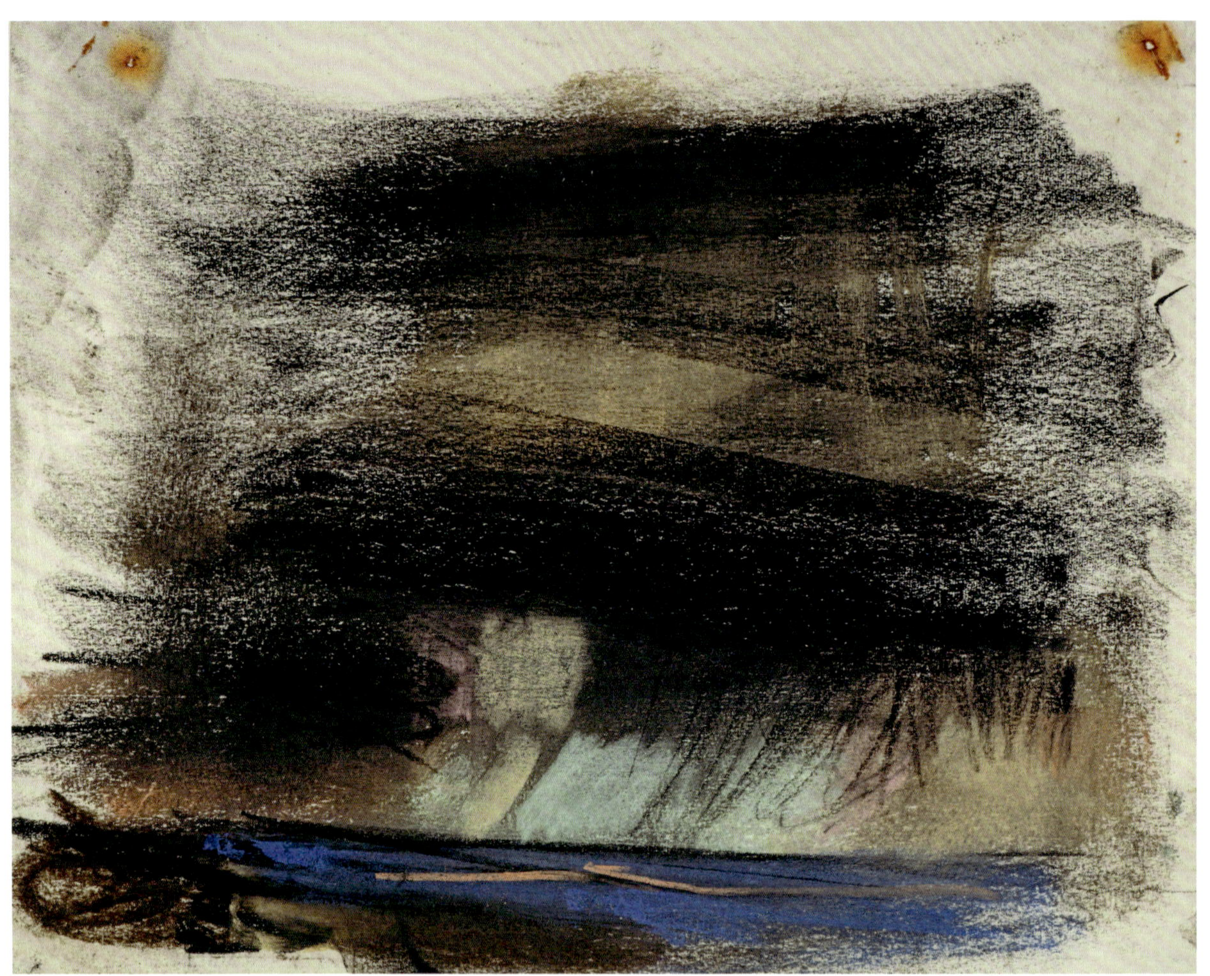

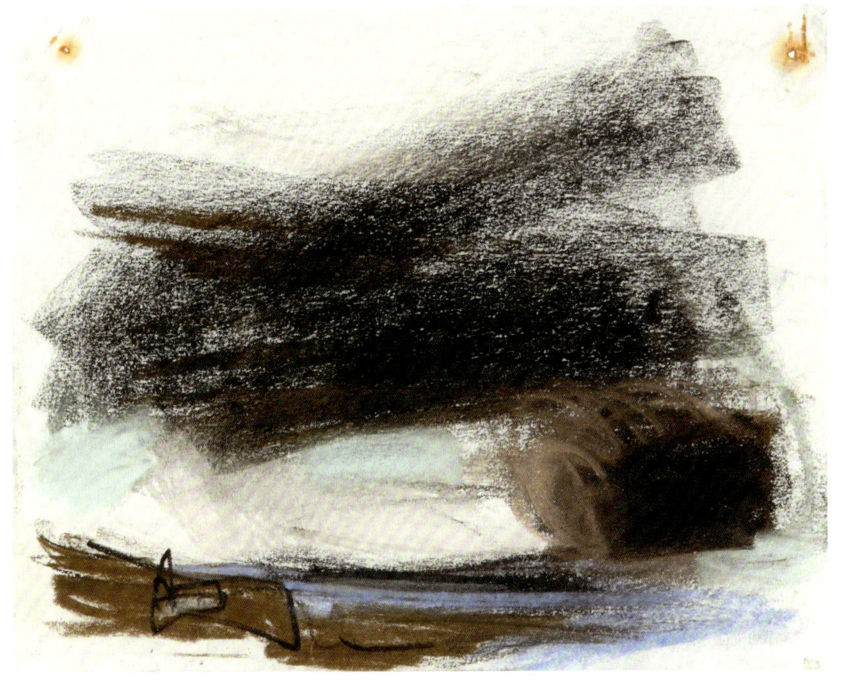
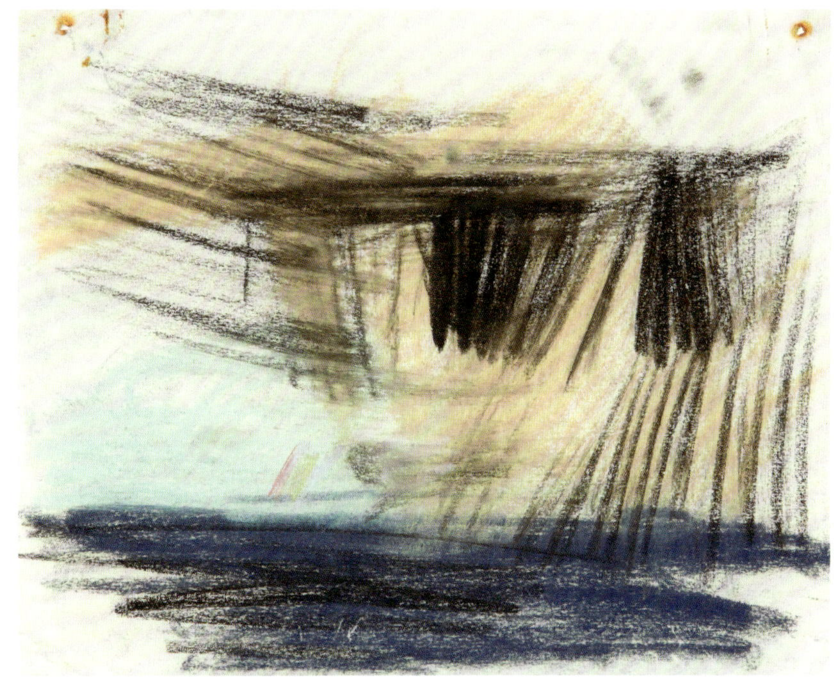
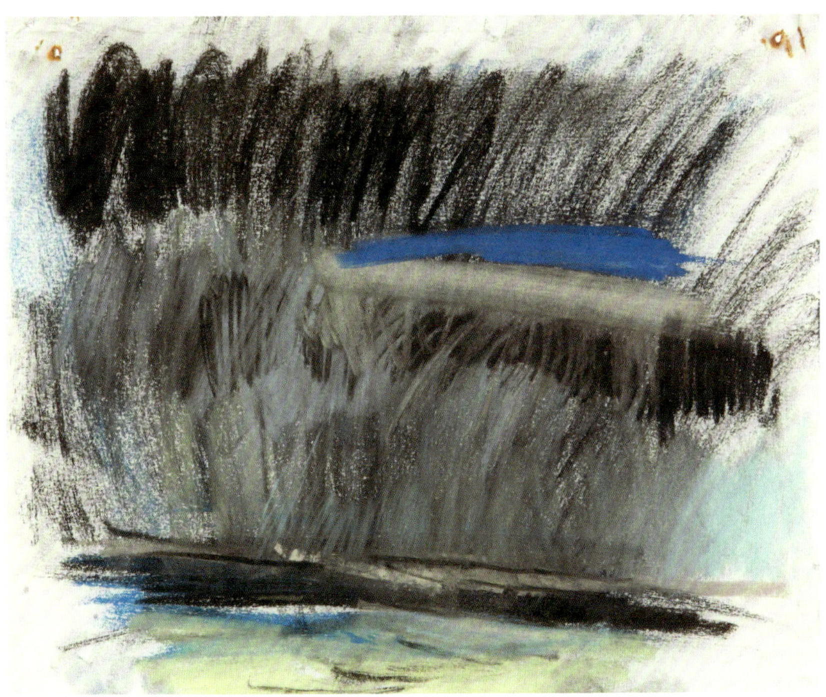
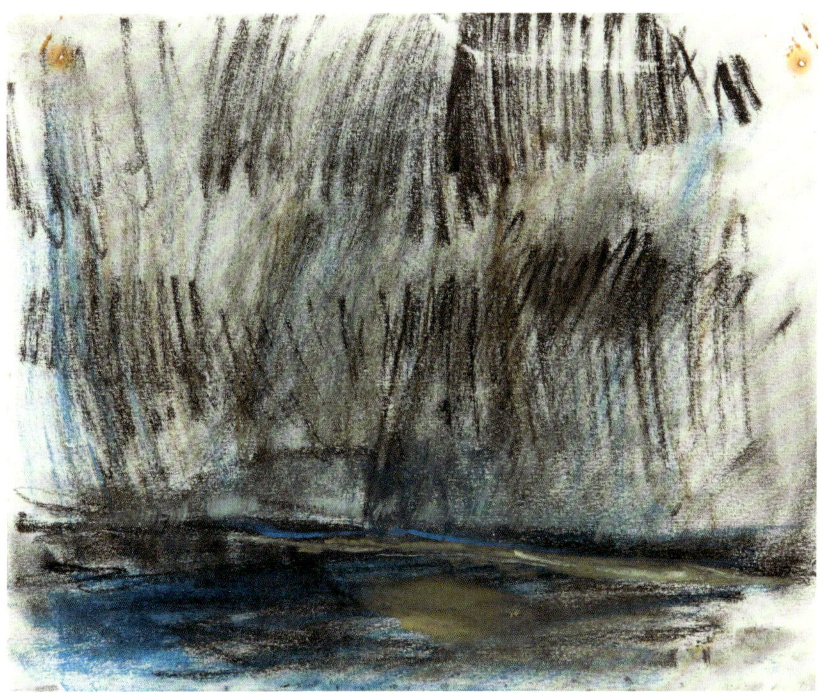

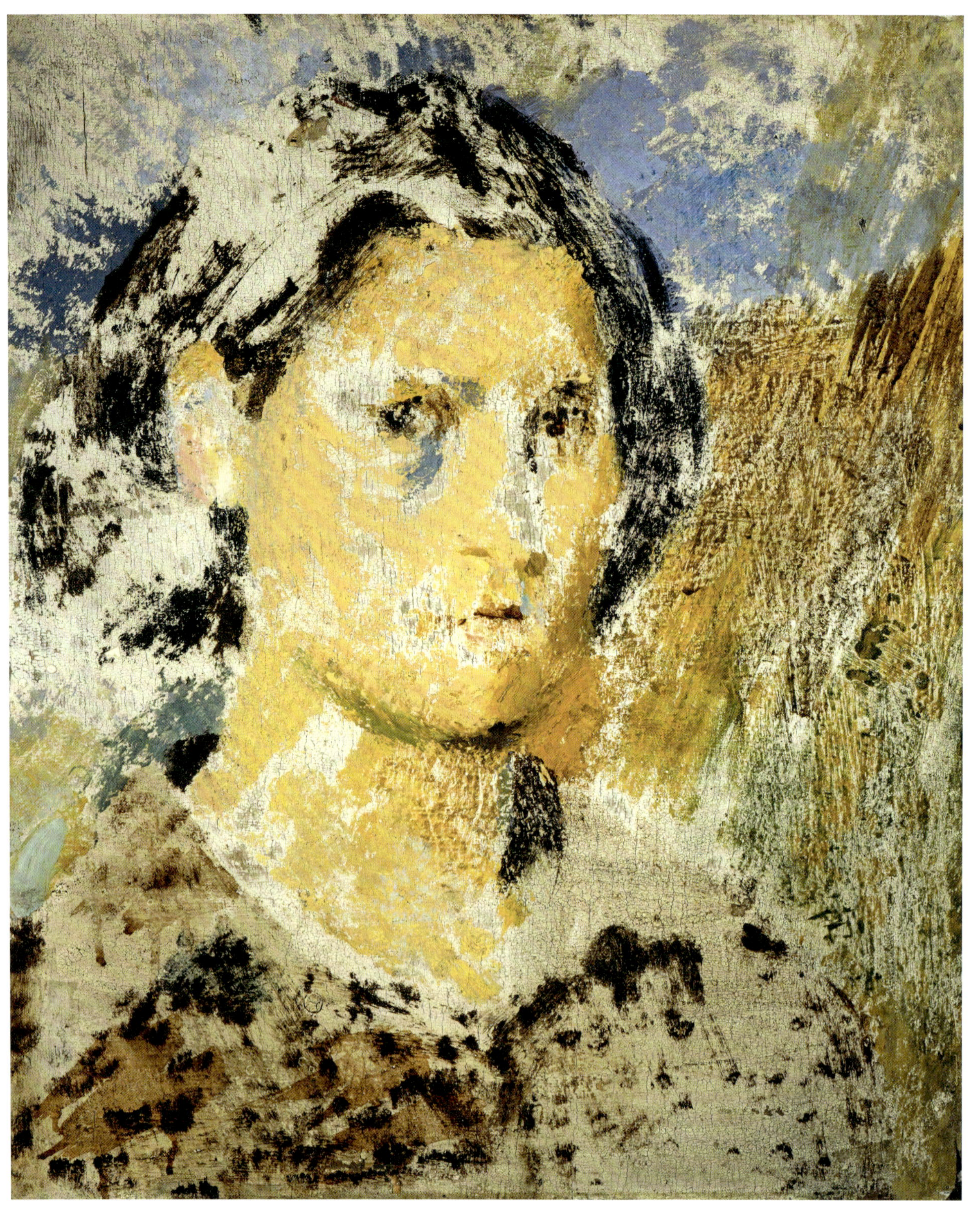

Fig.23 | *Self-portrait*, 1943
Oil on plywood, 53.4 × 45.7 cm
Scottish National Portrait Gallery, Edinburgh
Purchased 2001

Chronology

1921
Born 18 May 1921 at Bailing Hill Dairy Farm, Warnham, Sussex, to William and Irene Eardley (née Morrison), who was Scottish.

1922
Sister Pat born.

1926
The family moved to Blackheath, south-east London, staying with Irene's mother and an aunt.

1929
Eardley's father committed suicide.

1938
Spent two terms at Goldsmiths art school, London.

1939
The family moved to Auchterarder, near Perth in Scotland.

1940
The family moved to Bearsden, on the outskirts of Glasgow. Eardley studied at the Glasgow School of Art. Met fellow student Margot Sandeman, who became a lifelong friend. Met the Polish artist Josef Herman, who had recently arrived in Glasgow.

1943
Awarded diploma at the Glasgow School of Art, where she also won the Guthrie Prize for portraiture. In October, enrolled for one term at Jordanhill Teacher Training College, Glasgow.

1944
Worked as a joiner's apprentice in a small construction firm, John A. Russell, in Bearsden.

1946
Painted a mural at a girl's school in Lincoln.

1947
Spent time in London. From April to September studied at Patrick Allan Fraser College of Art, Hospitalfield, Arbroath, under James Cowie. Met Angus Neil, who became a lifelong friend.

1947–48
Post-diploma studies at the Glasgow School of Art. Won Royal Scottish Academy and the Glasgow School of Art travelling scholarships. Set off for Italy on 27 September 1948, spending much of her time in Florence, Venice, Assisi and Paris.

1949
Returned from her travels in the summer. Solo exhibition at the Glasgow School of Art in October. Rented a studio at 21 Cochrane Street, in the Townhead district of Glasgow.

1950
Solo exhibition at the Gaumont Gallery, Aberdeen, in April. Stayed with the Soper family in Stonehaven and with them visited the nearby fishing village of Catterline.

1952
Annette Soper bought the Watchie, a former Customs & Excise lookout cottage in Catterline; Eardley had free use of the cottage for the next two years and from this time on she had homes in Glasgow and Catterline. Met Audrey Walker, who became a close friend. Group exhibition organised by Arts Council of Great Britain, *Eight Young Contemporary British Painters*, includes *Catterline Coastguard Cottages* [plate 49].

1953
Moved out of the Cochrane Street studio and rented a top-floor studio at 204 St James Road, Townhead, which she kept until her death.

1954
Rented No.1 Catterline. Participated in a mixed show with five other artists at Parson's Gallery in Grosvenor Street, London. Eardley's first visit to Audrey Walker's house in Caverslea, near Selkirk, in October.

1955
First solo exhibition in London, at St George's Gallery in Cork Street. Solo exhibition at The Scottish Gallery, Edinburgh. Elected Associate of the Royal Scottish Academy.

1959
In May bought 'Sarah's Cottage', Catterline, for £30. In December bought No.18 Catterline for £250. She then sold Sarah's Cottage to the artist James Morrison the following year.

1960
Guest tutor at Patrick Allan Fraser College of Art, Hospitalfield, Arbroath, during the summer. Met Lil Neilson, a student at Hospitalfield, and invited her to Catterline; they became close friends. In August converted No.1 Catterline into a studio.

1963
In January bought No.1 Catterline, for £35. Solo exhibition at Roland, Browse and Delbanco, London. In February, elected Academician of the Royal Scottish Academy. Admitted to hospital in Aberdeen in June, then transferred to Killearn Hospital, north of Glasgow, where she died on 16 August 1963.

Maps of Townhead, Glasgow and Catterline, now Aberdeenshire

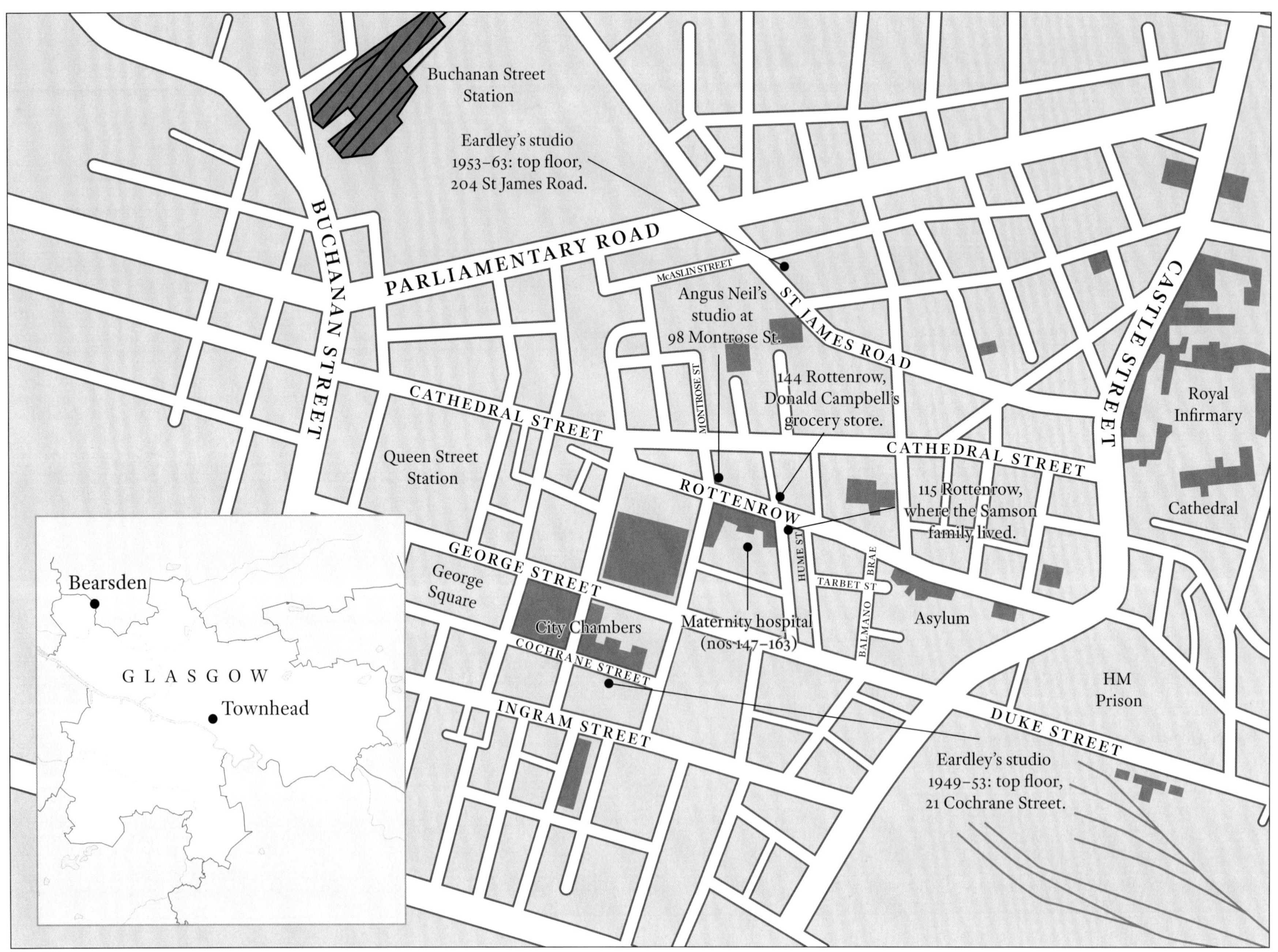

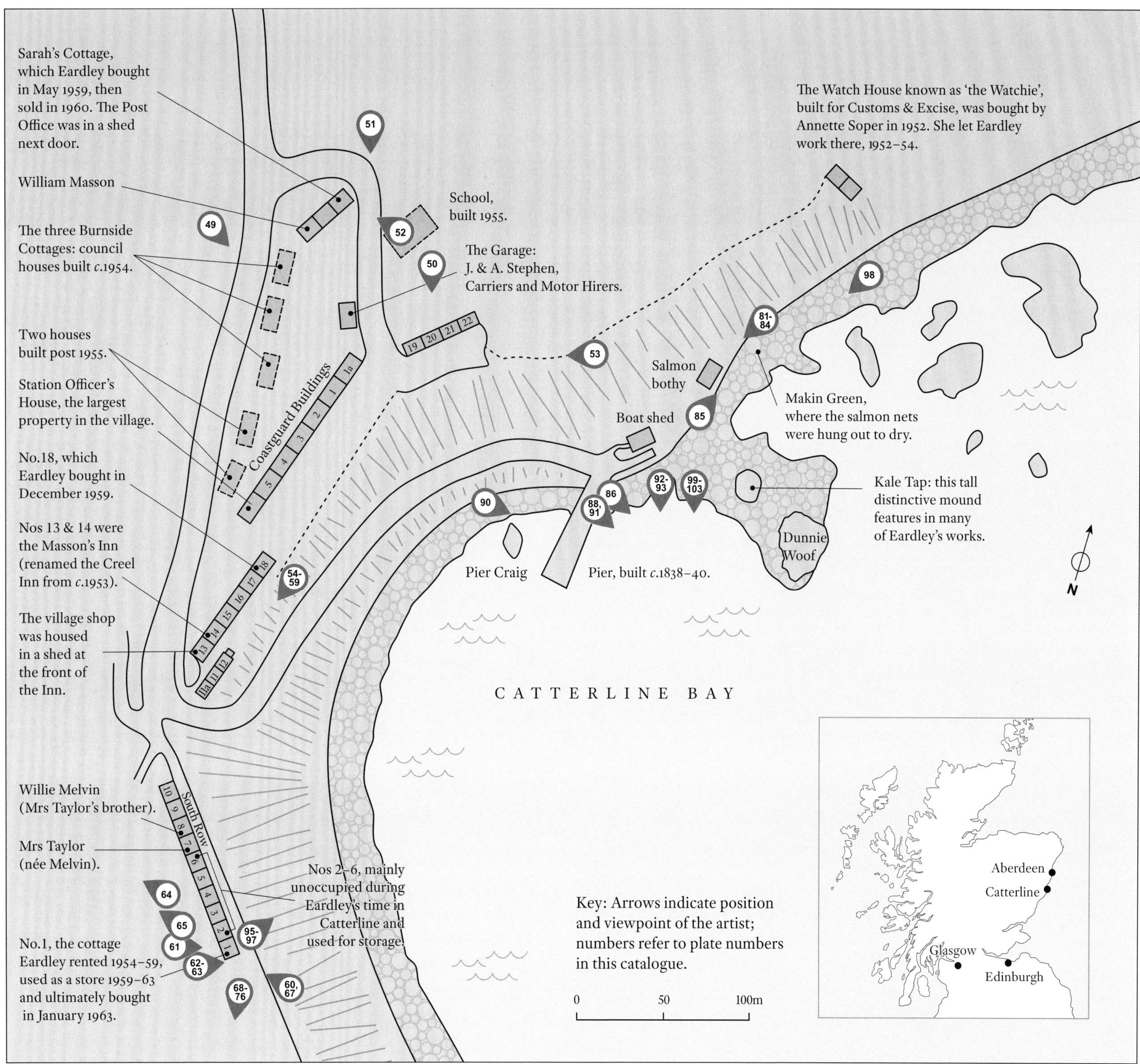
Sarah's Cottage, which Eardley bought in May 1959, then sold in 1960. The Post Office was in a shed next door.
William Masson
The three Burnside Cottages: council houses built c.1954.
Two houses built post 1955.
Station Officer's House, the largest property in the village.
No.18, which Eardley bought in December 1959.
Nos 13 & 14 were the Masson's Inn (renamed the Creel Inn from c.1953).
The village shop was housed in a shed at the front of the Inn.
Willie Melvin (Mrs Taylor's brother).
Mrs Taylor (née Melvin).
No.1, the cottage Eardley rented 1954–59, used as a store 1959–63 and ultimately bought in January 1963.
Nos 2–6, mainly unoccupied during Eardley's time in Catterline and used for storage.
School, built 1955.
The Garage: J. & A. Stephen, Carriers and Motor Hirers.
The Watch House known as 'the Watchie', built for Customs & Excise, was bought by Annette Soper in 1952. She let Eardley work there, 1952–54.
Coastguard Buildings
South Row
Salmon bothy
Boat shed
Makin Green, where the salmon nets were hung out to dry.
Kale Tap: this tall distinctive mound features in many of Eardley's works.
Dunnie Woof
Pier Craig
Pier, built c.1838–40.
CATTERLINE BAY
N
Key: Arrows indicate position and viewpoint of the artist; numbers refer to plate numbers in this catalogue.
0
50
100m
Aberdeen
Catterline
Glasgow
Edinburgh

Concise Bibliography

CHRISTOPHER ANDREAE, *Joan Eardley,* Farnham, 2013

MARTIN BAILLIE, 'Joan Eardley RSA', *The Glasgow Review,* vol.1, no.2, Summer 1964, pp.23–31

WILLIAM BUCHANAN, 'Painting the Richness of Glasgow', *The Listener,* vol.71, no.1823, 5 March 1964, pp.394–95

WILLIAM BUCHANAN, *Joan Eardley,* Modern Scottish Painters, no.5, Edinburgh, 1976

KEITH CLEMENTS, 'Artists and Places no.11: Joan Eardley', *The Artist*, vol.101, no.12, December 1986, pp.27–29

EMILIO COIA, 'Joan Eardley', *Scottish Art Review,* vol.9, no.3, 1964, pp.2–7

DOUGLAS HALL, 'Drawings by Joan Eardley, RSA (1921–63)', *The Connoisseur,* July 1965, pp.178–82

DOUGLAS HALL, *Joan Eardley 1921–1963*, Scottish Artists in the Scottish National Gallery of Modern Art, no.3, Edinburgh, 1979

DEREK HILL, 'A Tribute to Joan Eardley', *Apollo*, vol.71, no.27, May 1964, p.419

DAVID IRWIN, 'The Work of Joan Eardley', *New Saltire*, no.11, April 1964, pp.21–24

Joan Eardley, exh. cat., Roland, Browse and Delbanco, London, 1963

Joan Eardley, exh. cat., Royal Scottish Academy, Edinburgh, 1977

Joan Eardley in Context, exh. cat., The Scottish Gallery, Edinburgh, 2015

Joan Eardley, RSA *(1921–1963)*, exh. cat., The Art Gallery and Museum, Kelvingrove Glasgow and Royal Scottish Academy, Edinburgh, 1964

SARAH MacDOUGALL (ED.), *Refiguring the 50s*, exh. cat., Ben Uri Gallery, London, 2014

NIGEL MCISAAC, 'Private (Patron's) View of the RSA, II', *The Studio*, vol.154, no.773, August 1957, p.56

DUNCAN MACMILLAN, *Scottish Art in the Twentieth Century*, Edinburgh, 1994

CORDELIA OLIVER, 'Joan Eardley and Glasgow', *Scottish Art Review*, vol.14, no.3, 1974, pp.16–19

CORDELIA OLIVER, 'Joan Eardley and Catterline', *The Scots Magazine*, vol.112, no.2, November 1979, pp.133–42

CORDELIA OLIVER, *Joan Eardley,* RSA, Edinburgh, 1988

CORDELIA OLIVER, 'Through Women's Eyes: Women Painters in Scotland', *Modern Painters*, vol.12, no.4, Winter 1999, pp.93–94

FIONA PEARSON, *Joan Eardley 1921–1963*, Edinburgh, 1988

FIONA PEARSON AND SARA STEVENSON, *Joan Eardley,* Edinburgh, 2007

R.H. WESTWATER, 'Joan Eardley' *Scottish Art Review*, vol.6, no.2, 1957, pp.2–6

Notes and References

Directors' Foreword pages 6–7

1 Ronald Parkinson, *John Constable: The Man and his Art*, London, 1998, p.129.

Introduction · pages 9–11

2 *The Scotsman*, 25 May 1963, interview with Conrad Wilson.

3 Undated letter, later marked '1951', copy in the Joan Eardley Archive, Scottish National Gallery of Modern Art (SNGMA), Edinburgh (GMA A09/5/51).

4 BBC interview with Joan Eardley, 14 January 1963, tape recording in the Joan Eardley Archive, SNGMA (GMA A09/7/1/4).

I Townhead · pages 13–55

5 Glasgow Museums bought *Stack Yard* in 1948 and the Glasgow School of Art bought *Barn and Plough* in 1949.

6 'An Exhibition of Drawings and Paintings by Joan Eardley', leaflet for exhibition held at the Gaumont Gallery, Aberdeen, 7–28 April 1950.

7 Oliver 1988, p.38.

8 Typescript catalogue of *Four Centuries of Glasgow: An exhibition of views of the city by local artists*, The Provand's Lordship Society in collaboration with The Extramural Department of Glasgow University, 1959, copy in the Joan Eardley Archive, SNGMA (GMA A09/1/5).

9 Buchanan 1976, p.23.

10 Entry for 21 Cochrane Street in Valuation Rolls for City of Glasgow, 1953–54, National Archives of Scotland (VR102/2124/185).

11 Undated letters, copies in the Joan Eardley Archive, SNGMA (GMA A09/5/25; GMA A09/5/46).

12 Undated letter, but 1951, Joan Eardley Archive, SNGMA (GMA A09/1/1/72).

13 Although the date for Eardley's move to 204 St James Road is often given as 1952, her name first appears on the City of Glasgow Valuation Rolls for the year 1953–54 in the National Archives of Scotland (VR102/2123/251), and then again in subsequent years.

14 Buchanan 1976, p.25.

15 Robert Henriques, 'Eardley', leaflet for exhibition held at St George's Gallery, London, 1955.

16 Sydney Goodsir Smith, 'Joan Eardley: She Just Paints', *The Scotsman*, 19 August 1961.

17 The children were, in order of birth: Andrew, Elizabeth, Jimmy, Ian, Margaret, Brian, Mary, Pat, Ann, David, George and Robert.

18 'Woman Artist Takes Glasgow to Mayfair', *Evening Times*, 23 February 1954.

19 Andrew Samson, interview with Patrick Elliott, 1 September 2016. See also Andrew Samson's interview with Alan Taylor in *The Sunday Herald*, 21 October 2007.

20 Interview with Patrick Elliott, 5 May 2016.

21 Andrew Samson, interview with Patrick Elliott, 1 September 2016.

22 Buchanan 1976, p.27.

23 Valuation Rolls for City of Glasgow, National Archives of Scotland (VR102/2123/189; VR102/2162/189); Campbell's Licenced Grocer is recorded throughout the 1940s but is listed as 'empty' in 1954–55.

24 One of Walker's photographs and a related painting by Eardley were illustrated in the *Scottish Art Review*, vol.6, no.2, 1957, p.6.

25 Two uncredited newspaper clippings of 1957 in the Glasgow Museums acquisition file for the painting *Catterline Coastguard Cottages* [plate 49] mention the slipped disc.

26 Oliver 1988, p.71.

27 Letter to Lil Neilson, 22 May 1963, private collection.

28 Pat Black, interview for 'Street Kids and Stormy Skies', produced by Vivien Devlin for BBC Radio Scotland and first broadcast 18 August 1983.

29 BBC interview with Joan Eardley, 14 January 1963, tape recording in the Joan Eardley Archive, SNGMA (GMA A09/7/1/4).

30 Ibid.

II Catterline · pages 57–121

31 7–28 April; the show featured nineteen paintings and seventeen drawings.

32 Uncredited press clipping, Joan Eardley Archive, SNGMA (GMA A09/1/5).

33 Undated, but April 1950, Joan Eardley Archive, SNGMA (GMA A09/1/1/66).

34 She caught mumps while the exhibition was running (7–28 April) and must have returned to Stonehaven at a later date. From her home in Bearsden, she wrote that she wanted to return to Aberdeen or the vicinity 'in the near future – I felt quite an urge to paint which I think must be satisfied!' Letter to Bill Thomson, undated but 1950, Joan Eardley Archive, SNGMA (GMA A09/5/3).

35 The 'Old Watch-House' as listed on Search Sheet 3401, County of Kincardine, General Register of Sasines, National Records of Scotland.

36 Ron Stephen, interview with Patrick Elliott, 27 May 2016.

37 Ibid.

38 'Decay of the Northeast Fishing Villages', *Aberdeen Press and Journal*, 3 April 1928, p.8.

39 It was exhibited in the Arts Council's *Eight Young Contemporary British Painters* in 1952 (cat.21), where it is dated 1951. It was bought by Glasgow Museums in 1952.

40 There seems to be no firm evidence for the date of Eardley's move into No.1. Eardley's letters to Walker (National Library of Scotland, Acc. 11826) are mainly undated, but Walker's subsequent annotations suggest 1954 as the likely move-in date.

41 Letter marked '17 December 1957', National Library of Scotland (Acc. 11826). Eardley did not date her letters to Walker; dates given for this and all following letters from this archive were added later by Walker, possibly taken

from the postmarks on the envelopes, which are now destroyed.

42 Letter from No.1 Catterline, marked 'early days, 1954', National Library of Scotland (Acc. 11826).

43 Other sources note that 'Dunner' means a sound like thunder, and that it was not a silent dog, but that during heavy weather it seemed to be a very loud one.

44 Letter to Audrey Walker, marked '14 February 1958', National Library of Scotland (Acc. 11826).

45 'Too Sunny at Catterline', uncredited newspaper clipping, *c.*1960, Joan Eardley Archive, SNGMA (GMA A09/1/4).

46 Andrew Samson, interview with Patrick Elliott, 1 September 2016.

47 Letter marked 'August 1955', National Library of Scotland (Acc. 11826).

48 Letter marked '14 September 1955', National Library of Scotland (Acc. 11826).

49 Sydney Goodsir Smith, 'Joan Eardley: She Just Paints', *The Scotsman*, 19 August 1961.

50 Ron Stephen, interview with Patrick Elliott, 27 May 2016.

51 Letter to Audrey Walker, marked '18 or 19 November 1958', National Library of Scotland (Acc. 11826).

52 'Too Sunny at Catterline', uncredited newspaper clipping, *c.*1960, Joan Eardley Archive, SNGMA (GMA A09/1/4).

53 Letter to Audrey Walker, marked '14 February 1958', National Library of Scotland (Acc. 11826).

54 Undated letter, National Library of Scotland (Acc. 11826).

55 Ron Stephen, interview with Patrick Elliott, 27 May 2016.

56 Letter to Frank Stephen, an old artist friend (and unrelated to the Stephen families of Catterline), undated but *c.*1952–53, Joan Eardley Archive, SNGMA (GMA A09/3).

57 Ibid. The letter is undated, but since Annette Soper bought the Watchie in August 1952, it is likely the three-month summer stay referred to was in 1953.

58 'Bridgend, Catterline', known as Sarah's Cottage, as listed on Search Sheet 3734, County of Kincardine, General Register of Sasines, National Records of Scotland.

59 'House No.18 of the Village of Catterline', as listed on Search Sheet 3725, County of Kincardine, General Register of Sasines, National Records of Scotland.

60 'Building No.1 of the Village of Catterline', as listed on Search Sheet 5986, County of Kincardine, General Register of Sasines, National Records of Scotland.

61 In the *Aberdeen Press and Journal*, 23 June 1960, Angus Neil spoke of the need to save the cottages on the South Side 'which have been condemned'.

62 Letter marked '19 November 1959', National Library of Scotland (Acc. 11826).

63 Undated letter, Joan Eardley Archive, SNGMA (GMA A09/1/1/77).

64 Letter marked '5 August 1960', National Library of Scotland (Acc. 11826).

65 Undated letter, but possibly July 1962, Joan Eardley Archive, SNGMA (GMA A09/1/1/77). In the letter Eardley mis-spells her name 'Mrs Gardena'.

66 Undated letter in the Joan Eardley Archive, SNGMA (GMA A09/5/66).

67 Sydney Goodsir Smith, 'Joan Eardley: She Just Paints', *The Scotsman*, 19 August 1961.

68 She left an Estate valued at £19,909: uncredited newspaper clipping, Joan Eardley Archive, SNGMA (GMA A09/1/4).

69 Letter dated 17–18 May 1963, private collection.

70 Letter postmarked 22 May 1963, private collection.

71 Undated letter, National Library of Scotland (Acc. 11826).

72 Letter dated 10 September 1963, National Library of Scotland (Acc. 11826).

73 Letter marked 'Friday morning' by Eardley and '1956' by Walker, National Library of Scotland (Acc. 11826).

74 Richard Morphet's in-depth catalogue entry on Eardley's *Salmon Nets* painting in the Tate contains a detailed analysis of bag-net fishing: see *The Tate Gallery 1984–86: Illustrated Catalogue of Acquisitions Including Supplement to Catalogue of Acquisitions 1982–84*, London, 1988, pp.142–44.

75 Ibid.

76 Ron Stephen, interview with Patrick Elliott, 27 May 2016. See also 'Catterline on the Ebb-Tide', *The Weekend Scotsman*, 5 July 1975.

Copyright and Photographic Credits